An Economy of Strangers

JEWISH CULTURE AND CONTEXTS

Published in association with the Herbert D. Katz Center for
Advanced Judaic Studies of the University of Pennsylvania

Series Editors
Beth Berkowitz, Shaul Magid,
Francesca Trivellato, Steven Weitzman

A complete list of books in the series is
available from the publisher.

An Economy of Strangers

Jews and Finance in England,
1650–1830

Avinoam Yuval-Naeh

PENN

UNIVERSITY OF PENNSYLVANIA PRESS

PHILADELPHIA

Published by
University of Pennsylvania Press
Philadelphia, Pennsylvania 19104–4112
www.upenn.edu/pennpress

Printed in the United States of America on acid-free paper
10 9 8 7 6 5 4 3 2 1

Hardcover ISBN: 978-1-5128-2505-3
eBook ISBN: 978-1-5128-2506-0

A Cataloging-in-Publication record is
available from the Library of Congress

To Naomi, with love

In memory of Miriam and Moshe Schwartz, z"l

Contents

Introduction

One of the most persistent and powerful socioeconomic notions in the history of the Jews in the diaspora is the prodigious talent attributed to them in all things economic. From the medieval Jewish usurer through the early modern port-Jew and court-Jew to the grand financier of the nineteenth and twentieth centuries and contemporary investors, Jews loomed large in economic imagination. For capitalists and Marxists, libertarians and radical reformers, the Jews were inextricably intertwined with the economy. In fact, this association has become so natural in both non-Jewish and Jewish circles that to this day we often overlook the contingent dynamics behind the making and remaking of the complex cluster of notions about Jews and economy, emerging as they have within different historical contexts to meet a variety of personal and societal anxieties and needs.

Finance has always been a major axis of these associations. For centuries Christian societies have shunned finance and constructed a normative social system to avoid it, relying largely on the figure of the Jew as a foil. Yet during the long eighteenth century, in a process often designated as the Financial Revolution, finance became the hinge of national and imperial power. At its basis was the growing importance of credit instruments such as bills of exchange, stocks, and public debt, whose spread provoked intense debates. Could a Christian society and state not only accept but also depend on what had long been conceived as un- if not even anti-Christian practices? Moreover, in a deep sense the Financial Revolution was also about an economy made more abstract, more impersonal. This feature had traditionally marked the Jews, being perceived as set apart from and even essentially hostile to organic society. How then could financial economy be accommodated with the Christian notion of brotherhood?

As anthropologists have acknowledged, material exchange is a pivotal dimension of social interactions.[1] Societies vary in their systems of exchange, which are themselves multifaceted. The early modern shift of exchange relations from a personal credit system based on face-to-face social networks and unmediated trust to a system of large-scale, mediated, anonymous credit has also entailed change in the cultural regulation of credit: from the dominance of social obligations and moral considerations to that of legal regulation and formal institutions. As sociologist Niklas Luhmann put it, it was a shift from personal trust to system trust.[2]

From the latter part of the sixteenth century, England—later Britain—experienced these shifts with particular intensity, undergoing a profound process of commercialization that transformed the nature of both state and society. Gradual as they may have been, these socioeconomic changes did not go unnoticed by contemporaries. Key to their concerns was the problem of social attachment: If the force of informal moral obligations declines, what could replace them in holding society together? This backdrop lends an acute historical sense to what is perhaps the most celebrated cultural piece dealing with the issue—Shakespeare's *Merchant of Venice*, composed at the turn of the seventeenth century when this movement began gaining momentum. Its dramatic tension pivots around the notion of the bond, a term that recurs forty-one times in the play. Shylock argues for the absolute power of the contracted, formal bond, while his adversaries plead for a social bond based on friendship and mercy.[3] Shylock is defeated, yet paradoxically it is by hyper-legalism, not by a Christian ideology of compassion. Which, then, is the normative bond that could hold society together? Or, more precisely, how could the two kinds of bonds be accommodated?

The question becomes more complex considering Shylock's arguments, which are unsettling for citizens pursuing the benefits of a commercial society. If pure law could not establish a society, neither could mercy. Commercial prosperity requires legal infrastructure, extending to more and more aspects of social life in tandem with commercialism itself. Shylock convincingly declares to the court that the denial of the contract would mean the collapse of "your charter and your city's freedom."[4] Consequently, the Venetians—or Londoners—resemble the Jews not only in their commercial inclination (as Portia wonders when she enters the court: "Which is the merchant here? And which the Jew?"),[5] but also in their need of a formal legal system. *The Merchant* is thus interweaved with the contemporary confusion of commercialism.[6] What is the bond that underlies relationship within society, and how should one accommodate the expanding formal law and traditional communal obligations? How should credit—both financial and social—be negotiated in a society that is becoming increasingly dependent on capital and legislation for economic growth and prosperity?

When *The Merchant* was written, England was taking early yet decisive steps toward becoming a market society. Market forces came to swallow more and more segments of the material and social domains, taking under their wings fields regulated until that time by customs, including trading in money (usury), grain, and land. Subsistence agriculture and small-scale manufacture waned in favor of commercialized large-scale operations. By the eighteenth century England featured a capital-intensive economy, large-scale market relationships, increased production and consumption, and the majority of its population became dependent on the market.[7] These gradual shifts culminated with the establishment of new financial institutions around the turn of the eighteenth century—primarily the Bank of England, the national debt, and a thriving market of securities, which enabled the state to obtain vast amounts for waging its wars. Many English people were now entangled in credit relations not only with their fellow countrymen but with the state as well, via various securities investments. Larger sections of society enjoyed a surplus of resources, invested in financial ventures, and at the same time increased their consumption. All these factors coalesced into a contemporary sense of transformation that triggered enduring public debates.

At the same time these socioeconomic shifts impelled the English to negotiate the way they imagined their social and political institutions and, at times, to adapt their religious and cultural worldviews to the new structure. The impact of the economic changes was not limited to economic institutions, structures, and thought—it reverberated in popular print, literature, and visual and material culture, and deeply affected political discourse. No wonder then that the rise of finance in the eighteenth century attracted extensive and multidisciplinary research.[8]

The issue of Jews and Jewishness integrated within these concerns not only as signifying precarious financial practices but also as a concrete historical case. Parallel with the economic shifts, English society experienced the resettlement of Jews after their expulsion in 1290. The 1650s saw intense public controversy around the readmission of Jews, which generated a persisting debate on their status and role in English history. Eventually, they began resettling openly in England, a process that triggered further polemics well into the nineteenth century.

Notwithstanding their concurrence, the Financial Revolution and the reemergence of a Jewish community in England were two independent historical phenomena. This book aims to reveal, however, that contemporaries commonly projected one upon the other, imbuing them with interrelated meanings. Jews came to emblematize the moral discontent with modern finance, expressing most sharply the religious and social concerns evoked by it. Consequently, concerns regarding the status of Jews and Judaism in England fused with fundamental contemporary problems that erupted at the same time regarding the balance of economy, religion, and cultural heritage. Contemporaries conceived the establishment of the new financial order as endorsement of "Jewish" characteristics and approached the question of the Jews' status as instrumental in English economic life. When they contested these questions, they negotiated the development of the capitalist system and the nature of their own modernizing society.

The resonance of the Jewish issue in England was amplified by the thriving Hebraist discourse of the time, shared by intellectuals across the entire Republic of Letters.[9] In England, however, the interest in matters Jewish went beyond the intellectual sphere: It was a widespread preoccupation, also touching on millenarian expectations. As demonstrated in the last decades by various scholars, early modern English people employed conceptions of Judaism for reconstructing their own identity: Individuals imbued the Bible in their private lives to frame their experience; political authority was imagined and defended in biblical terms; a religious worldview was grounded on a parallelism between the biblical Jews and contemporary English people; and perhaps most markedly, the self-conception and rhetoric of all sides in the enduring religious and political struggles culminating in the civil wars were saturated with biblical images.[10] The seventeenth century was the heyday of the English Bible.[11]

* * *

In a simplified manner, the moral engagement with the market in premodern Europe could be encapsulated by the question of usury, which hinged on the biblical prohibition. The productivity of money, the value of risk, the nature of partnership, and social justice and obligation were all subsumed under this ancient preoccupation. Unlike today's "interest," medieval and early modern "usury" was more than a purely financial term—it was also a cultural concept laden with significance.[12] Central in its network of meaning was the biblical phrase, "Unto a stranger thou mayest lend upon usury; but unto thy brother thou shalt not lend upon usury" (Deuteronomy 23:19, KJV). The biblical differentiation between brother and stranger captured the aforementioned conflicts embedded in commercialization.

As implied in its title, the current book resonates with two historio-graphic discussions on the dynamics of alienation, association, and identity on the seam of the modern era. As Francesca Trivellato demonstrated in her seminal work, *The Familiarity of Strangers*, early modern commercial life entailed intricate dynamics of trust between people of different ethnoreligious groups, as strangers found ways to trustfully collaborate on the one side, while on the other, belonging to the same group did not guarantee absolute trust.[13] While Trivellato dwelled on the global relations of commerce, it is the national perspective that constitutes the core of the current book, for the issue at hand reflected the very nature of social unity. Was early modern English society composed of brothers or strangers?

Indeed, estrangement was a defining feature in the experience of mod-ern societies, as aptly conveyed in James Vernon's recent book on nineteenth-century Britain. Britain became the first modern society in the nineteenth century, argues Vernon, after reaching a critical mass of change in core dimen-sions of social life that rendered traditional social organization obsolete.[14] Late-seventeenth-century England did not experience such changes to such a degree and was not a society of strangers in Vernon's sense of the term. However, the notion of spreading strangeness was gaining ground, and the changing economic experience was central to this process.

Usury was the nexus of the changing credit relations, the biblical import, and the enduring conflation of finance with Jews—who were themselves con-ceived as the embodiment of alienation. (Shylock, again, neatly encapsulates these preoccupations.) For a long time usury had been identified with Jewish-ness, cast as the diametric opposite of the true spirit of Christianity.[15] Despite the biblical prohibition, Jews practiced usury against Christians because—so it was commonly believed—they were an exclusive fraternity, which under-mined the universal brotherhood heralded by the Gospel. The fact that there was practically no Jewish community in England from 1290 to the last third of the seventeenth century did little to blunt this notion in the English imagi-nation.[16] This was distinctly apparent in Shakespeare's time. Usury is one of the most acute concerns of our age, stated the historian William Harrison in his *Description of England* (1587), and is "now perfectly practised almost by every Christian and so commonly," despite being actually "a trade brought in by the Jews."[17] Thomas Wilson, an MP and a diplomat and civil servant in the Elizabethan government, who dedicated a whole treatise to the problem of usury, phrased this critique much more harshly: "The Jewe, that hath used thys horrible sinne [of usury] most aboue all others . . . hath so robbed the christians wheresoeuer hee came, that his evill lyuinge seene, hee is banished out of the most places in christendome, and worthily; for surely that common weale and country cannot long stande in prosperous estate and welfare, wher merchants and all others become usurers. And no better do I call them then Iewes, yea, worse than any infidel, that wittingly lyue by the onely gayne of their money."[18] Yet increasingly it became apparent that lending with interest had become prevalent in multiple forms throughout English society. Not only did English people lend and borrow frequently with interest, but from the eighteenth century, it came to undergird an elaborate national financial system. The problem of distinguishing between the right Christian practice and the deceptive Jewish one, the "Judaizing critique" in David Nirenberg's terms, became an obsessive concern, which grew alongside the rapid commercial developments since the latter part of the sixteenth century.[19] The tension between the Shylockean foundations of commerce, profit, and contract and Christianity as self-attributed by English society was painfully present.

The development of the market in England during the sixteenth century was a gradual process. Beginning in the 1520s, England's population, which stagnated after the Black Death, began a steady growth: From around 2,400,000 in 1520, it reached 3,900,000 by the 1590s—a remarkable rate by early modern standards. This growth propelled economic activity, which in turn enhanced demographic growth, but it also caused a drastic rise in the demand for goods that the manufacturing infrastructure could not meet.[20] Alongside other factors, it resulted in chronic inflation, a phenomenon new to early modern people. By the turn of the century, the average price of foodstuffs was five times higher than a century earlier.[21] These rates seem fairly low by modern standards, but in those days they were not only a cause for concern but also incomprehensible. The growth of demand was not the sole factor in the soaring of prices. It is assumed that the oversupply of bullion (gold from Latin America and silver from German mines) was one of the major causes of inflation in Europe; in England, however, this effect was not as decisive. Yet as Craig Muldrew demonstrated, it was not only bullion that mattered, but all means of exchange. As cash was used in fewer than 7 percent of economic transactions, credit constituted the lion's share of exchanges. Consequently it was the amount of credit, not only of specie, that mattered. The expansion and increased complexity of the market required the extension of credit, leading to a rise in prices but also bolstering the market itself, in mutually reinforcing dynamics.[22]

The expansion of credit was associated with growing indebtedness. Most early modern English households were both creditors and debtors.[23] The pervasive form of credit was sales credit, which consisted of an informal contract that did not carry interest. These small debts accumulated to vast amounts in a complex social network, and they were eventually reckoned against one another, leaving the smallest possible net amount to be paid in cash. Both trust and moral reputation were indispensable for this complex system to function. All participants had to rely on each other, thus increasing their interdependency and mitigating the growing competitiveness of the early modern market. The latter, claims Muldrew, should be understood in terms of trading in reputation no less than in material goods.[24]

From the late sixteenth century, however, the use of formal forms of credit expanded, especially from the mid-seventeenth century.[25] This was directly connected to the legal changes regarding usury. Until the mid-sixteenth century, the legal approach to usury in England was traditionalist. Attacks on the scholastic doctrine of usury by fifteenth-century thinkers such as Konrad Summenhart and Gabriel Biel, and later John Eck and Martin Bucer, did not gain acceptance in England, where the limitation on moneylending was reinforced by the Act of 1487.[26] In 1545, however, Henry VIII's Parliament licensed interest loans of all sorts with a maximum rate of 10 percent. The statute was revoked in 1552 and revived again in 1571. In 1624 the interest-rate ceiling was reduced to 8 percent, in 1651 to 6 percent, and in 1713 to 5 percent.[27]

These repeated attempts to regulate usury might create the misleading impression of a steady, progressive process. Behind the legislative scenes, however, was a series of intense public controversies, and the legal bottom line did not necessarily represent the parliamentary, let alone the public, approach to the issue.[28] This setting is the focus of Norman Jones's study on the parliamentary discussions on usury between 1571 and 1624. Jones points to a gradual but profound shift between the acts of 1571 and 1624. In the late sixteenth century, the question at hand was the manner of applying the word of God to human law. Eventually, the pragmatic approach prevailed, yet its concern was still religious. During the early seventeenth century, the legal permission to lend with interest given in 1571, which implied an undesired option, became understood as sheer acceptance. Consequently, Jones demonstrates, the parliamentary discourse of the 1620s stressed the secular and economic reasoning that should undergird legislation, with hardly any concern with squaring divine with human law. The difference between the acts was more rhetorical than substantial—both permitted the practice—but this change of rhetoric marked the shift of the cultural perception of usury.

What occasioned this discursive shift? Clearly, economic changes were in play. The late sixteenth century saw the emergence of the great trading companies, the increase in domestic investment, and the spread of credit relations.[29] It was clear that not only the poor borrowed money. But what was the cultural underpinning that facilitated this shift? Jones, and before him Richard Tawney and Benjamin Nelson, emphasized a Protestant revolution in religious ethics, along lines similar to Max Weber's thesis. Protestantism's emphasis on individual conscience made sin a private matter; accordingly, they suggested, the defining element of usury also shifted from action to intent, and the sin moved from the social to the mental sphere. As this could not be policed by the state, social utility remained the only moral standard in the public domain. Economy, according to this explanation, began its divorce proceedings from theology, never to be reunited again.[30]

Despite its conceptual elegance, the Weberian explanation is not borne out by history, as many have shown. If we focus on the debate over usury in England, we see that the promoters of a liberal attitude were not necessarily Puritans, while several of their fiercest opponents were. Moreover, few justifications for usury were made on the ground that it belonged to an inner mental realm.[31] Scholars of continental Europe have demonstrated the inconsistency of the theory with concrete settings, both Catholic and Protestant. Furthermore, as Jones has shown, opposition to the traditional prohibition on usury developed long before the Reformation.[32] Yet criticism of the grand theory does not exclude other possible connections between Protestantism and the development of capitalism. As Johann Sommerville suggested, Protestants' breach with the scholastic heritage eased the intellectual challenges confronted by those who did adopt a progressive stance, compared to their Catholic peers. In other words Protestantism was a supportive condition, not an exclusive historical cause for the growing acceptance of usury.[33]

Lending with interest was not merely culturally accepted. By the turn of the eighteenth century, with the establishment of the Bank of England (1694) as a shareholders' company aimed at funding the ever-growing government expenditure on warfare, interest became "the basis of the whole system of credit," to quote Sir James Steuart.[34] This facilitated an unprecedented national debt, parceled into bonds of government loans. A negotiable commodity, they quickly became the pivot of a prosperous securities market. The national debt kept expanding. It is estimated that from £6.1 million in 1694, lent by five thousand creditors, it swelled to £78 million in 1750, lent by sixty thousand. More and more people became involved and affected by state finance. The number of Jewish stockholders and their invested capital also grew. While the contribution of Jewish investors to the first borrowing of the bank in 1694 was negligible, in the 1710s they figured in the top section of stockholders (10 out of the 74 holders of £5,000 and more). This trend only increased during the eighteenth century.[35]

The new political-economic condition in England during the long eighteenth century imbued the traditional tendency to associate Jews with economy with distinct meaning. The rise of the British Empire to world domination, the consequent increase of the public debt and the centrality of finance, and the rise to prominence of several Jewish financiers have converged to create a particularly fertile ground for a new, modern economic stereotype of the Jew. This book contends that the English association of Jews with finance, and particularly with the modern financial economy, has been boosted by a parallel religious significance of both economy and the Jews in Christian eyes. Economic relations have shaped the vision of society and its boundaries and the map of social communication—and vice versa. Jews have had an indispensable eschatological role in Christian belief, also manifested in the material world: Their economic conduct has been interpreted as revealing contesting notions of trust and belief, of hostility toward Christianity, and of their own ideas of redemption. This turned notions of Jews and Judaism, as well as of Jewish history, into conceptual keys with which to rework contemporaries' own moral and legal attitudes to commercial reality. Consequently, these notions offer a distinct analytical perspective for understanding how eighteenth-century people made sense of that reality.

This book focuses on the rise of finance and the apprehensions that accompanied it. Yet another dimension was entwined to this story—the debate over luxury. In the long eighteenth century, with the dramatic expansion of global commerce, luxury goods reached broad sections of society. New foods and consumer goods encouraged the development of new forms of sociability and civility, heralding social and intellectual shifts. Eighteenth-century culture saw luxury as a positive progressive force that promoted the arts, culture, and politeness, let alone the economy; at the same time it was seen as a force that threatened the cultivation of both society and the individual. Thus during that period both the definition of luxury and its moral evaluation became contested. In the words of Maxine Berg and Elizabeth Eger, "luxury was no less than the keyword of the period, a central term in the language of cultural transformation."[36]

This book argues that in its rhetorical and cultural levels, the debate about luxury had much in common with the debates about finance and the status of the Jews in the long eighteenth century. All three were construed as a force that "feminized" society; as an urban force that thwarted the genuine national spirit; as economically unproductive; as a peril to religion; and as essentially related to foreign forces that defied the national interest.[37] The overlapping of the three issues made the Jews a "thick concept" for contemporaries, whose importance went beyond its bounds and became a vehicle for broader deliberation. In the English context of the long eighteenth century, one's approach to the Jews could plausibly project on the questions of luxury and finance, and vice versa.

The braiding of political-economic concerns with the development of Anglo-Jewish society dovetails with the growing scholarly interest in Jews' economic life—which some refer to as an economic turn in Jewish history. In general this body of works explores the ways economic discourses and practices have shaped Jewish identities and experiences, especially in their passage into "modernity." Derek Penslar's classic work and more recent ones by Cornelia Aust, Adam Teller, Rebecca Kobrin, and others demonstrate this trend.[38] Conversely, my book looks at the relationships between Jews/Judaism and the economic discourse as a means for understanding more subtly the development of the latter and does not engage with its influence on the intra-Jewish world. Thus, although the book resonates with this growing body of works, it does not dialogue with it directly.

The current book is inspired particularly by two recent works in the field—Jonathan Karp's *The Politics of Jewish Commerce* (2008) and Francesca Trivellato's *The Promise and Peril of Credit* (2019). Both take the early modern economic discourse about the Jews as a pathway for delving into the profoundly shifting European economic thought of the time. Central for both projects is a subtle analysis of the relations between ideas and the changing concrete realities. Consequently, they reveal the impact of notions and images of "Jewish commerce" in the development of protomodern political and economic paradigms and mechanisms.[39]

Like these works, the present book demonstrates that Jews are a revealing key for understanding the tensions through which capitalism has developed in Europe. It departs from them however on two levels—perspective and methodology. Karp provides a broad European account of the early modern development of the political and economic discourses on the Jews. To maintain such an overview, he focuses on the nexus of the political and economic, and on select writers whom he uses to represent different national settings. Trivellato's book has a similar geographical scope, and it too focuses on economic writers (in the inclusive sense). The geohistorical breadth of both works, I believe, comes at the price of narrowing the thematic scope. In contrast, by focusing on the English case (with auxiliary comparisons), I wish to provide a more subtle analysis of the cultural dynamics behind the historical changes. This focus also allows a broader thematic view, exploring diverse discursive settings rather than concentrating on distinct economic or political figures engaged directly with the status of the Jews. Many of the texts studied in the current book—biblical commentaries, travelogues, popular print, and drama—are seemingly peripheral to the political-economic tensions of the time. Yet bringing them together uncovers the underlying engagements with these tensions that permeated contemporary discourse.

Shifting the focus away from intellectual history to the broader economic and political culture, the book thus advocates a broad and culturally oriented approach to the economic field as organically integrated with other social activities and beliefs. Economic culture in its full sense, it premises, is expressed not only in economic thought and policy but in a broad array of cultural productions. Accordingly, it highlights the dependencies of the economy and social norms and imagery, implying a broader conception of the pool of sources historians may employ to understand economic culture.[40] This broader outlook could better guide us, I suggest, in discerning the concerns of ordinary contemporaries and the contested reception of economic ideologies and practices. Beyond that, unlike "proper" economic writing, these diverse discourses are essential for understanding Jewish-Christian relations as well, and the operating of economy in them. As illustrated in the following chapters, this different perspective reveals the shifts, conflicts, and frictions within contemporary conceptions of the relations between Jews and finance, which often do not feature a clear and predictable correlation between one's approaches to commerce and to the Jews.

While scholars of Jewish history have focused on the Continent, it was England that laid the groundwork of the modern economy. Understanding the modern ties of Jews and economy—both concrete and symbolic—must involve an in-depth study of this setting. This focus allows subtle scrutiny of the economic imagery of the Jews and the intricate ties of pro- and anti-Jewish attitudes, and may shed new light on the conflictual relations of economic liberalism and the civil and economic evaluation of the Jews. It also allows a deeper look at the social functions these sets of images and notions fulfilled. As this book will demonstrate, concerns and discussions on economy and on the Jews were imperative in the broader process of the formation of British identity in the long eighteenth century.

The focus on the English setting carries advantages, as I hope to convince, but also a price: It might veil the imperial context that was building up during the long eighteenth century and which gradually became a fundamental factor in British economy. An increasing portion of the capital invested in the financial market came from colonial trade profits. Conversely, companies whose stocks were traded on the market were increasingly involved in that trade. Capital, credit, and colonization were thus intrinsically connected. So was slavery: From the mid-seventeenth to the early nineteenth century, it is estimated that more than three million Africans were transported to British colonies.

Jewish merchants and investors have played a key role in all these developments. In recent years scholars have increasingly explored this involvement after long years of neglect. Unfortunately, comprehensive engagement with this topic is beyond the scope of the current book. The theme is engaged with sporadically in the book, and the reader may draw on other existing works for that purpose. Indeed, an integrative account of Jews' role—both real and imagined—in the development of modern finance, and in the colonial trade in commodities and human beings, has yet to be published.[41]

* * *

A terminological note regarding my use of "England" and "Britain" and their derivative adjectives is in order. The political entity studied here underwent fundamental transformations during the period under study. In 1535 Wales was annexed to the Kingdom of England, and in 1707 Great Britain was formed with their union with Scotland. In 1801 the union with Ireland formed the United Kingdom. While the book begins with seventeenth-century England and ends with the early nineteenth-century United Kingdom, most of the sources, figures, and historical settings studied here are English, not least due to the fact that Jews concentrated in London and several other major towns in England. Accordingly I will refer to England rather than Britain, unless when referring to a formal state apparatus or in a quote.

Relatedly, note that the historical account set here is an *Anglo*-Jewish history. Its focus is not on the development of the Jewish community but rather on the way it figured in English imagination and on the functions it played over the long eighteenth century.[42] Perhaps unsurprisingly, Judeophobia was expansive in this matrix of shifting attitudes. Accordingly this book is embroiled in the history of antisemitism, a theme on which intensive critical discussion has been going in recent years, in both academia (the *American Historical Review* and *Zion* have dedicated special issues to it) and the public sphere. The debate, first of all, is conceptual. Is there a definition of antisemitism that can describe the broad range of historical phenomena of Judeophobia without losing its analytical force? While the dominant voice advocates the use of the term and its analytical importance, others have been increasingly criticizing it. Holocaust historian Yehuda Bauer admitted that the concept blurs scholarly efforts to make distinctions between phenomena, but that its use is yet warranted for lack of a better one. Conversely, Jonathan Judaken proposed using the term *Judeophobia* instead.[43]

The question here is not merely terminological but one that projects dramatically on other issues of high public profile and even political implications. Are the phenomena of Jew-hatred distinctly different from other historical and current forms of xenophobia, and if so, how? Was the Holocaust the "natural" culmination of this history or a radical divergence within it? What is the relationship between traditional and contemporary forms of Jew-hatred? The terminological policy one follows implies certain approaches to these dilemmas, with methodological implications relevant to the present book. Using the terminological lens of antisemitism encourages comparisons within Jewish history and emphasis on continuities; its avoidance invites comparisons with other sorts of xenophobia and emphasis on discontinuities. The chosen term thus encapsulates a debate between "eternalist" and "historicist" approaches to phenomena of Jew-hatred, the former affiliating them together as essentially "antisemitic," while the latter tends to see them as a series of distinct, contextually embedded cases.

In this book the term *antisemitism* is deliberately avoided. As I hope to convince in the following chapters, the historical developments analyzed are characterized by changes and idiosyncrasies more than by continuities. Thus, in contrast with works on early modern Anglo-Jewish history stressing the persistence of antisemitic traditions,[44] I propose that a more adequate way to make Judeophobic incidents comprehensible is by contextualizing them within the shifts in English society during the long eighteenth century. Here I run the opposite risk of being biased to see phenomena as discrete and similarities as superficial, overlooking the alternative analysis of continuous traditions.

Avoiding the term allows a more subtle observation of the intricate and varied relations between manifestations of Judeophobia and Judeophilia.

"Philosemitism" is only a little less fraught with tensions and dilemmas than its counterpart. Indeed, some critics have argued that it is analytically useful to see both phenomena as offshoots of the same root.[45] Zygmunt Bauman usefully developed the concept of "allosemitism" (coined by Artur Sandauer) to denote the practice of "setting the Jews apart as people radically different from all the others, needing separate concepts to describe and comprehend them and special treatment in all or most social intercourse." Allosemitic discourse is essentially exceptionalist but does not imply a specifically negative or positive approach (although it does imply a radical approach of some sort). Rather, in a deeper sense, it implies the inherent ambiguity of Jews, their being a stumbling block to the attempt of making order in the world. It is thus, according to Bauman, the primary impetus underlying both anti- and philosemitism, making the Jew an abstract, ahistorical concept, detached from concrete social life.[46]

The allosemitic disposition contradicts the approach of "normalizing" the Jews. Yet, as the historians Adam Sutcliffe and Jonathan Karp wonder, the latter is probably an inherently unattainable aspiration in a Christian civilization and therefore an ahistorical yardstick for the evaluation of non-Jewish attitudes toward Jews—at least in the past. Indeed, Sutcliffe and Karp's revitalizing approach to the study of philosemitism demonstrates the need for an analysis of the varied historical manifestations of this phenomenon in their unique contexts, as a fundamental stage in such metadiscussion.[47] As the following chapters demonstrate, the shifts between pro- and anti-Jewish positions in the long eighteenth century were nuanced: Similar images or accounts had different meanings and implications in different contexts and served different aims.

Taking this conceptual deliberation into account, I will proceed with terminological caution and resume this discussion in the Epilogue.

* * *

The book is arranged both chronologically and thematically, spanning the period from the mid-seventeenth to the early nineteenth century. Commercialization was a long historical process, stretching beyond this book's chronological scope. Instead, it is concerned with what could be loosely termed the long Financial Revolution. Carl Wennerlind recently claimed that focusing on the institutional novelties of the 1690s obscures previous innovations in political economy that preceded them and served as their theoretical support.[48] This book shares this perspective and stretches the Financial Revolution back to the early seventeenth century. Yet it also stretches it forward in time, to the early nineteenth century, when—after Britain's temporary withdrawal from the gold standard and the following Bullionist controversy—the age of paper money began.[49] This periodization also fits the basic framework of Anglo-Jewish history: from the polemic on Jewish readmission in the 1650s to the onset of the campaign for emancipation in the 1830s.

This book is structured in three thematic parts: "Usury," which deals with the period between the middle of the seventeenth century to the middle of the eighteenth century, and elaborates on the dismantling of the traditional ethics of usury and the new perceptions of the Jews it entailed; "Finance," which deals with the eighteenth century and delves into the new political-economic circumstances that evolved during the so-called Financial Revolution and the heated discussions on the Jews in its wake; and "Reform," which focuses on the late eighteenth to the early nineteenth century, and investigates the polemical public discourse on the improvement and emancipation of the Jews in England during this period.

Part I, "Usury" (Chapters 1–3), focuses on the earlier period of the Financial Revolution in the second half of the seventeenth and the beginning of the eighteenth century, and examines the persistent ethical problems of usury. Usury effectively epitomized the cultural conflicts embedded in commercialization, and at the same time the problem of integrating Jews within Christian society. This part proposes that the idea of usury was entrenched not only in economic ideology but also in historical imagination. I illustrate the complex and interrelated discussions about Jews and usury through different themes and demonstrate how far they are from a simple continuation of medieval prejudices. Chapter 1 investigates the repercussions of the debate regarding usury on the public controversy over Jewish readmission in the 1650s. It demonstrates that the polemic implied a historiographic debate over the place of usury in Anglo-Jewish medieval history. The traditional historical account associated Jews and usury and explained the expulsion against that backdrop. Remarkably, however, this proved to be a side issue in the attack against the Jewish cause. Counterintuitively, staunch opponents of readmission sought to revise and belittle the association between Jews and usury, while supporters of the readmission accepted the traditional narrative. I explain this anomaly by demonstrating the critical role played by the historical narrative of the expulsion in the debate, and its mutual relations with the changing conception of lending with interest.

Chapter 2 demonstrates the profound contemporary shifts in the understanding of the biblical prohibition on usury. English Bible commentaries of the seventeenth and eighteenth centuries reveal a profound change in the way usury was understood and narrated from the last third of the seventeenth century. Earlier biblical discourse had made sense of usury by associating it with the postbiblical history of the Jews as undermining Christian society through their economic practices. From the latter part of the seventeenth century, however, the focus turned to an imagined account of the ancient Israelites, which implied a novel understanding of usury: Historical descriptions of this society as an encapsulated rural autarky became a basis for explaining usury as an irrelevant prohibition. This became a stock description among English writers and facilitated the detachment of the biblical ethics of usury from contemporary English society.

Chapter 3 ties together contemporaries' engagement with past and present Jews through the genre of ethnography. The seventeenth century saw a growing interest in the ethnography of the Jews, involving both their ancient past and present. This chapter demonstrates the decline of the idea of usury as an organizing principle of contemporary Jewish economic life in English eyes. It was replaced by a growing preoccupation with the socioeconomic characteristics of the ancient Jews, whose organizing structure was depicted very similarly to the shift described in Chapter 2. The last section of the chapter ties Part I together, fleshing out a feature that played an essential role in the shifts that marked the different genres and cases: the evolution of a historical analytical perspective on Jewish economic life. This move entailed a historical reimagination of the Jews, which undermined the cultural force of usury.

Part II, "Finance" (Chapters 4–7), focuses on the bulk of the eighteenth century and dwells on the anxieties inflamed by the success of the new public credit system. These related to the modern concept of national debt, commonly seen not only as ever-burgeoning but also as having transformed social and political relations into creditor-debtor relations and subjected the state to speculation. The chapters in this part demonstrate how these concerns became mediated through contemporary discourse on the Jews. While Part I reveals how the traditional concept of usury was dismantled during the second half of the seventeenth century, here I argue that the setting of the mid-eighteenth century nurtured a new association of Jews with finance: as undermining not private finance (through usury) but public finance and the very integrity of English society and politics. The need to fund the wars of the 1740s–1760s fostered the rise of several spectacularly successful Jewish financiers. During this belligerent period, which shaped the future trajectories of British nationality, public concerns over empire, politics, finance, and religion meshed. This setting incited the consolidation of a new stereotypical figure of the Jewish financier, which proved a compelling lightning rod for all these concerns.

Chapter 4 explores the expanding discourse against finance from the 1690s to the early eighteenth century. It investigates the involvement of Jews in the financial market and shows that, on the one hand, it was significantly increasing, yet on the other hand, notwithstanding the intense public critique against the expanding market, Jews were not seen as a special target. The association of the financial market and Jews was not a natural transition from the traditional image of the usurious Jew, as often portrayed; rather, as demonstrated in the following chapters, it was a new notion that evolved in the particular concrete context of mid-eighteenth-century England.

Chapter 5 addresses the public agitation over the 1753 Jewish Naturalization Bill—the most consequential episode between the readmission of the Jews and their mid-nineteenth-century emancipation. The bill offered Jews a private act of naturalization without the sacramental test. A costly and cumbersome process, the measure could have had only minor practical impact; however, it ignited public clamor through hundreds of newspaper columns, pamphlets, and prints. What made it so resonant, and why were its opponents so successful? It is commonly argued that the affair was an instance of partisan conflict in which the Jews themselves played an incidental role. Alternatively, this chapter argues that a central reason for its resonance was that the discussion about the Jews evoked concerns with the expanding financial market and its sociopolitical implications. By the 1750s the linkage of Jews in public imagery with destructive aspects of finance was gradually taking shape, lending the opposition to the bill an effective polemical vocabulary.

Chapter 6 explores the development and consolidation of a new stereotypical Jewish figure, tightly related to finance. Against the backdrop of the decline of the traditional emphasis on Jewish usury charted in Part I, new patterns of representation evolved in the eighteenth century. The chapter concentrates on drama and popular print and demonstrates a development of two stages. While at the beginning of the century it became common to portray the Jew as threatening to defile the English woman, around midcentury this representation combined with the charge of financial manipulation. This move is reflected by the shift in the productions of *The Merchant of Venice* and in their public resonance throughout the century, from low-key references in the first decades to a powerful motif in the public discourse from the midcentury.

Chapter 7 reveals two dimensions that rendered the new Jew so effective for engaging socioeconomic concerns: the linkage of finance with gender, and the framing of the discourse within eschatological rhetoric. These facilitated scapegoating the Jew as a financial demoralizer. In contrast to other historians, I argue that the trigger for this move was not a counter-reaction to financial developments but rather the establishment and cultural acceptance of finance—the image of the Jew was used not to denounce finance but to distinguish between its "right" and "wrong" uses. Accordingly, the changing representation of the Jew illuminates contemporary ideas about English society and economy not less, and perhaps even more, than the light they throw on Anglo-Jewish relations.

Part III, "Reform" (Chapters 8–9), discusses the mental convergence of Jews and finance during the early Age of Reform (c. 1790s–1830s), when anxieties about the power of finance and the paper economy blended with new agendas of reforming English society and the Jewish community alike. These trends resulted in new modes of discourse about both the Jews and the economy and on their mutual entanglement. Chapter 8 engages the perceived nexus of Jews and the economy through the intensifying discourse on Jewish criminality. In the second half of the eighteenth century, a growing preoccupation with Jewish crime developed into a conception of a Jewish illicit counter-economy of trade in stolen goods. This added to their perception—illustrated in Part II—as manipulators of the poorly regulated credit market who capitalized on its anonymity and exploited its deficiencies. Both were conceived as orchestrated, collective maneuvers undermining and corrupting the very bases of England's prosperity: commerce and credit.

Chapter 9 explores the emerging discourse on Jewish emancipation in the early nineteenth century. The civil status of the Jews became a much-discussed issue in France and Germany in the years around the French Revolution, and the public debates over it provoked a parallel discussion in England. This controversy was decisive not only regarding the question of church-state relations but also as it resonated with contemporary deliberations on the moral, social, and political implications of the financial system. The chapter begins in the 1790s and ends when this discourse enters Parliament in 1830, straddling the blurry boundary between the early modern and modern periods. It illustrates the intricate relations among the varied attitudes to the bourgeoning financial network and between those and the civil status of the Jews. By the time the issue becomes a parliamentary debate, the linkage between Jews and finance has lost its cultural force. The last part of the chapter aims to explain this shift in terms of the shifting attitude of English society to the financial market and the cultural ramifications of this shift.

* * *

The shadow of Karl Marx's 1844 essay, "On the Jewish Question," still hovers over discussions of Jews and the economy. Marx equated the spirit of Judaism with capitalism. Money, "the jealous god of Israel," has commodified everything, robbing the worlds of nature and man of their distinct value and estranging the essence of man's work and existence. It has become the god of the world. In Marx's view, capitalism was inherently Jewish. His premises were elaborated by German sociologist Werner Sombart, who argued, in his 1911 *The Jews and Modern Capitalism*, that not only was capitalism essentially Jewish, and not only did the Jews benefit uniquely from its development, but that the Jews set it in motion and, consequently, reshaped the trajectory of world history. These basic ideas were adopted by the antisemitic critique that saw Jewish economic activity as the basis for Jewish power and became a backbone of Nazi propaganda. It is therefore no surprise that the discussion of Jews and capitalism became highly charged after the Holocaust, and that historians largely avoided it for half a century.

However, circumventing the issue meant throwing the baby out with the bathwater. With little in the way of an alternative discussion, shunning it entrenched the Marx-Sombart thesis as a common intuition. The new interest in Jewish economic history, broadly construed (as touched on earlier in this Introduction), in the early twenty-first century began filling this gap. The new wave of studies offers—for most cases—fine-grained contextualized investigations that reveal both the inadequacies of essentialist grand theories and the pitfalls in a presumed linkage of Jews with capitalism.[50]

This book joins this project, but rather than exposing distinct Jewish economic lives, it aims at the tortuous history of the cultural association of Jews with modern finance itself. If you will, it is an attempt at revealing one of the histories of the modern essentialist approach to the relation of Jews and economy. Digging into the context of English society on the seam of the early modern and modern periods, it delineates the contingencies and conflicts through which these sets of images and notions ebbed and flowed, and at times were discarded tout court.

PART I

Usury

Chapter 1

Jewish Usury, Jewish Historiography, and the Readmission Polemic of the 1650s

Interest in Jews and Judaism increased consistently through the first decades of the seventeenth century and burst into public attention in the 1650s. Under the Cromwellian Commonwealth, theological issues were remodeled as political questions, and the relation between Jews and revolutionized England became a central topic. The Jewish readmission polemic broke out in September 1655 with the arrival in England of the Amsterdam-based rabbi Menasseh ben Israel and his appeal to Cromwell and the Parliament for the readmission of the Jews. In December Cromwell convened the Whitehall Conference to discuss the issue, but it dispersed after two weeks without reaching any conclusion.[1]

For an abortive scheme with seemingly no direct political significance, the polemic ranked high in historical memory. Apparently, it was unique in relation to other seventeenth-century discussions on similar questions elsewhere: The discussion on Jewish resettlement in England had surfaced long before Cromwell and Menasseh ben Israel triggered the formal debate and continued afterward; it was also not confined to the political realm but extended to the public sphere, interlacing with broader religious and national sentiments.[2] Much ink has been spilled on the topic in the last two centuries, interpreting the event from various perspectives and employing it for different goals. In the nineteenth century, when the growing Jewish community was pressed to prove its Englishness, it was recast into a teleological heroic narrative of growing religious tolerance, culminating in emancipation.[3] This was sidelined by the mid-twentieth century when the focus shifted to the polemic's theological aspects, emphasizing the role of persistent English involvement in Hebraism and millenarian philosemitism.[4] Most recently, in the vein of placing the question of English identity at the center of scholarly attention, the controversy was framed as partaking in the discourse of England as a divinely chosen nation,[5] and conversely in larger political-legal debates crucial in establishing new citizen-state relations at that time.[6]

What all these approaches share is downplaying the economic dimensions of the discourse. Seemingly, there is a good case for that. As far as the accounts of the Whitehall Conference testify, economic arguments were not the central thread. Baptist minister Henry Jessey, who attended the conference and published an account of it, introduced the merchants' arguments without elaborating on the deliberation. Nathaniel Crouch, who included an account of the conference in a compilation of texts concerning Jewish matters, noted the merchants' objection as the chief cause of the plan's failure, yet he did not elaborate any further on the actual economic controversy.[7] As David Katz argues, mercantile interests were mentioned by the supporters of the Jewish cause only reluctantly and in passing, nor did its opponents employ it as a central argument.[8]

This reluctance was unexpected, at least for Menasseh ben Israel, who sought to hinge the discourse on the economic issue. As Benjamin Braude has illustrated, he intended the specific version of *Hope of Israel* that was to be translated into English to convey that message.[9] He opened his argument in the *Humble Addresses*, the petition he handed to Cromwell and the Council of State, by stressing the Jews' economic utility, merchandizing being their "proper profession." This view was underpinned by a historical-providential narrative: Banished from their land, the Jews were given by God a "natural instinct" for commerce as compensation for the lack of land; and until the end of times, when they shall return to their land, must they commit to merchandize. This makes them an "infallible profit" for their hosting countries, much more than any other minority, for the Jews' dedication to exchange and innovations promote commerce wherever they dwell.[10]

To prove the Jews' mercantile advantage, Menasseh ben Israel saw it crucial to exonerate them first from the accusation that they undermine Christian material wellbeing by their usury (alongside threatening Christian lives with ritual murder and Christian souls by conversion). Seeking to demystify Jewish usury, he argued that it was far from being a Jewish preoccupation, as most of them "hold it infamous to use it." True, many Jews invest their money in banks for interest, yet they do so with a small profit and with the borrower's consent. And although they are allowed by Scriptures to lend on interest to non-Jews, they are nonetheless forbidden to defraud them, and because high interest is considered robbery, it is proscribed. The few Jews who do lend at excessive rates "do it not as Jews simply, but as wicked Jews, as amongst all nations there are found generally some Usurers."[11]

As far as the sources we have testify, Menasseh ben Israel was seemingly fighting on the wrong front. Not only did the documentation we have from the Whitehall Conference, as I have noted, refrain from economic discussion, but the public polemical material mostly downplayed it as well. This is not to say that economic arguments were absent; rather, they were minor in importance. Paradoxically, while opponents to readmission did not find such accusations effective, as I shall soon show, advocates of the Jews—such as John Dury and Thomas Barlow—accompanied their support, which was based on millenarian expectations, with traditional economic prejudices. What facilitated this odd constellation? My argument here is that economic questions did not fade out of the polemic; rather, they received a different and somewhat unexpected focus. It was not the economic features of contemporary Jews at stake—but their economic *history*. Underpinning the polemic was a debate on the account of medieval Anglo-Jewish relations. And usury was a crucial component in it.

* * *

The trigger to this debate was inadvertent and initially did not at all pertain to the question of readmission. Although written evidence of the 1290 expulsion decree was never found, the common belief in the seventeenth century and before was that the major reason for the expulsion had been Jewish usury. King Edward I, who banished the Jews, stated in a letter to the Barons of the Exchequer on November 5, 1290 (about two months after the last Jews had left) that, whereas the Jews transgressed the prohibition to lend on usury to the Christian, and afterward "maliciously deliberating amongst themselves, changed the kind of usury into a worse, which they called 'courtesy' (*curialitatem*), and depressed the king's people under colour of such by an error double that of the previous one; wherefore the king, by reason of their errors and for the honour of Christ, has caused the Jews to leave his realm as perfidious men."[12]

This became a common thread in early modern historical accounts of the event.[13] It was most marked in the account of the distinguished jurist and politician Sir Edward Coke (1552–1634). In his magnum opus, *Institutes of the Laws of England*, published partly posthumously, he argued that the Jews' immersion with usury was central to Anglo-Jewish history and the fundamental reason for their departure. Against this backdrop, he added, Edward I decreed the *Statutum de Judaismo*, designed to place a total ban on Jewish usury. The decree, accordingly, suppressed their fundamental livelihood and had consequential outcomes: "[It] struck at the rout of this pestilent weed, for hereby usury itself was forbidden; and thereupon the cruell Jews thirsting after wicked gain, to the number of 15,060 departed out of this Realm into foreign parts, where they might use their Jewish trade of usury."[14]

As it was known that the Jews left England in 1290, Coke dated the undated *Statutum de Judaismo* to the same year. Coke had died twenty years before the readmission became a political question and did not refer to such an eventuality, yet his writing was highly significant in the polemic. Despite his blunt Judeophobia, within one generation its effect turned about-face.[15] For if the denial of the Jews' livelihood made them leave England of their own will, this obviated any parliamentary or royal edict, and if so, there was no legal impediment to their readmission.[16] Moreover, although Coke referred to usury as an act against the laws of God, nature, and the ancient constitution, he admitted that all prohibitions against it were void by the acts of Henry VIII (1545) and Elizabeth (1572), which had allowed it under certain limits.[17] Consequently, if one applies Coke's thesis to the readmission question, the key factor necessitating the withdrawal of the Jews could paradoxically serve their readmission.

Indeed, Coke's anti-Jewish account was employed by supporters of readmission. The lawyers in Whitehall agreed that there was no legal impediment to readmission, basing this claim on Coke's historical account, as presented to the committee by Lord Chief Baron of the Exchequer William Steele (1610–1680). Steele argued that before the Jews were banished in 1290, King Edward I had "restrained their excessive taking of Usury," attaching, like Coke, the decrees installed in the *Statutum de Judaismo* to the expulsion itself.[18] This view was promoted by a pamphlet on tolerating the Jews in England written by the Oxford scholar and librarian Thomas Barlow (1608/9–1691), which presumably was available to the delegates. Relying on Coke's historical narrative, Barlow argued that, because the main objection to the Jews was their harmful usury and because nowadays usury was accepted in Christian polities, not letting the Jews settle in England was "irrational."[19] The Jews' "being the greatest Usurers in the World" did not entail a legal impediment but was rather a matter for close government attention.[20]

Coke's narrative retained its influence for more than a century, as is apparent in various and unrelated texts on Jewish and medieval English history. Some of these were staunchly anti-Jewish, others addressed the Jews benevolently, while still others had a mixed approach. All conflated the question of usury with that of readmission, yet each judged the nature of usury differently.[21]

This somewhat odd move was observed by the sharpest opponent of readmission, lawyer and antiquarian William Prynne (1600–1669). His *Short Demurrer to the Jewes* was hastily published in December 1655 and reached the delegates just before the final meeting. Plausibly, it was a significant factor in the failure of the readmission advocates.[22] Prynne also offered a historical account, and Jewish economy was central to it, too. He argued that "Jewish money" played a fundamental role in history in general, and in medieval Anglo-Jewish history particularly. Through it, the Jews maneuvered Christian rulers, not only for their own interests but also against Christianity—inducing them "to perpetrate most unchristian, and antichristian actions."[23]

Yet despite this metaphysical conception of Jewish money, Prynne diminished the role of usury in the historical account. He painstakingly minimized the moneylending role played by Jews in medieval England, arguing that only an elite minority of Anglo-Jews held this profession. Moreover, he argued that usurious practices were only a subsidiary reason for their expulsion in 1290. Usury had been universally prohibited in England long before, to Christians and Jews alike, and any Jewish usurer in medieval England was under a decree of banishment without any need for a further general edict. Accordingly, as far as it related to usury, the *Statutum de Judaismo* only confirmed former laws. Relying on archival materials, Prynne dated the act to 1275 and not 1290, discarding the very basis of Coke's historical account. For all these reasons, Prynne argued—in contrast to Coke and to most other historiographers—usurious practices could not have been a central factor leading to the final expulsion.[24]

It is precisely the unintended implications of Coke's narrative and their use by supporters of readmission, I suggest, that pushed Prynne to offer a historical narrative with an alternative balance of factors. He dedicated a significant portion of his text, which was doubled by the second edition, as well as in other works, to refute Coke's thesis.[25] The most crucial part of the expulsion Prynne sought to prove, against Coke's account, was that it derived solely from a formal edict—a "new special Act," rather than a voluntary departure of the Jews. Such a source was never found, yet Prynne insisted that a parliamentary and royal edict of expulsion did exit, stating that the banishment "was by the unanimous desire, Judgement, Edict, and Decree both of the King and his Parliament; and not by the King alone: and this Banishment, total, of them all, and likewise final, Never to return into England. Which Edict and Decree though not now extant in our Parliament Rolls (many of which are utterly lost) nor in our printed Statutes; yet it is mentioned by all these Authorities."[26]

Prynne sought to establish the legal status of the Jews' banishment, which Coke himself undermined by emphasizing the charge of usury. Instead of usury, Prynne underscored that "the Jews were all judicially really expelled & banished the Realm in 18 E. 1. [1290] both by the King and Parliament, and that principally for their infidelity not Usury."[27]

This is not to say that Prynne diminished the economic features of the Jews tout court, but only their usury. In his account, "Jewish money" provided effectual means for undermining English society and polity: It enabled the Jews to intrude into and damage the Anglo-Christian constitution. They did so in medieval times; and they will do so with much greater damage, Prynne argued, in our own erratic times.[28]

Mid-seventeenth century England was changing not only politically and socially, but also economically. The English financial sector was developing significantly. Private goldsmith banks began functioning not only as custodians of money but as investors, thus greatly expanding credit. The elaborate system of face-to-face credit that dominated the English economy from the sixteenth century—as skillfully analyzed by Craig Muldrew—was giving way to a growing use of formal credit modes such as bonds, bills, and moneylending, which involved an additional payment over the principal.[29] As portrayed earlier, in the Introduction, the parliamentary discourse was moving from traditional disapproval of usury, to its pragmatic acceptance (as seen in the Act of 1571), to its ideological approval marked by the 1624 act. By the mid-seventeenth century, the intense public polemic on these issues was waning, leaving usury as an accepted practice.[30] As we have seen, some advocates of the Jewish cause used the anachronism of usury to prove that not letting Jews into England was nonsensical. This was latently implied in Coke's own account that usury had been legally approved from the mid-sixteenth century.

To neutralize the inadvertent explosive Coke had set with his usury-based narrative, and foreseeing that this was no longer an effective charge against the Jews, Prynne had to decouple the longstanding compound of Jews and usury—against both early modern and medieval historical accounts. This was an odd move in what could otherwise be seen as a vehement anti-Jewish attack. This oddity was all the more highlighted by his relying on none other than his opponent, Menasseh ben Israel, for confirmation that the Jews did not depend on moneylending for their livelihood. Swallowing this bitter pill was necessary for undermining the traditional usury account, a move that in the final balance paid more.[31]

While other adversaries of readmission shared Prynne's narrative, not all of them did so.[32] Another harsh adversary of readmission, William Hughes (1587/8–1663?), argued that the Jews are noted "for that practice of Usury of which our adversary [Menasseh ben Israel] would clear them," and that "usury with great extortion" was their predominant practice in England.[33] He rejected Coke's emphasis on usury as an exclusive cause for the expulsion, yet argued that nonetheless it was a major one among others. Apparently, Prynne's approach was more influential. Only one writer who replied to the attack against the Jewish cause found it necessary to defend the Jews from usury, and, moreover, did that in a minor way.[34] Possibly, they all conceived the issue to be rather insignificant in the overall attack on the Jewish cause. Indeed, when Menasseh ben Israel replied to his adversaries in his *Vindiciae Judaeorum* (1656), he hardly mentioned usury anymore.[35]

Presumably, Prynne's alternative medieval historiography had another goal: sidelining Menasseh ben Israel's attempt to direct the discussion to economic issues by focusing on the Jews' religious and social rather than economic features. He correctly observed that Menasseh ben Israel mostly insists on the commercial benefit England would obtain from readmission, profit being "a most powerfull motive and which all the world prefers before all other things." Accepting the Jews on this ground, he argued, would be "a sign we love their money better than their souls or our own."[36] This last contention was shared among supporters of the readmission, the only difference being that they would argue a very different case for the progress of Christianity. At the end of the day, as David Katz demonstrates, the readmission polemic focused not on economic but religious issues.[37] However, this contention must be qualified: Indeed, for most writers the economic features of the Jews did not matter much; yet their economic *history* was of particular importance.

* * *

It was not only the Jews' medieval economic history that was re-narrated in the mid-seventeenth century. In the rest of this chapter and in the following one, I illuminate another change of perspective regarding Jewish economic history and argue for its significance in English economic culture. At the center of this historical exploration was none other than the ancient Israelite society and its regulation of usury. This was a marked shift, for medieval and early modern discourse on usury was infused with notions about *present-day* Jews (or, as I have shown in this chapter, about recent Jewish history). The shift to ancient Jewish history evolved from the new intellectual tendencies of European humanists from the late sixteenth century forward, a context to be discussed shortly. Meanwhile, let us delve into an early English elaboration of this conceptualization.

In 1656 James Harrington's republican magnum opus, *The Commonwealth of Oceana*, a benchmark of political thought, was published. Almost nothing is known of Harrington's activities and political opinions before this publication. *Oceana* was a utopian text with a concrete context: an ideal program for a republic that referred specifically to English conditions and history. Like the Jewish readmission polemic, *Oceana* was an offshoot of the English Revolution. Yet the connection of the book and the historical events went deeper.[38]

Jews turn up in the work in a double manner. First, in direct relation to the readmission polemic, Harrington proposed in the introduction to *Oceana* to establish a Jewish settlement in Ireland, which would foster England's wealth. He added this scheme shortly before publication, in the wake of the readmission polemic and concurrent with Cromwell's plantation of Ireland.[39] Notwithstanding such acceptance, Harrington excluded Jewish settlement in England proper. Receiving the Jews in England would maim the commonwealth, "for they of all nations never incorporate but, taking up the room of a limb, are of no use or office to the body, while they suck the nourishment which would sustain a natural and useful member." The peril is made clearer later, when he criticizes current magistrates as being driven by "such a selling, such a *Jewish* humor" [Harrington's italics], namely a commercial spirit, against the interest of a commonwealth.[40]

However, the critique of the Jews was ambiguous. They were hyper-commercialized ("altogether for merchandise"), yet at the same time, argued Harrington, they maintained their age-old agrarian traits (when they were "altogether for agriculture"). Accordingly, they could excel in both and contribute to England's expansion in both commerce and agriculture. This passage resonated with Menasseh ben Israel's claim in the *Humble Addresses* that the Jews were originally rural people and that they would resume that occupation in the (messianic) future. Similarly, Harrington also drew a line of continuity between the ancient agricultural Israelites and contemporary Jews who still possess the hereditary rural trait that makes them fit as colonizers.[41]

This leads to the second and main dimension of Harrington's relation to Jews. His entire goal was to establish a sociopolitical organization modeled after the ancient Israelite social constitution. Large portions were dedicated to articulating this polity, which he regarded as founded on both natural and divine laws, hence as the purest political model.[42] The essence of this model was the Israelite agrarian law, which constituted a stable and enduring republican commonwealth. Prima facie, such a model of pure agrarianism stood in contrast to the commercialization of present-day Jews. Yet as we have seen, Harrington's conception of the economic characteristics of modern Jews was more complex than mere denunciation. First, he saw them as still bearing their admirable ancient features of Commonwealth people; but second, his general disdain for commerce was mixed. This conflict was fleshed out by Adam Sutcliffe, who argued that Harrington's attitude to the Jews, as that of other republican thinkers, was grounded in the indeterminate stance of republican thought regarding commercial values.[43]

Here again, usury provides a valuable entry point into economic ideology. Harrington did not relate to usury in *Oceana*, but in his defensive elaboration of the work, *The Prerogative of Popular Government* (1658), he advances an innovative approach to it, one hardly addressed by scholars.[44] One of *Oceana*'s main and innovative arguments is that the system of political power in any given society is determined by its economic structure. As the distribution of land regulates economic power, the formula for a stable government lies in the equilibrium between political and economic power. Thus, in a monarchical government, most of the land is owned by the king; in an aristocratic one, by nobles; and in a popular one, by the common people. As long as the distribution of land is definitive—namely, most of the land is clearly concentrated in the hands of the king, the nobles, or the people—the regime will be stable. Yet stability does not mean perpetuity. Perpetual political balance could be achieved only by a relatively equal distribution of land, which would limit the possible shifts of economic relations. Accordingly, insufficient land risks political imbalance, for where the economy cannot be based on land, money will become a more important factor, destabilizing the delicate economic-political balance.[45]

In *The Prerogative of Popular Government*, Harrington follows up and provides an illustration of a polity that succeeded in maintaining stability despite land shortage—that of the Israelites in Canaan. Although their (equal) lots were remarkably small, they took special measures to prevent the uncontrolled growth of the economic power of money by regulating usury. Lending on usury to foreigners was approved but was prohibited toward a fellow Israelite. Drawing on the concept of stability, Harrington deduced that the biblical prohibition on usury should be understood as unique to the Israelite context rather than universally unlawful. Accumulation of monetary gains—by usury, for example—would jeopardize the Israelite stability in a way that would not risk that of a different polity. In the Israelite case of insufficient land, monetary accumulation could easily outbalance the economic power of land. As usury was conceived to be a primary means for such accumulation, it was "of such a nature as, not forbidden in the like cases, must devour the government." It was forbidden by God, therefore, only because and wherever "it might come to overthrow the balance or foundation of the government."[46]

Harrington thus rationalized the prohibition of usury not as a moral precept but as a political one, part of his view on the evolution of regimes. As the economic base of society determines the political structure and legislative system—including rules regarding economic conduct such as usury—different societies pursue different economic precepts. The prohibition of usury is therefore a relative precept and should be judged in political terms. And although the Israelite social constitution was the most perfect system, some of its elements were based on distinct social and geohistorical conditions— such as their shortage of land: "Where a small sum may come to overbalance a man's estate in land, there, I say usury or money, for the preservation of the balance in land, must of necessity be forbidden, or the government will rather rest upon the balance of money, than upon that of land."[47]

However, in the geosocial conditions of countries such as England, with territories large enough for land not to be "overbalanced by money," there was no need to outlaw usury. Moreover, in a commercial country usury is not only not destructive, but also necessary, enabling "mighty profit to the public and a charity to private men," which otherwise would be hindered. Thus, argued Harrington, "we may not be persuaded by them that do not observe these different causes, that it is against Scripture. . . . Had usury to a brother been permitted in Israel, that government had been overthrown: but that such a territory as England or Spain cannot be overbalanced by money."[48]

It should be emphasized that this was a novel argumentation in the years-long deliberation on usury. Traditionally, arguments for both the restriction and relaxation of moneylending on interest orbited around the definition of the transaction and around what it entailed.[49] In sharp contrast, the outlook offered by Harrington moves from the personal to the overall social structure and its historical changeability. This move challenges the accentuated agrarianism we tend to ascribe to early modern republican thinkers. Harrington's analysis of usury demonstrates how republicanism could be integrated with commercialism.[50] Lastly, it problematizes our conception of the scope of uses of the Bible and the Jews in early modern discourse. The polity of the ancient Israelites was not necessarily used as an ideal model of agrarian virtues for direct adoption. Rather, its apparent idealization could convey a very different idea—the distance of biblical society from contemporary early modern social conditions. Consequently, the binary opposition between (creditable) Israelites and (corrupted) Jews, often used by historians as emblematic of early modern attitudes toward Jews, seems to lose much of its force.[51]

* * *

At the center of Harrington's analysis of usury, then, was the notion of the autarkic agrarian ancient Israelite society. Harrington was not an expert Hebraist, as he himself testified, and his ideas about the ancient Israelites relied on other scholars' works. To appreciate these influences, a Dutch detour is required. From the latter part of the sixteenth century, the Old Testament was becoming a central resource for European humanist political thought. The United Provinces centered much of this movement, as best articulated in the work of the Dutch philologist and jurist Petrus Cunaeus (1586–1638), *The Hebrew Republic* (1617). Cunaeus analyzed the ancient Israelite society as hinging on agrarian-egalitarian stabilizing principles. An important component of this order was the social isolation of the Israelites from their neighboring peoples, which owed much to the abstention from commercial relations with them. Commerce was the strongest force of communication, hence of change and innovation of all sorts, which would have shaken the foundations of the Israelite commonwealth. It was the source of corruption. Under Cunaeus's pen, the Israelites were rendered as an extrahistorical encapsulated society, self-sufficient in its simplicity.[52]

Cunaeus did not relate directly to the question of usury, though given his anticommercialist view, it seems plausible that he had no reason to justify it. Yet his detailed historical description of the Israelite society needed just a twist to reach a totally different outlook. Perhaps the most renowned contemporary scholar to investigate the question of usury was a colleague of Cunaeus in Leiden, the French-born scholar Claudius Salmasius (1588–1653), who dedicated three lengthy books to the subject. Salmasius's main argument was that the ban on usury has no natural or moral basis, hence moneylending is not different from any other business and should not be constrained under unique limitations. In his last book on the subject, however, he deviated from the legalistic reasoning and introduced a new kind of argument: that the ban on usury was meant to operate only among the Jews themselves and only with respect to their unique agrarian, enclosed social structure. The fact that the ancient Jews, in contrast to their neighboring nations, did not conduct commerce was the historical rationale for banning usury.[53]

The two scholars from Leiden had a significant influence on Hugo Grotius (1583–1645), another Leiden-schooled intellectual. A pioneering thinker of international and natural law, Grotius was one of the most influential seventeenth-century critics. He was a close friend of Petrus Cunaeus, from whose book he developed his own use of the ancient Hebrew commonwealth as a republican source, as well as of Salmasius (though the two later became bitter foes). Grotius's attitude to usury is especially telling, for it underwent a significant change. Despite his high regard for commerce, he conceived usury along traditional lines. In chapter 12 of the second book of *De Jure Belli ac Pacis* (1625), he presented arguments from both sides of the matter but concluded that because neither could refute the other on the basis of natural law, "we ought to be satisfied with the Law given by GOD to the Hebrews." The usury prohibition must be observed toward all, as "all Distinction of People being entirely taken away by the Gospel, and the word *Neighbour* of a much larger Signification."[54] Not long after, however, he changed his mind—probably following a correspondence with Salmasius.[55] An instructive reflection of this change, which will loom large in the following chapter, was in his commentary on the New Testament. Commenting on Luke 6:35, Grotius clarified that the biblical ban was not a moral but rather a civil law peculiar to the Jews. The ban was "founded on the particular State of the People of Israel" who were "for the most part shepherds or husbandmen" while most of their neighbors "inriched themselves by Trade." Accordingly, the distinct social structures necessitated different economic ethics; the biblical ban on usury, therefore, did not apply to modern Christian society.[56]

This intellectual background illuminates Harrington's discussion on usury. Cunaeus's analysis of the Israelite agrarian law had a profound influence on the construction of Harrington's own model.[57] Harrington also relied extensively on Grotius, especially in his works following *Oceana*,[58] and it is also hardly imaginable that he was unaware of the works of an intellectual of the caliber of Salmasius. The three writers built on the historical construction set by Cunaeus, while adapting it for a contrary use: Instead of employing it as a role model, they emphasized the historical distinctiveness and distance of the Israelite society from contemporary European societies. For Harrington this historical construction fitted well within his elaborate theory of sociopolitical balance. As seen in the next chapter, the adaptability of the notion of the historical Israelites increasingly informed discussions about contemporary economic questions.

How did it project on the attitude toward contemporary Jews? This was also a flexible matter that could go both ways. Salmasius employed the uniqueness of the ancient Israelite society to justify usury in contemporary European society, yet nevertheless stated that modern Jews "always stood out as restless usurers" who believed they had authorization to practice it against Gentiles and indeed widely practiced it.[59] His vindication of lending on interest crumbled in front of this enduring prejudice. Harrington, too, does not seem to have had a benign conception of present-day Jews, though, as illustrated earlier, it was a complex one.

* * *

Let us return to the historical context of the middle decades of the seventeenth century, which was briefly drawn in the Introduction. The predominance of the commercial market system in English society was an evident reality. This had intellectual, cultural, and ethical implications, for it became clear that the traditional economic-moral system could not retain its grip on a commercializing society. Usury was emblematic of this tension, as aptly articulated by John Selden (1584–1654), who wondered, "Would it not look oddly to a stranger that should come into this land and hear in our pulpits usury preached against and yet the Law allow it? Many men use it, perhaps some churchmen themselves."[60] Engaging these cultural conundrums was unavoidable.[61]

The cases presented in this chapter resonate this tension. Each had its idiosyncrasy: distinct triggers, goals, and discursive contexts. Seemingly, the connection among them was loose—Harrington did relate to the readmission polemic, but it is unlikely that his discussion on biblical usury was influenced by it. Yet they also demonstrate what I argue to be a shared preoccupation regarding usury: the (re)narration of Jewish history. These versions of Jewish history—one medieval, the other ancient—offered ways of dealing with the problem of usury.

Moreover, from the perspective offered here, the moves made by the principal writers presented had another common feature: a detachment of the long-held association of Jews and usury. What is all the more telling is that they arrived at comparable positions while pursuing very different objectives. The deconstruction of the usury-Jews compound was not consensual, of course, nor univocal. As noted, during the readmission polemic several controversialists of both parties retained the long-conceived association of Jews and usury, and throughout the following decades, different English writers continued tapping it. Yet it marks the emergence of a new alternative for imagining Jews and economy that was facilitated around the mid-seventeenth century. This alternative did not necessarily entail a pro-Jewish approach, as seen in Prynne's virulent pieces. Yet it could also indicate a reevaluation of the Jews' role in a commercial society as mutually beneficial. Such a position was aptly expressed by lawyer Charles Molloy (1640–1690), known mainly for his best-selling legal textbook *De Jure Maritimo*. Molloy hinged the 1290 expulsion on usury and consequently claimed that withdrawing from it was a sufficient justification for readmission. Writing in 1682, he argued that "Commerce and Traffick having now taught [the Jews] a more exquisite way of enriching themselves, than by that cruel biting trade of Usury," so that the newly settled Jewish community in England could now "flourish in as high a manner as of old."[62] Yet the present-day Jews were not the center of interest following these developments. Far more resonant was the new historical conceptualization of the ancient Israelites. The following chapter engages the arena where it struck roots most decisively: English biblical discourse.

Chapter 2

Usury and the Re-narration
of the Ancient Israelite Society

The new historical narration of ancient Israelite society depicted in the previous chapter found a receptive and fertile ground in English biblical discourse and became a hotspot for thinking on the shifting socioeconomic setting of the latter part of early modernity. In a way, this comes as a surprise. Biblical discourse is usually conceived as tending toward traditionalism, conventionalism, and continuity. As this chapter demonstrates, however, from the second half of the seventeenth century to the eighteenth century, this was an arena where diverse opinions about current pressing matters circulated.

One cannot overemphasize the cultural significance the Bible had for all social strata in early modern England. In the words of Christopher Hill, it was "the foundation of all aspects of English culture." In the 1630s alone, 76 editions of the Old Testament (OT) and 16 editions of the New Testament (NT) were published in English. During the following decades, the Bible was present in almost every English household.[1] By the early seventeenth century, after the vernacular English Bible was well entrenched, commentaries came to the front of biblical scholarship. The seventeenth and eighteenth centuries saw a proliferation of commentaries, most of them appealing to the lay public in the vernacular.[2] Bibliographies of English commentaries, published around the mid-seventeenth century, testify to this genre's growing interest and importance.[3] At least 123 editions of full Bible commentaries and at least 71 editions of NT commentaries were published during the eighteenth century. As Thomas Preston illustrates, Bible commentaries were a central component of the stock reading in long eighteenth-century England. Samuel Johnson, for example, advised James Boswell to accompany his reading of the Bible with a commentary, adding specific recommendations.[4]

This genre's volume and broad reception make it an effective indicator of the confrontations early modern English men and women had between their religious world and their changing social reality. Such questions, of course, were not confined to usury. Yet usury was a uniquely effective issue, for it touched on the core of contemporaries' concerns over their commercializing environment—moving from an economic system based on direct familiarity and interpersonal obligations to one based on faceless mechanisms. Aiming to illuminate the clash between growing commercialism and biblical discourse, this chapter is informed by an examination of all available Bible commentaries written in English and published in the seventeenth and eighteenth centuries that referred to the usury prohibition in the Pentateuch. It focuses on commentaries on the proscriptive verses regarding usury (Exodus 22, Leviticus 25, and Deuteronomy 23). It also relates more extensively to commentaries on other pertinent passages (Ezekiel 18 and 22, Proverbs 28, Psalms 15, and Nehemiah 5).

This symbolic significance of usury hinged on a specific biblical verse: "Unto a *stranger* thou mayest lend upon usury; but unto thy *brother* thou shalt not lend upon usury" (Deuteronomy 23:20; KJV; my emphasis). Applied literally, this verse implied that late seventeenth-century England, where usury was legal and broadly practiced, was—at least symbolically—a society of strangers. This was a disturbing notion. It is worth reiterating James Vernon's concept of the modern social experience discussed in the introduction. Vernon defines modernity as a phase wherein the fundamental societal condition is that of ubiquitous strangeness. Britain became the first modern society in the nineteenth century, argues Vernon, after reaching a critical mass of change in core dimensions of social life (geosocial mobility, urbanization, and political and economic organization) that rendered "traditional" social organization obsolete. Late seventeenth-century England did not experience such changes to such a degree. It was in no way a society of strangers in the concrete sense. What was new and shattering, however, was that the notion of spreading strangeness was becoming conceivable. This notion, I suggest, was an underlying preoccupation of contemporaries, and as demonstrated in this chapter, one of the main channels for thinking it through was biblical usury. Usury symbolized social estrangement due to the Deuteronomic verse and its cultural history, and its legal and social acceptance was therefore often conceived as a stimulant of this process. Ironically, the same verse, I will soon show, came in the late seventeenth century to neutralize the very essence of the biblical challenge to the early modern credit market. The historical image of the ancient Jews was paramount in that development.

What was tricky about the phrasing of the Deuteronomic ban on usury was its decisive limitation. It seemed to permit usurious lending to a "stranger"; yet who should be so defined? This was a haunting question with far-reaching implications. Saint Ambrose offered a constitutive interpretation of the term in the fourth century: The permission to take usury from the stranger pertained only to the Canaanite nations whom the Jews had been commanded to destroy. Everyone else, particularly after Christ, was to be considered a brother. Thus, usury became entrenched in the fundamental Christian call for universal brotherhood. This interpretation persisted well into early modernity, in England as elsewhere in the Western Christian world.[5]

In this vein, the Douai English version of the Old Testament, published in 1609–1610, annotated on Deuteronomy 23 that only enemies were meant by the "stranger," hence usury was permitted only in relation to them and only in a just war.[6] This was reiterated by Andrew Willet (1562–1621), a senior clergyman and religious controversialist, and perhaps the most extensive of Jacobean exegetes, who commented that this privilege was invalidated by Jesus when he eliminated the distinctions among men. Both added that the fact that contemporary Jews continued to rely on this permission confirmed their blindness and depravity.[7] This interpretation was also entrenched in lay polemical writing on usury. Roger Fenton (1565–1616), for instance, argued in his *Treatise of Usury* (1611) that, because nowadays the Canaanites no longer existed, usury was simply unlawful without any qualifications. In his renowned *Lex Mercatoria* (1622), Gerard Malynes (1586–1641) claimed that usurers were like Jews who justified their lending on interest with the pretense that all Gentiles were considered strangers, as if they were of the Canaanite nations. To name one final example among many, Sir Edward Coke, the great authority on legal history and our secondary hero from the previous chapter, also noted that the biblical permission applied only to Canaanites.[8]

Another common argument was that the biblical permission to take usury from the Gentiles was meant to be avoided in the first place, just like the permission to divorce, and that only the hard-heartedness of the Jews made God permit it. As David Hawkes demonstrated, the associating of usury with divorce was prevalent in early modern England in diverse genres. The prolific exegete and religious separatist controversialist Henry Ainsworth

(1569–1622) pointed out that failing to understand this was an inherent flaw in the Jewish interpretation of usury, by which they supported their double standard against Gentiles. Instead, Ainsworth and others—among them Bishop Joseph Hall (1574–1656), Arthur Jackson (c. 1593–1666), and the *Assembly's Annotations* for the *Authorized Version* of the Bible—interpreted "stranger" as applying only to infidels beyond the fold of faith.[9]

The traditional interpretation of usury was expressed most pronouncedly by midcentury puritan commentator John Trapp (1601–1669), whose full biblical commentary was issued in parts between 1646 and 1662. Trapp emphasized both the sin of usury and the Jews' distinct economic characteristics in the harshest manner found in seventeenth-century England. Commenting on Deuteronomy 23, he likened usurers to the demonic nation of Amalek, falling upon the borrower like cormorants, sucking his blood and devouring him with an open mouth. The Jews, he maintained, practice exorbitant usury against Christians—whom they regard as "strangers"—to this day, wherever they reside. Remarkably, Trapp does not base his radical charge on textual analysis but rather on a somewhat crude ethnography of contemporary Jews, whom he considers the continuers of biblical history. His reference to Amalek inhabits the same semantic field of the traditional explanation that usury was permitted only toward the Canaanite nations, but the other way around: He who lends on interest to people whom God does not doom for annihilation becomes himself a member of that category. This rhetoric highlights another point: Usury is the working of collectives no less than of individuals—it is an issue of national dimensions.[10]

Trapp's harsh reproach of both Jews and usury was not emblematic. Neither was the traditional interpretation of the ban univocal. Despite the prevalence of years-long interpretive conventions on usury in the seventeenth century, there was also a tendency to relax the scope of the ban. Andrew Willet, for one, shifted the center of gravity of usury from the objective action to its circumstantial conditions: the characteristics of the specific lender and borrower and the manner of lending. The scope he dedicated to the discussion demonstrates how painstaking this task was.[11] Elizabethan bishop Gervase Babington (1549/50–1610) offered a more exceptional approach. He concluded that as long as the lender charged moderate interest and had empathy for his debtor, lending on interest could be permitted—usury was a matter of the heart, not of objective regulations, which only God could, and would, judge. Babington's approach strikingly fits Weber's renowned thesis on the Protestant ethic and its emphasis on inner conscience and intent-oriented judgment. Yet this remained an isolated voice not picked up by succeeding English commentators, who mostly retained conventional articulations of usury. [12]

At about the same time Trapp published his commentary, the Cambridge-educated parish priest John Mayer (1583–1664) published his own, aimed for those who "not being professed Divines, yet, are studious of the Scriptures."[13] His comments on usury are telling, for his definition of the terms *brother* and *stranger* are blurred. Whereas in his commentary on Exodus 22 he argues that only members of the nations "appointed to destruction" may be defined as strangers (to whom the Jews "might lend upon usury to waste and to weaken them"), he also defines the "brother" exclusively as a fellow Israelite or proselyte. Where does the common Gentile fall? This becomes clearer—or perhaps even more confusing—in his commentary on Leviticus 25, where he argues that the "stranger" is the ordinary Gentile. The Jews were commanded to exercise charity toward the Gentiles, but "that is elsewhere injoyned"—not regarding the taking of usury.[14]

Why did Mayer contradict himself, and why did he deviate from the traditional line of interpretation? I want to speculate that it was a Freudian slip—an emblematic expression of the lingering tension around usury typical of the period and of which we have seen different illustrations in the previous chapter. His remark that charity toward the Gentiles was "*elsewhere* injoyned" attempts to separate moneylending from other kinds of social interactions. This inconsistency was entrenched in the seventeenth-century discourse on usury. And as we shall see presently, subsequent English writers made new interpretive efforts to address it.

* * *

The Cambridge educated nonconformist theologian Matthew Poole (1624–1679) is a good starting point. Poole's magnum opus was the five-volume *Synopsis Criticorum* (1676), which summarized views of dozens of biblical commentaries, including rabbinical and Catholic sources. Having completed it, he embarked on its adaptation for the broader English public. His *Annotations upon the Holy Bible* were published posthumously in 1683 and 1685 and gained enormous popularity: By the turn of the century, four editions were sold, to the point that one eminent clergyman testified that it "got into most hands."[15]

Poole claimed that all writers who understand the "stranger" as the Canaanite do so "without any solid or sufficient grounds."[16] It is not the "brother" who is universal and the "stranger" who is particular, but the other way around.

Poole supported this interpretation with a new logic, already encountered in the previous chapter:

> Because the Israelites generally employed themselves in the management of land and cattle, and therefore could not make any advantage of borrowed money to ballance the use they should pay for it, and consequently it may be presumed that they would not borrow money upon use but for want and poverty, and in that case, and principally for that reason, usury seems to be forbidden for them. . . . But the strangers made use of their money in way of trade and traffick with the Israelites, which was more gainful, and could much better bear the burden of usury, and reap advantage from money so borrowed.[17]

This historical-structural reading hinged the ban of usury on a universal rationale that acknowledged the difference between different societal economic structures. From this perspective, the ancient Israelite society was exceptional, and in turn, all who were not Israelites were "strangers," whether "proselyted to the Jewish religion or not." This explanation neutralized the religious and ethnic conflict embedded in the verses and dulled their identity-politics edge: Rather than implying one's identity, "brother" and "stranger" came to signify social structures or functions.

I will soon dig into the socio-intellectual context of this new interpretive schema, but first I wish to linger on its practical and intellectual implications. The core of this interpretation is the historical contextualization of the ban, which implies a distancing of contemporary from biblical reality. Just as we have seen with Harrington, the next inference that derives from it is that the ban is irrelevant to seventeenth-century England, whose distance from the autarkic-rural Israelite economy cannot be overstated. Poole himself evades contemporary implications, noting that "whether all usury be unlawful to Christians is too great a question to be determined in a work of this nature." Ingenuous or not, at least some contemporaries attributed such intentions to him. Scottish pamphleteer James Hodges (fl. 1695–1705), for one, called on Poole to prove that usury itself was not contradictory to charity, saying that Poole did "plainly argue for taking Usury, tho' not in the same Words, yet in the proper Sense here pleaded, as a just Recompence for a Benefit."[18]

No less significant than its practical implications is the reasoning behind the new interpretation. Shifting from the moral language of sin and virtue, it adopts a sociological viewpoint that examines the socioeconomic system rather than the individual. Note that this new reasoning is profoundly different from the "Weberian argument" offered by scholars such as Norman Jones and Benjamin Nelson, who stressed a new and growing focus on inner consciousness—a mode of thought that was rare in English Bible commentaries.

The significance of the dismissal or acceptance of the interpretation that the biblical term *strangers* meant only Canaanites was decisive. It was understood by contemporaries to indicate one's stand on the practical question of usury. As noted by the anonymous writer of *Usury Stated* (1679), "None, I dare say, understands Stranger in this place, barely of the Canaanite: but as respecting all other Nations." In response, the pamphlet *The Case of Usury Further Debated* (1684) noted that "there are divers Persons of great Eminency, if not the greater number of Expositors, who understand that place to be meant of such Strangers [i.e. Canaanites] only." Since it is impossible to judge between the contrasting arguments, and "there is no manifest Evidence that the word Stranger in Deut. 23.20. takes in all others besides the Jews," we better be "afraid of meddling with Usury" and leave the ban in force.[19]

The new interpretation tapped into the Dutch-English intellectual backdrop depicted in the previous chapter. It was through Hugo Grotius's work that the argument that the ban on usury was based on the Israelite social structure entered English exegetical discourse. Grotius had a tremendous influence on English intellectuals, who were clearly acquainted with his annotations.[20] Poole incorporated Grotius's annotation on Luke 6:35 in his *Synopsis Criticorum*. Most likely, he also adapted it into his *Annotations* on Deuteronomy.[21] Some of the subsequent English exegetes who used the historical explanation in their commentaries referred explicitly to Grotius on Luke.[22] As I will soon show, Poole was not the only English religious scholar to use this interpretation, nor was Bible commentary the only field where it was employed. The new structural history of the ancient Israelites was becoming a hotspot, and now it entered religious writing itself.

An examination of English Bible commentary following Poole reveals the conspicuous reception and entrenchment of the new interpretation and how the practical implications that derived from it became increasingly explicit. Bishop Richard Kidder (1633–1703), a Cambridge fellow of Poole, defined the stranger as "opposed to *Brother* . . . [as] one who is not an *Israelite*, and consequently one who by Traffick and Merchandise, might be better able to pay interest for Money, than the *Israelite*, who did not drive that Trade" (italics in original). Notably, this "Israelite" was defined not merely by his religion or ethnicity but no less importantly by his structural features of not practicing "Traffick and Merchandise." Another Cambridge fellow, Bishop Simon Patrick (1626–1707), went a step further and explicitly denoted economic structure as the criterion for applying different economic norms: "there was nothing more rational than this, that their Neighbours making great gain by Merchandize . . . they should not borrow Money of the Israelites for nothing; so it was no less reasonable, the Israelites themselves, whose chiefest Profit was by Husbandry and Breeding of Cattle, should have Money lent them freely by one another, without any Interest; their Land not being a Country of Traffick, whereby Money might be improved." Accordingly, a "Country of Traffick, whereby money might be improved"—such as late seventeenth-century England—should apply different precepts than the biblical polity.[23]

Succeeding commentators applied this interpretation to current economic reality more overtly. Presbyterian minister Matthew Henry (1662–1714), one of the century's most renowned evangelical preachers and the author of a highly popular and esteemed commentary, explained that God permitted lending on interest to a stranger because he was "supposed to live by trade, and (as we say) by turning the penny, and therefore got by what he borrowed, and came among them in hopes to do so." Hence, Henry concluded, "usury is not in itself oppressive; for they must not oppress a stranger, and yet might exact usury from him." Similarly, he argued in his commentary on Exodus that "it seems as lawful to receive interest for my money, which another takes pains with and improves . . . as it is to receive rent for my land, which another takes pains with and improves."[24]

English commentators pursued this rationale in the next generation. Robert Jameson explained that "whatever some casuists of the Romish church may pretend . . . there is nothing absolutely unlawful in the nature of the thing. . . . In a trading commonwealth, where the industrious merchant may make great advantage by the use of money . . . in that case, where is the hardship or injustice to make him pay five or six per cent. for the use of that money, which the proprietor might have turned to account by using it himself."[25] Likewise, John Gill (1697–1771), a leading dissenting theologian and commentator, emphasized that the prohibition on usury related exclusively to the rural and autarkic ancient Israelite society. Accordingly, "it was lawful to take interest" from people who profited from money, "as it was but reasonable, when they gained much by the money they lent them, and as it is but reasonable should be the case among Christians in such circumstances."[26]

This line of interpretation continued throughout the eighteenth century and beyond. Similar theoretical and practical observations were noted by most commentators, among them clergyman Thomas Haweis (1734?–1820); William Dodd (1729–1777), the extravagant clergyman and writer who was eventually executed for forgery; and clergyman and biblical scholar Thomas Scott (1747–1821). Perhaps the only exception to the historical structural rule was Thomas Pyle (1674–1756), a Church of England clergyman and religious controversialist. Nonetheless, Pyle explained that usury was prohibited only among the Israelites, "Whatever *Israelite* lends Money to another *Israelite*" (italics in original). Overall, the new interpretive model struck deep roots in English biblical discourse.[27]

Another angle of the historical image of ancient Israelite society was developed by stressing the connection between the Israelites' economic system and their geographic organization. Simon Patrick, Matthew Henry, and Thomas Scott all emphasized that not only were the Israelites not engaged in commerce, the Law prevented them from doing so by dividing their land equally and strictly forbidding them from alienating their inheritance. Consequently, they did not need significant sums of money to invest in trade to expand their estates. In Henry's words, God forbade interest among them, as it would be "little or no loss to the lender, because their land was so divided, their estates were so settled, and there was so little of merchandise among them."[28]

Another remarkable variation was made by Simon Patrick and John Gill, who ascribed the traditional interpretation that usury was allowed only toward the Canaanite nations to Jewish exegetes. (Only two Jewish writers, Isaac Abravanel and Leon de Modena, referred to this model.) Jameson ascribed this same interpretation to Catholic writers. What is telling about them all is that they overlooked the prevalence of this explanation among English Protestant exegetes until the middle of the seventeenth century. This somewhat odd feature attests not only to the deep-rootedness of the new interpretation but also to the profound abandonment of the traditional one—that had to be ascribed to one's antagonists, whether Jews or Catholics.

The shift in the understanding of usury is apparent also in commentaries on narrative, prophetic, and poetic passages of the Bible. Let us see first the early ("traditional") interpretive model at work. Commenting on Ezekiel 18:8 ("He that hath not given forth upon usury, neither hath taken any increase"; KJV), Trapp offers an extensive and vehement condemnation of the practice, remarking that no distinctions of types of interest whatsoever can be made:

"Interest we call it now, after the French, who first helped us to that fine word. But let the patrons of usury consider that what distinctions soever they bring for it, God alloweth here of no usury." In a similar vein, the *Assembly's Annotations* on Psalms 15 noted that "the common distinction of *biting*, and more moderate usury, hath no ground at all in Scripture," and on Ezekiel 18 brought forth Aristotle's thesis of the barrenness of money. On Nehemiah 5, when the majority of the Jewish population in Palestine becomes subjugated to their moneylenders, we find Trapp once again highlighting the demonic features of usury and blaming the Jews for a "presumptuous violation of the law . . . a sin that they had soundly smarted for." Given the volatile situation of the budding Jewish population, he writes, this was nothing less than a national betrayal. Trapp takes this as a model story for England's history: In the thirteenth century, usurers cunningly entrapped the king and nobility, just like usurers in Nehemiah's time subjugated the Jews to the king of Persia.[29] Finally, in his commentary on the Parable of the Talents (Matthew 25:14–30 and Luke 19:12–27), where the slothful servant is condemned for not lending on usury the talent he received from the master, he notes that Scripture's intent is that the servant should profit not by usury, but by a honest way of trade. Trapp stresses that Jesus only used the term metaphorically, similar to the case with other idioms.[30] Usurers, he reminds the reader, are "the most pernicious pests of mankind."[31]

Shortly after the middle of the seventeenth century, English commentators began referring to these passages very differently. Poole's *Annotations* abridge the discussion on Ezekiel by stating that "the whole will amount to this, he that in his lending hath truly weighed the borrower's case, and used him with kindness as he would be used himself, this man is no usurer."[32] Similarly, Mayer and Henry state that defining a loan as usury depends on intending a "damage of the borrower"—otherwise it is a lawful contract. Referring to the story of Nehemiah, the later commentators emphasize that the transactions were a clear transgression of the prohibition of an Israelite to lend on interest to a fellow Israelite but do not indicate anything on lending on interest in general.[33]

Perhaps the most telling are the later comments on the passages from the New Testament. On Luke 6:35 ("lend, hoping for nothing again"; KJV), Poole's *Annotations* advocate an elaborate pro-commercial outlook. Instead of interpreting it as a warning against usury, it suggests reading it more broadly as a command for acts of charity. Usury itself was never "absolutely forbidden to the Jews," who were allowed to take it of strangers. Rather than a universal moral rule, the ban on usury is a Jewish political precept derived from the Israelites' unique social structure: They had less need of moneylending "partly in respect of their years of jubilee, and partly in regard their employments were chiefly in husbandry, and about cattle, which called not for such sums of money as merchandising doth." Accordingly, lending on a moderate interest could be "helpful and relieving to our neighbor . . . nor can there be any injustice in it."[34] Commenting on the Parable of the Talents, the nonconformist divine Richard Baxter (1615–1691) states that it does speak of gains made by exchange "with seeming approbation," and Henry claims that usury "was a common practice at that time, and not disallowed by our Saviour."[35]

* * *

The new historical outlook for analyzing usury was not invented by any of the English exegetes I have dwelled upon here. As suggested in the previous chapter, it was probably adopted from the works of Dutch writers. What is nevertheless striking about the English side of the story is the unequivocal reception of this idea. What made it so acceptable and transmittable? The first part of the answer lies in the social characteristics of the first generation of writers who promoted and naturalized this new idea.

Matthew Poole was the first writer to apply historical thinking on usury as part of Bible exegesis, but contemporaneously with him, other religious writers expressed it in other contexts. Richard Baxter and the latitudinarian theologian Edward Stillingfleet (1635–1699) articulated very similar ideas.[36] When we add to them Poole's younger peers—Simon Patrick and Richard Kidder—whose commentaries I have discussed earlier, the social picture behind the conceptual shift of biblical usury starts taking shape. Despite their apparent theological divisions, this group shared social connections and a Whig inclination. They were all moderate Dissenters or Low Churchmen who promoted comprehension and religious toleration. Politically, they opposed absolutism and eventually came to be firm supporters of the post-Glorious Revolution settlement; some of them (Stillingfleet, Patrick, and Kidder) were nominated bishops by the new regime. They shared social connections and political views and were an important part of the Whig faction in the English Church, which Steve Pincus calls the "Williamite bishops." Poole died before this politically oriented faction consolidated, but his social connections and religious approach related him strongly to it. He and Baxter commented on each other's works and corresponded considerably. Together with Stillingfleet, who was also a trustee for Poole's *Synopsis*, they engaged in 1675 in discussing a comprehension bill.[37]

The foregoing analysis of biblical exegesis renders it plausible that this group also took part in a Whig ideology of political economy. As Pincus portrays it, this ideology maintained that national wealth derived from labor, not land. Arguing that the key for promoting industry was the national circulation of money and credit, supporters of Whig economy advocated the financial innovations that comprised what came to be termed the Financial Revolution. Apparently, the English exegetes promoted this ideology by contextualizing and limiting the biblical ban on usury.[38] Moreover, the new interpretation of usury also debunked the opposing Tory political-economic ideal of the self-sufficient landowner, which insisted on an intrinsic relation between wealth and land, and that the landowner was the only potential political agent.[39] By alienating the model of the ancient self-sufficient and agrarian Israelite society, they demonstrated the irrelevance of this ideal to seventeenth-century England. As noted by historians, the English autarkic landowner (in contrast to other settings on the Continent) was an extinct social creature by the midcentury.

This demands some qualification. I do not mean to indicate that the exegetical shift we have seen was part of a conscious and concerted attempt to promote a political-economic agenda; plausibly, at least some of the writers might not have been fully aware of the political consequences of their new readings and expressed ideas that were in the air. What is clearly important here, however, is that the new reading resonated within the political and political-economic context of the turn of the eighteenth century.

* * *

The reconceptualization of usury rested on a new ethnological reading of the history of ancient Israel. Its importance and novelty did not lie solely in providing a justification for lending on interest.[40] What was new in the mid-seventeenth-century version was that a profoundly new outlook was at work—not legalistic or moralistic, but historical. This was based on a new ethnological sense of the Israelites as distinct from Jews. This distinction itself, of course, was not new. Yet while it usually signified spiritual and moral distance between the Israelites and the Jews, it now came to mark a socio-economic one.[41] This was not a distinctly English endeavor, moreover. From the late sixteenth century, the historical Jewish commonwealth captivated scholars across Europe, who applied the study of ancient Jewish society to their own early modern settings. This intellectual phenomenon has been extensively studied in recent years, mainly pertaining to questions of religion ("Christian Hebraism") and political science ("political Hebraism"). The discussion here illustrates that the Hebraic tendencies also resonated in early modern discourse of political economy.

As elaborated in the previous chapter, the ideas that drove this rethinking of usury originated in works published in the Dutch republic. Petrus Cunaeus developed an extensive model of the ancient Jewish society, which became an elastic resource in the hands of later writers who adopted it for different purposes. I demonstrated how these ideas took new and different shapes in the works of Claudius Salmasius, Hugo Grotius, and James Harrington. The open-endedness of the uses of the historical model is abundantly demonstrated by the way it was applied across the Channel, by contemporary French biblical commentators.

Les moeurs des Israélites was published in 1681 by the prominent ecclesiastical historian Abbé Claude Fleury (1640–1723) and was soon translated, becoming highly influential. Fleury's primary goal was to offer a new exegetical device on a systematic ethnographic base. The quintessence of the Israelite society, he claimed, was its self-sufficiency and simplicity. The Israelites were "entirely addicted to agriculture," and, consequently, most trades were useless to them. This was a very similar notion to the model we have seen in use so far. But behind the similarity of imagery lay a very different way of addressing this historical distance.[42]

While the English and Dutch writers I have explored used the historical distance as a buffer between modern society and scriptural economic teaching, for Fleury the distance from the Israelites needed to be overcome. He dedicated his first chapter to this problem and insisted on the relevance of the Israelite polity to contemporary society as an ideal to be pursued—an "excellent model of that way of living, which is most conformable to nature." Underlying his work was the idea that "most of the difference betwixt us and them does not proceed from our being more enlightened by Christianity, but from our being less guided by reason."[43] By virtue of their "noble simplicity," which is "much preferable to all refinements," they managed to avoid many of their contemporaries' defects. Thus their customs illustrate the "most rational method of subsisting, employing one's self and living in society," hence serving as a moral model "both in publick and private life."

Fleury's ethnographic model of the ancient Israelites was part of a comprehensive anti-Colbertist political agenda, designated by Lionel Rothkrug in his classic study as Christian agrarianism.[44] It arose against a model that based French national political economy on production and consumption of luxurious fashion. The opposition disputed this model because it prioritized commerce motivated by glory over commerce that provided for everyday needs. Alternatively, the opposition promoted a communal, local commerce and the privileging of the countryside over the city. Fleury was a significant figure in this opposition, along with his close friend François de Salignac de la Mothe-Fénelon (1651–1715), who was the preceptor of Louis XIV's grandson and made Fleury his deputy. Fénelon's most famous work, *Les aventures de Télémaque fils d'Ulysse*, a kind of sequel to the Odyssey, was a reformation model for purging a corrupt state of despotism and luxury. His critique was directed at Louis's regime and particularly Colbert's economic policy, which favored the luxury industry. He modeled his alternative society (Boetica) on Fleury's Israelite society.[45]

Fleury's model had a great impact also on French religious writers, Bible commentators among them. A strong case at hand where this was expressed was the question of usury. Antoine Augustin Calmet (1672–1757) was the most prominent French Bible exegete of the period. He is considered one of the first to depart from moral and allegorical interpretations in favor of a literal one, and he recommended Fleury's book as an important introduction for the reading of the OT.[46] His discussion on usury is infused with Fleury's utopian conception of the ancient Israelite society. Very differently from the English exegetes for whom this was an alternative to traditional interpretations, Calmet integrated the two. The uniqueness of the Israelite social organization did not entail a separation between them and us but rather the exact opposite. Accordingly, Calmet maintained the traditional scholastic arguments that the Israelites were allowed to lend on interest only to the Canaanite nations—"a mere condescension given to the hardness of their heart, and rightly revoked by the Gospel which forbids any kind of usury." By the Gospel, all people were made "brothers" and the very category "stranger" was eliminated, making the total ban on usury the new percept. The same approach was reiterated in his *Dictionnaire historique, critique, chronologique, géographique et littéral de la Bible* (1722–1728), under the term *usury*.[47]

The centrality of Fleury and Calmet in the French intellectual setting of the eighteenth century makes them ripe for comparison with the English writers. The social model of the ancient Israelites became prevalent in both intellectual settings, yet the two differed profoundly in their approach to the historical distance from it. Fleury and Calmet sought to overcome this distance and employ the Israelite model as a utopian criticism of modern economy and social relations. This was accompanied, as Francesca Trivellato recently demonstrated, by a French obsession with both usury and its association with Jews, which endured throughout the century.[48] The English commentators drew the opposite meaning from a similar historical model. The apparent historical differences between the Israelite and modern societies made it impractical for the modernizing English society. For English writers the suitable biblical entity to identify with, if any, was the Gentiles neighboring Israel, the "strangers." In a figurative vein the expansive English interpretation of the biblical "stranger" was consistent with the methodological focus on the "strangeness" or unbridgeable difference of the Israelites. Note that Fleury, Fénelon, and Calmet were influential also among English religious writers. However, their take on biblical political economy did not gain much resonance. Fénelon's *Télémaque* is a telling case of the English reception of the French version of the Israelite model. Istvan Hont demonstrates that the work quickly acquired great popularity in oppositional Jacobite circles averse to commercialism as part of their ultra-Tory political stance.[49] This accentuated the English commentators' Whig and pro-commercial approach, advocating a social ideal different from that of the self-sufficient landowner.

This short French detour again exemplifies the claim that the myth of the autarkic ancient Israelites became a common idea shared across the Republic of Letters. Dutch, German, French, and English intellectuals all employed it, borrowing themes from each other. Its uses, to reiterate, were diverse, at least on certain issues. What is telling about the Anglo-Dutch use of the story is its application in making what Jonathan Sheehan called the "Historical Bible"— an attempt at a Bible cleansed of contested confessional paradigms. The means to this end was the "principle of knowledge through alienation": defamiliarizing the biblical text by disassociating it from the European world and mentality and locating it in an Oriental context. Sheehan traces this development among German intellectuals in the second half of the eighteenth century. I suggest that the historical model of the ancient Israelite society in its Anglo-Dutch version anticipates this shift.[50]

What was new about this version of biblical historicism was not the practice of historicizing itself but the management of historical distance. As Richard Ross lucidly demonstrated, historization was a central means in the hands of a school of Protestant religious-legal thinkers that flourished around the turn of the seventeenth century and attempted to discern those biblical laws that were eternal and universal from those particular to biblical society. The signature feature of the "Mosaic legalists," as he terms them, was their caution about destroying the bridge spanning the biblical and contemporary worlds. When historicizing biblical society, they were attentive not to historicize their own contemporary society, thus maintaining a theoretical link between them. It is precisely the stabilizing factor of the historical exegesis that was lacking in the undertaking of the English commentators from the late seventeenth century: By comparatively historicizing both biblical and contemporary societies, they offered a radical reading of the Scriptures—at least on usury.[51]

The shift of approach to the Bible is also evident in the essential difference between the English commentators studied here and the great translation movement a century earlier. Naomi Tadmor illustrates how the various English translators of the Bible emphasized through their work the *affinity* of English society with the biblical text. The English Bible was made in light of the English social universe, a project she calls the anglicizing of the Bible, thus rendering it comprehensible and relevant—and extremely popular.[52] The new historical reading of usury, as well as of other commercial questions, distanced English readers from biblical reality and thus maintained the Englishness of the Bible in an opposite manner: By detaching biblical socioeconomic teaching from early modern society, it made the Bible fit for English society. Instead of being rejected, these teachings were identified as historically irrelevant.

* * *

Having concluded this circuit, I would like to make explicit some arguments implied throughout this chapter. Presumably, the historical interpretation of biblical usury did not shape social reality. Lending on interest was a ubiquitous practice in England for a century before the spread of the new biblical reading. At the same time, we may suspect that many of the people who lent and borrowed on interest did not delay their transactions waiting for an effective justification; if they did, they had other qualified scholastic approvals with a long history of their own. Also, the gradual religious relaxation of usury was underway at that time, independent of the change of viewpoint I demonstrated.[53] Where this new reading intervened was in broadening the intellectual possibilities for thinking about the Scriptures, society, and history.

Three big questions hover above the discussion, and it is time to revisit them. The first is the adequacy of Max Weber's thesis on the Protestant ethics and capitalism. The doctrine of predestination, argued Weber, made

the individual's inner conscience the core of ethics and created an environment in which mundane work and success became religious hallmarks. This
radically new ethics supported the development of later capitalism. The question of usury in the English setting seems to be a particularly appropriate
case for testing the thesis. Indeed, several works attempted to validate it by
examining the changing approach to usury in England, demonstrating a shift
of emphasis from social action to one's inner conscience.[54] However, the current examination indicates that during most of the seventeenth century, most
English exegetes adhered to traditional concepts.[55] Furthermore, and more
important, the interpretive shift that eventually occurred was triggered not by
a Protestant ethic or any other Protestant content but through a new historicist viewpoint. It should be stressed, however, that the tendency for histori-
cization itself was a Protestant inclination of the seventeenth century and that
this heritage greatly impacted the intellectual development discussed here.

The other haunting question is that of secularization. The sociological secularization thesis—that is, that modernization inherently entailed a linear process of the ebbing of the social power of religion—has been severely criticized
over the last decades. Indeed, the story of this chapter—whose protagonists
are all leading clerics—does not seem to indicate any weakening of religion.
Quite to the contrary, it demonstrates the vitality and power of the Scriptures
in negotiating pressing political-economic issues. Yet this vitality was dialectic.
The historical contextualization depicted here implied a reconceptualization
of society as a specific system constituted according to relations that vary in
time and space. This loosened the dependency between the economic sphere
and religion, promoting, perhaps, a kind of semiautonomous economic logic.
The perspective offered in this chapter, however, stresses that religion was
not in decline; rather, its relations with society were being restructured. Put
differently, this was a change in religious *sensibilities*. Whereas usury was traditionally bound with the question of identity, whose core was religious, the
new commentators replaced this organizing principle with an analytical view of
society as a system determined by its economic and social parameters. This was
not achieved by discarding the authority of Scriptures—as in a "hard secularization" schema—but through it. The chapter thus echoes Sheehan's reflection
that the dialectic recess and return of religion are inherent to modernity.[56] In a
sense it also resonates the claim that in settings where the established church
accommodated the separation of the religious from other civil spheres, we tend
not to see antireligious upheavals. The disparity between the English and the
French writers is revealing of this broader pattern.[57]

With the third question, I want to tie the threads of this chapter to the preceding and following discussions. One channel for handling socioeconomic questions in seventeenth-century England, this book suggests, was through the discourse on the Jews. Here I sought to reveal how the shifting of focus from modern Jewish history to the ancient one, and the re-narration of the latter, operated in reshaping the approach to usury. Was this in any sense related to contemporary questions regarding the recently settled Jews in England? Was it in any way encouraged by the new situation and the public controversy of the 1650s over the Jewish settlement, or did it affect the approach to concrete Jews? Put differently, what was the relationship between ancient and contemporary Jews in the English cultural matrix? It is hard, perhaps impossible, to prove a direct link between the two. And it might be unlikely that the readmission debate encouraged the shifts in biblical thinking, or that these conceptual changes affected the approach to real-life Jews. Yet the historicized vision of biblical usury had at least one discernible impact. It shifted the perspective on the Jews from an ahistorical to a historical one, thus breaching the allegedly homogenous continuum of Jewishness, or, more specifically, of the Jewish economic character. This detachment was conceived not along the theological lines of the disconnection of the Jews from holy history after rejecting the Gospel, but by an analysis of changing historical conditions. It bestowed on the traditional Christian dichotomy of Israelites versus Jews a new meaning grounded in a historical-anthropological rather than theological conception.[58]

The changing discourses on the ancient and contemporary Jews were related in another, perhaps self-evident, way. They were both parts of broader changes in patterns of thinking that developed at the time. The following chapter demonstrates how the anthropological outlook changed the perception of Jewishness—this time not of ancient but of contemporary Jews.

Chapter 3

English Ethnography
and the Economy of the Jews

The observations about the economy of the Jews explored in the preceding two chapters were pieces in the broad early modern puzzle of knowledge about people. This consisted of a mixture of genres, interests, and methods, encompassing what later became geography, history, ethnology, and sociology. The encounter with the New World confronted writers with the challenge of describing and explaining heretofore unimaginable peoples, cultures, and landscapes. These led the way to a new conceptualization of society and culture. By the seventeenth century, the Science of Man was beginning to professionalize.[1]

Although ethnology as a field, let alone a term, is anachronistic to early modernity, I employ it here to capture the concern with other people's social and cultural characteristics. Like much of early modern intellectual culture, many ethnographic works crossed national borders and languages, becoming influential in different places and contexts, sometimes in very different ways than their original ones. Accordingly, the important question is that of the audience, not necessarily the writer. English readers received ethnological information about the Jews through two main channels: travel literature and ethnographies. As a genre, travel literature was less frequently translated, so readers read mostly original English material. As one would expect, these works focused on present-day conditions. In contrast, systematic ethnographies, namely texts directly intended to address the manners of diverse peoples—which were more often translated—engaged a broader historical spectrum.[2]

This chapter places the growing English interest in Jews and their economic characteristics in the context of the emerging early modern ethnography. What distinguished them in comparison with other Others that attracted ethnological interest was that they were a target for a double analysis, as both ancient and contemporary objects. This chapter demonstrates that it is precisely this move, at times tension, between historical and present-day Jews that marked the English use of Jewishness in thinking about socioeconomic concerns. Moneylending and usury embodied this cross-historical linkage and, as in the previous chapters, serve as my focal points.

Jews became the object of English ethnological inquiry in the late sixteenth century as both historical and contemporary people. The translation of *Josippon*, the medieval adaptation of Josephus, by clergyman Peter Merwen, marked the rise of a new interest in Jewish history.[3] In the same period, English travel literature gained popularity as a channel for examining the manners of contemporary Jews. Both branches consolidated in the seventeenth century. The interest in biblical and classical Jewish society was articulated in works by eminent English Hebraists such as John Selden, Thomas Hobbes, and James Harrington. They were followed by a tide of ethnological works on contemporary Jews, most notably around midcentury, as Jews became salient Others in the English imagination. As demonstrated by Eva Holmberg, English people examined the different aspects of Jewish life to make sense of the Jews' place in the world. Such examinations formed notions about their own identities as well as the Jews.[4] Holmberg's work on early modern English ethnography of the Jews joins Yaakov Deutsch's broader study of the same in early modern Europe.

This chapter draws on both, but navigates differently in the ethnographic ocean, asking different questions: How were the Jews economically described, and how did this inform English people's concerns about their own economy? It demonstrates a two-stage process. During most of the seventeenth century, English ethnographers studied contemporary Jewish economic practices and tended to view them in a derogatory manner. By the latter part of the century, this interest waned. In its place, there developed a new interest in the economic system of ancient Jewish society. The move along the historical timeline and the shifting moral evaluation that it entailed are the main thrusts of this chapter.

The Economic Ethnography of Modern Jews: A Narrative of Degeneration

Early modern travel literature facilitated the generic transition from medieval to modern ethnological inquiries.[5] Perhaps the most significant English-language travel publication was the *Pilgrimes* by Samuel Purchas (c. 1577–1626). Educated in Cambridge and Oxford, Purchas was ordained deacon in 1598 and served as a clergyman in various positions and parishes. Though he himself never traveled out of central England, his compilation of travel accounts, first published in 1613, could be considered the contemporary English textbook of world knowledge. Purchas's work was the fruit of almost twenty years of compilation and editing, and amounted to four folio volumes, encompassing both the Old World and the New World.[6]

Purchas maintained a common claim that the Jews were an instrument in the hands of despotic rulers—mainly Catholic and Ottoman, but also historical English overlords—for exploiting their own subjects. They were given privileges to extract extortionate usury so that they could be taxed by the local chiefs and provide them with capital. Describing the Jews in Italy, he noted that they were privileged by the pope to live and practice their religion in Rome and to engage in intensive usurious moneylending. Sometimes they even had special magistrates to mediate controversies with Christians, "with particular direction to favor them in their trade." Their "cruel trade" was suffered for gain, as they paid an annual poll tax, "besides other meanes to racke and wracke them in their purses at pleasure, they being vsed as the spunge-like Friers, to sucke from the meanest, to be squeezed of the greatest."[7]

This pattern recurs conspicuously in sixteenth- and early seventeenth-century accounts. In *Historye of Italye* (1549), William Thomas describes with astonishment the gain that the people of Venice receive from the Jews' usury.[8] The prominent traveler-writer Fynes Moryson illustrates a pattern of cyclic exploitation in his account of travels in Italy and Germany (1617), as does Robert Fage (1658).[9] The same explanation is invoked in the geographical books of Samuel Clarke (1657), G.H. (1670), and Peter Heylyn (1625),[10] who epitomized the economic character of the Jews as "a people which know how to comply with the times, and the condition which they live in; especially if their profit be concerned in it. . . . A Nation which will thrive wheresoever they come, but most by usury and brocage."[11]

The predominance of Jewish usury in Europe in the works of English travel writers reflected not only an anti-Jewish but also an anti-Catholic aspect. Because Jews were seen as enriched by usury, the Catholic Church decreed that converts' property be confiscated. English travelers saw this as another instance of the despotic exploitation of Jewish usury and a major hindrance to conversion, noting that there were fewer converts in Italy than in any other Christian country.[12]

Jewish usury was no less central in travelers' depictions of the Muslim world. According to George Sandys's account of his travels in the Levant (1615), the Jews live everywhere as hated aliens who are suffered as a "neces-sary mischief," their occupations being "Brocage and Vsurie." They accom-modate themselves to contemporary profitable opportunities and are generally "worldly wise and thrive wheresoever they set footing." William Biddulph, the Levant Company chaplain in Aleppo in the early seventeenth century, described them as "very great Vsurers," and suggested that the Turks use them to extort the public.[13]

The most elaborate discussion of the Jews in both the Christian and Mus-lim worlds was offered by Sir Henry Blount in his account of his journey in Italy and the Levant (1636). As noted by Holmberg, Blount sought not only to describe but also to explain the ostensible Jewish preoccupation with interme-diary trades. This was part of his overall intellectual endeavor of travel, which he saw as a means to obtain knowledge through immediate encounters with other cultures, transcending the restraints of religious and national biases.[14] Blount claimed that because modern Jewish society was "more condemned than understood," its analysis was inescapably flawed. Instead, he explained the Jews' socioeconomic condition historically, arguing that they have undergone a degeneration from their original professions as husbandmen and shepherds into the "Merchants, Brokers, and Cheaters" they are nowadays. The Jews' desperate fortunes and frequent captivities have brought them into "forreigne conversation" with the corrupted Gentiles that "did extreamely debauch their old innocence." Blount bases this explanation on the premise that changes in social manners derive from shifting necessities; hence, "desperate fortunes" are the primary cause of social decay. Accordingly, this condition, along with the inherent particularism of the Jewish religion, has made them odious and led them to rely on machinations for survival. Thus a self-sustaining loop has been formed, branding the Jews as a "faction against the rest of Mankinde." The persisting exclusion made them highly cunning, gaining excessive riches. In the Orient they have also gained extraordinary political influence, applied to a large degree against Christendom.[15] At the same time, their deceiving spirit is the force that prevents them from uniting into one nation and holds them in exile; for the love of private interest that they have developed operates also among themselves, so they lack the "justice and respect to common benefit without which no civill society can stand."[16]

Around the same time Blount published his account, other writers were developing a similar explanatory model. Here we make a generic move from travel writing to systematic ethnographies, starting with one of the most important of such works in early modernity: *The History of the Rites, Customes, and Manner of Life, of the Present Jews* by the Venetian rabbi Leone de Modena (1571–1648). Modena was Jewish, but his book was aimed at a non-Jewish audience. Indeed, it was translated into several languages and had a substantial impact on the discourse regarding Jews in Europe. As we shall see, it became a central reference point also in the English ethnographic discussion and served as a counterforce to the anti-Jewish momentum described earlier. Accordingly, it should be included in the early modern map of English ethnographies of the Jews. It is assumed that the work was written in 1616, after the English ambassador implored Modena to write a treatise on the Jews for King James I. It was first printed in Italian in 1637 (with a revised edition in 1638) and translated into English in 1650, at a time when the status of Jews in England became a prominent political and religious question.[17]

Modena sought to promote the social emancipation of European Jews by stressing the benevolence of their customs and behavior toward their Christian neighbors. In the second edition, he also offered historical reasoning for their supposed contemporary socioeconomic degradation. He accepts the claim that the Jews have degenerated from their "ancient *Israelitish* Sincerity" (italics in original) to the pursuit of uncreditable occupations but argues that this situation has evolved from "the narrowness of their circumstances that their long Captivity has reduc'd them to" and the economic and occupational limitations placed on them. This Jewish "debase of spirits," he argues, is the source of their inclination to moneylending. Having taken the liberty to obtain usury from Gentiles, they transgress the Deuteronomic precept that allows lending with usury only to the "stranger" (taken to refer only to the anathematized Canaanites). Yet because modern Jews are excluded from creditable means of employment available to Christians, their "Brethren by Nature," they wrongfully contend that they may lawfully lend them upon usury. However, Modena claims, defining Christians as "strangers" is against both the written law and the law of nature.[18]

Modena's apologia for Jewish commercialism is remarkable primarily in acknowledging the basic Christian critique. As seen in the previous chapter, the understanding of the biblical allowance to lend on usury to strangers as pertaining only to Canaanites has been an enduring polemical Christian interpretation mainly directed against the Jews. At the heart of his defense one finds a similar historical model to that proposed by Blount, which I would call a circumstantial explanation of Jewish economy. Yet despite their agreement on the fundamental premise that Jews' affiliation with financial trades derives from historical circumstances, each reaches very different conclusions with this historicism. Historical circumstances, according to Blount, debased Jews' character to such an extent that it became incurable: Only complete emancipation could rehabilitate them, yet their profound debasement prevents them from developing the required solidarity needed for achieving that. Modena, in contrast, sees this as an amendable situation that has nothing to do with the Jews' essential character. Should the circumstances change, he implies, so would their economic inclinations.

Two other notable contemporary Jewish writers also promoted a historical-circumstantial rationale. As we have seen in Chapter 1, Menasseh ben Israel applied it for apologetic purposes, but in a different manner. He related the Jewish condition not to social dynamics but to providence and emphasized the *positive* aspect of their degraded situation: The Jews indeed lost their authentic social features, yet in promoting their commercial aptitude, divine providence provided them with a new system of solidarity, suitable to their exilic condition. A third version was proposed by Modena's younger contemporary, the Venetian rabbi Simone Luzzatto (1583–1663), who explained the Jewish social condition along similar lines but emphasized its practical implications instead of judging it morally. In his 1638 political-economic treatise, Luzzatto refrained from portraying Jews' "authentic" condition as utopian or their current one as debased, but rather sought to convince that their commercial inclination and their detachment from agrarian occupations disengaged them from civil ambitions and made them distinctly more useful and reliable to the local societies.[19]

Menasseh ben Israel and Luzzatto's narrative of the commercial usefulness of the Jews highlights Modena's argumentative idiosyncrasy: He offered a model of Jewish economic *degeneration*, in accordance with both the Christian historical view and traditional moral economy. This is remarkable because he held very different views in internal Jewish discourse. As Benjamin Arbel demonstrates, by the early seventeenth century Christian merchants and financiers were using elaborate and effective means of credit via bills of exchange, while Jewish merchants were still using cumbersome means to circumvent—at least in principle—the limitations of Jewish law. As a chief rabbi of Venice, Modena was asked whether Jews could use bills of exchange, and he responded favorably: He was one of the first Jewish decisors who pushed for a pro-commercial adaptation of the usury prohibition and the acceptance of bills of exchange as a means of credit extension.[20] Why was his view on Jewish usury in *Rites* so different, then?

Seemingly, both the genre and the intended readership shaped his ethnographic rhetoric. Modena engaged with an attack aimed at the cultural core of Judaism. In a personal letter he referred to the recently published and highly influential ethnography of the Jews by the Basel Hebraist Johannes Buxtorf (1564–1629), *Juden Schul* (1603).[21] In the first comprehensive study of its kind and the most authoritative ethnography of the seventeenth century, Buxtorf dwelled on the Jews' customs as proof of both their inherent evil and their theological failure.[22] Modena composed his treatise, the first modern ethnology written by a Jew for a non-Jewish audience, to correct that reputational damage. Buxtorf denigrated the Jews' customs without referring to their economic behavior, whereas Modena aimed to vindicate them by illustrating the general benevolence of the Jews and avoiding any hint of Jewish commercial distinctiveness. And for that, I suggest, he was ready to bite the bullet of the traditional Christian critique against Jewish usury.[23]

What was the significance of this critique for contemporary readers? Here, a comparison with the French reception of Modena is illuminating. Modena's book was translated into French by the seventeenth-century priest and biblical scholar Richard Simon (in 1674, with an expanded edition in 1681), and this translation disseminated Modena's work around Europe.[24] Simon used Modena's discussion of usury and its implied criticism of the Jews as a springboard for elaborating on Jewish economic evil. He dedicated an essay to a comparative study of Judaism and Christianity in which an entire chapter related to differences in questions of morality, and he included extensive references to usury.[25] In his introductions to both editions of Modena's book, moreover, Simon took a long note of medieval French Jews, as illustrative of Modena's formula. Before their banishment from France, Simon argued, the Jews exceeded all the rest in riches and power, thanks to the usury they were allowed to exercise under the pretense that it was of benefit to the public. Finally, it became necessary to destroy them.[26] Notably, English writers made no parallel denunciation of English Jews, despite the available anti-Jewish historiography that could stress that point (as mentioned in Chapter 1). A recent English translation of the text rendered from Simon's French by Simon Ockley (1707) kept the economic discussion and particularly the economic critique to a minimum.[27]

Modena's *Rites* via Simon's translation had an expansive intellectual impact. Two outstanding works by exiled Huguenots on the history and manners of the Jews relied on it: Jacques Basnage's *History of the Jews* (1706) and *The Ceremonies and Religious Customs of the Various Nations of the Known World* (1723–1737) by Bernard Picart (engraver) and Jean Frederic Bernard (author).[28] Basnage went further in complicating the case of Jewish usury laid out by Modena and Simon. During the Middle Ages, he describes in a Modenan vein, the Jews were excluded from all occupations and "made themselves amends by the excessive Usuries they extorted from the Christians." Measures taken by the church had little effect, and because moneylending was essentially necessary, both sides could not but violate the ban. Accordingly, he concludes, "Usury is still, as it has been in all Ages, an abundant source of Riches to this Nation [the Jews]." Basnage's main criticism is targeted toward the church; ultimately, however, and much different from Modena's sympathetic explanation, he figures the Jews as almost essentially perpetual usurers.[29]

Notably, among the English texts that followed and engaged with contemporary Jewish ethnography, only one picked up on Modena's discussion, and that only for a side reason. In his *Ceremonies of the Present Jews* (1728), the convert Moses Marcus mentioned in passing Modena's circumstantial explanation of the Jews' usury as demonstrating the potential power of historical circumstances in mending much of the dated religious conduct of the Jews. Other writers who dwelled on Jewish customs and ways of living showed no interest in Jewish economic life whatsoever.[30]

From Present Back to the Past: The Rise of the Economic Ethnography of Ancient Israel

From the latter part of the seventeenth century, the harsh approach of English writers to contemporary Jewish economic life—and especially toward usury—diminished. This change of mood might explain the markedly different attitudes in England and France to Modena's text, as explored earlier. Lancelot Addison (father of the renowned Joseph Addison) provides an apt example. Addison was a chaplain of the English stronghold of Tangier in the 1660s; on his return to England in 1671, he published a reportage portraying the civil and religious conduct of the North African Moors and Jews. He noted that usury was so rampant among Jews that the Moors—who strictly forbade it—believed it to be the reason the Jews were "oppressed of God and live Exiles from their own Canaan." Four years later, after consulting the available literature in England, Addison published a new text focused on the Jews of North Africa, which offered a different take. Along with their thriving merchandize, he states, the Jews practice their "darling Brokage and Usury, in which they are very serviceable both to Christians and Moors."[31] Geographer John Ogilby remarked at about the same time that Jews "bring no small advantage by the liberty of their Usury" to the great wealth and merchandise of Barbary.[32]

From around the beginning of the eighteenth century, fewer English travel writers criticized Jewish economic conduct, and those who did ignored the issue of usury. Examples of the latter include Aaron Hill and Lady Mary Wortley Montagu, wife of the British ambassador, both of whom traveled the Ottoman Empire, as well as Thomas Nugent, who toured Germany.[33] Many others manifest disinterest in Jewish economic traits in general, even in texts that deal extensively with Jews.[34] Samuel Sharp's *Letters from Italy* (1767) is revealing in that regard. Like many travelers in Italy, he describes the Mount of Piety—the public bank in Bologna providing low-interest loans to the poor. Standing in front of the building, which holds an ancient inscription that states its goal to eradicate Jewish usury, Sharp ponders the traditional association of Jews and usury as an explanation for the inherent detestation of moneylending itself. If the Jews were the only moneylenders in Europe in the past, he writes, no wonder that "what was a *Jewish* practice, should be held in such detestation by Christians; but, with the times, we see the modes of religion totally alter, and good Bishops now make no scruple to receive five *per cent.*" (italics in original).[35]

While interest in the economic life of contemporary Jews was declining from the late seventeenth century, a parallel one, having to do with the economic life of *ancient* Jews, was rising. The historical ethnography of the Jews was an important branch of early modern Hebraism (whose background was explored in Chapter 1), including works by John Selden, Thomas Hobbes, James Harrington, and John Locke.[36] These writers were mainly interested in the political and social order of ancient Jewish society, perceived as a normative basis for early modern polities. With the exception of Harrington, none found interest in the economic aspects of the ancient Jewish society. Yet by the eighteenth century, this issue emerged as a new point of reference, revolving around the myth of the autarkic agrarian Israelite society. As shown in Chapter 2, from the 1680s on, this portrayal became a univocal explanation of the biblical usury prohibition by English Bible commentators. Soon enough, it became a central component in the expanding genre of ancient Jewish ethnography.

Origines Hebrææ (1724–1725) by Thomas Lewis is a good example. In his discussion of the laws of mercy, Lewis elaborates on the nature of the biblical regulations regarding usury, which he explains as a set of norms that differentiate according to socioeconomic distinctions. Usury was banned toward an insider Jew because the ancient Jewish social order was established on autarkic agriculture, while it was permitted toward the Gentiles because their social order was based not least on commerce. The similarity to the ideas expressed in the corpus of biblical commentaries is not coincidental of course: Lewis borrowed entire passages from Simon Patrick's commentary on Deuteronomy. What is notable is Lewis's ideological profile: a High Church polemist and vehement opponent of latitudinarianism, which Patrick himself, as well as the other writers in the circle of commentators who pushed this interpretation, aptly represented. As it becomes clear, the ideas of the biblical Jewish economy, and their contemporary moral implications, were no longer confined to Whiggish-leaning writers.[37]

In contrast to Lewis's ideological profile, the eminent natural philosopher and radical theologian William Whiston is another example of the historicizing interpretation of usury. In *The Horeb Covenant Reviv'd* (1730), Whiston compares the ancient Jewish and Christian systems of conduct and defines usury as a distinct obligation within the former. As the ancient Jews could not increase their wealth by trade or by buying lands (as these must be returned by the jubilee), they never borrowed money for an extended period, except under conditions of extreme poverty. This is demonstrated, he argues, by the permission to take usury from aliens only and not from proselytes living among the Jews (in this case, the term proselyte designates not a convert but a non-Jew who settles among the Jews in the land of Israel), proving it was not a question of religious affiliation but of social-structural characteristics.[38]

Moses Lowman is another nonconformist minister who joined our set of socially oriented writers. In *A Dissertation on the Civil Government of the Hebrews* (1740), he analyzes the Hebrew society and polity as constituted by a complex and comprehensive system of checks and balances aimed at preventing the accumulation of land, wealth, capital, and hence power. Peculiar to the ancient Jewish society until its dissolution, this system maintained equality and immobility. The prohibition on usury was distinct to this social system, designed to curb extreme financial power.[39]

Because ancient Jewish society hinged on subsistence agriculture, some writers argued, it lacked any circumstances of luxury or personal ambition, and it was only in such a social framework that the ban on usury could prevail. This claim was expressed in the popular gigantic historical compilation *An Universal History, from the Earliest Account of Time to the Present* (1745). Mosaic law, it argued, was designed for a noncommercial society, a structure that was dissolved by the Jews themselves since the time of Solomon, when trade and manufactures were introduced, generating pride and luxury and enticing commercialization.[40]

These ideas were not limited to English writers. Scottish jurist James Home defined in his *Scripture History of the Jews and their Republick* (1737) the prohibition on usury as a social law unique to the Jewish commonwealth, implying that Christians are allowed to lend on interest as long as it is in accord with civil law.[41] Similarly, Church of Ireland clergyman Edward Ryan, in *The History of the Effects of Religion on Mankind* (1788), locates the prohibition on usury in the larger economic system of the ancient Israelites, implying the peculiarity of the prohibition: "The law relative to usury was founded on their polity with respect to property, and absolutely unjust with respect to other nations; a man having as just a right to what his money produces by trade or otherwise, as to the rent made by the industry of others. The prohibition of usury being founded on an equal division of land, there could be no reason for it in countries where that equality did not subsist."[42]

Abbé Claude Fleury's *Les moeurs des Israélites* (1681), discussed in the previous chapter, had tremendous influence over eighteenth-century ethnology.[43] As we have seen in the biblical discourse, in this context, too, we can identify descriptions similar to those of the English writers, bearing contradictory implications. All these writers have shared the utopian analysis of the ancient Jewish society as self-sufficient. Almost none of the trades was of use to them, and the same was true regarding the growing use of money that we see in early modern Europe, which had very limited relevance for the Israelites. For Fleury this made the ancient Israelites the perfect role models for mending the flaws of contemporary commercializing and globalizing societies. English writers, in contrast, never made this conjecture. They either avoided applying the ancient model to current appraisals or emphasized the unbridgeable distance between the two worlds.[44]

Whereas, as we have seen, the eighteenth century in England saw the rise of interest in the economy of ancient Jews and a decline of interest in that of contemporary Jews, one exceptional work attempted to connect the two—the popular encyclopedic compendium *New Universal History of the Religious Rites, Ceremonies, and Customs of the Whole World* (1780) by William Hurd. Hurd devoted two sections to the Jews—ancient and modern—with which he opened the colossal work.[45] He had a marked concern with the modern Jewish preoccupation with moneylending. Following a social-historical explanation similar to Modena's, he describes their inevitable recourse to "usury and commerce" that brought on them endless miseries. In response to their demand for repayment, their "merciless unprincipled debtors" stigmatized them as usurers and "let loose upon them the whole rage of civil and ecclesiastical power." Hurd then expounds on historical examples from England and other countries, which forever bring dishonor "upon those concerned in the persecution."[46] Like Modena, he justifies the Jews' inclination to moneylending by the severe circumstances they confronted in Europe. Yet he adds a twist: The fact that Jews were constrained to the occupation of moneylending in itself bolstered the negative perception of the practice. The (just) repayment demanded by the poor Jew became "usury" in the public mind. Despite relying on a similar historical explanation for vindicating the Jews, Modena and Hurd's approaches to usury are oppositional. Hurd interprets the entire history of European Judeophobia within the framework of the economic tension between progressive and backward elements. Jewish economic success was the hinge of the regrettable Christian- (and specifically English-) Jewish relations, leading to accusations against Jews for "crimes they never committed." He explains how a person who owed the Jews money could exhume a dead boy's body to falsify a charge and nullify his debt. The whole set of anti-Jewish accusations, like the blood libels and ritual murders, derived from the Jews' financial advantage. In the same vein, he describes their prosecution by Edward I (r. 1272 to 1307) as carried out "under the stale pretence of their being usurers."[47] The accusation of usury, a pivotal justification for the expulsion, becomes for Hurd a political excuse.

Hurd's account of the ancient Jews complements his view of modern Jews. There, he has another goal: to demonstrate, against Deist attacks, that biblical law is both rational and moral. He does so mainly through the historical contextualization of biblical law, constantly referring to the "circumstances of time." Some biblical proscriptions, including usury, he demonstrates, derived from the ancient Jews' agrarian, autarkic, and anticommercial economy. Being "people living without commerce, confined to agriculture," the ancient Jews were different in their social circumstances from contemporary English people "who live in a commercial land of real liberty."[48] The association of commerce and liberty stands in contrast to agrarianism's infringement on people's rights, as expressed most notably in the biblical endorsement of slavery. For Hurd, the prohibition on usury and the approval of slavery are both characteristic features of the particular ancient Jewish society and derive from its radical agrarianism; consequently, they do not pertain to modern European societies. Although biblical law as a whole provides an epitome for the divine natural law, it should be critically understood as, in some cases, pertinent to specific social circumstances, a principle that eighteenth-century commentators fail to realize.[49] Ironically, throughout history the ban on usury, which should have been a particular law of the ancient Jews, became the source of Christian oppression of modern Jews.

Historicizing Jewish Societies

This is an appropriate point to tie together the threads laid out in the preceding chapters. Early modern English writing on the question of commerce was somewhat traditional in its approach to the Jews, locating them as an explanatory and rhetorical hinge of the problems of commercialism. Central to this rhetoric was usury. However, from the second half of the seventeenth century, this entrenched tendency was beginning to wane. As demonstrated in these chapters, in different genres and for different reasons, either the effectiveness or interest in the notion of Jewish usury was losing its grip. These different moves shared an essential feature: a *historical* analytical perspective on Jewish economic life.

Instead of the obsession with modern Jewish economy, the economy of ancient Jewish society was becoming a prevalent theme. At the heart of this new concern was the myth of ancient Jewish society as an autarkic and encapsulated entity. This was not a uniquely English intellectual trend: Historicizing the ancient Israelites was an essential feature of humanist political thought around the beginning of the seventeenth century. Most notable was Petrus Cunaeus's influential treatise, discussed in Chapter 1, which was presumably the basis for subsequent seventeenth-century writers.[50] Yet English writers found in this model an exceptionally fruitful resource. By stressing the historical distance if not incommensurability of modern society and the ancient Jews, the new paradigmatic analysis discharged modern commercial society from the social norms set by the Scriptures. This was profoundly different from other approaches to mitigate the prohibition on lending on interest, whose arguments were entirely extrascriptural.[51] Consequently, while traditional criticism of usury retained some effectiveness,[52] its influence became limited mainly to sermons and other moralistic genres.

The increasing preoccupation with the ancient Israelites from the late seventeenth century co-occurred with the growing presence of real Jews in England. It is tempting, though purely speculative, to connect the two. The writers who promoted the historical reading of usury were all in their twenties and thirties s when the readmission polemic occurred. Harrington, for one, explicitly referred to the question of readmission, to Bible exegesis, and to the historical ethnography of the ancient Jews. However, the use of the model of the ancient Israelite economy seemingly did influence the perception of modern Jews—yet indirectly and contingently. As we have seen, the shared concept of the autarkic Israelites, and the shared method of historicizing the Jews, endured across the Republic of Letters, serving contradictory purposes. For French writers the essential notion determining the status of the Jews was their *degeneration* from this state of authenticity. This was apparent in late seventeenth-century works but still held sway a century later in classical enlightenment works such as the *Encyclopédie*.[53] This model—in line with the Christian supersessionist paradigm—was built on a semantic distinction between modern Jews and ancient Hebrews or Israelites. In England, however, these semantic designations were fluid.[54] Perhaps this difference explains the motivation of modern French Jews to refer to themselves as *Israélites*, something English Jews were never inclined to do.

The continental emphasis on Jewish degeneration, along with the semantic distinction between Israelites and Jews, did not necessarily entail hostility, nor did the ambiguity of the English terms connote sympathy toward the Jews. Prominent French writers, as we have seen also with Modena, promoted a new, sympathetic understanding of the Jewish condition, which they argued derived from their historical circumstances. English writers, on the other hand, were not necessarily bent on justifying Jews. Instead, they were more interested in justifying commercial practices. Perhaps inadvertently, the vindication of usury in the mainstream English version delineated here also vindicated present-day Jews from traditional accusations. Inadvertently, because what was at the focus was not the conduct of the Jews but the biblical prohibition of usury itself. This was a much more radical move than the one sought by Jewish apologists such as Modena and Menasseh ben Israel, for it provided an entirely new perspective on usury, not merely on the behavior of the Jews. Schematically put, then, while sympathetic continental writers (Jews among them) often implied the conclusion that the base condition was not the Jews' fault, the English use of the ethnological analysis tended to downplay the fault itself.

This shift in understanding biblical usury was the gradual outcome of an increasing tendency of historization, especially in Protestant settings. The intellectual history of this idea from the early seventeenth century, demonstrated in Chapter 1, seems decisive in its adoption among English writers. Yet beyond the Dutch-English intellectual exchange, a deeper cultural shift appears to underlie this story: a profound change in religious sensibilities. Philosopher Marcel Gauchet described what he called the end of "Christian history," God's gradual retreat from direct terrestrial involvement in human affairs into the position of a remote celestial creator. In the wake of God's withdrawal, man was left to make sense of the world on his own terms, empowered to understand his influence on the world and on history in new ways. The human order was gradually becoming understood as autonomous and self-regulating. Infusing these insights with historical substance, Keith Baker, David Bell, and Dror Wahrman illustrated different facets of this grand process in early modern French and English history.[55] One profound shift they all illuminated was the emergence of "foundational concepts" for understanding the world. A central concept was "society," designating a universal system of interrelations within human collectives that adhere to a set of common structural principles. This was the basis for the rise of new proto-social scientific approaches to communities, cultures, and religions, soon reaching its pinnacle with the systematic ethnographical explorations of the eighteenth century.[56]

Why did the new intellectual conceptualization of the ancient Israelite society find such fertile soil among English writers? I suggested that it resonated effectively with the increasing commercialization of English society and the growing sophistication and prominence of finance, a process that historians now call the Financial Revolution. The conception of the Israelites could serve as a vocabulary by which to address—at varying levels of explicitness—questions of commercialism, including usury, in a changing reality.

The seventeenth century was a period of accelerating changes in the economic order in England, on both the material and discursive levels. Scholars often indicated a process of secularization of the economic discourse, from its immersion in theology as late as the end of the sixteenth century to growing independence in the budding seventeenth-century field of political economy. Prominent in this development in England were early economic writers Edward Misselden and Thomas Mun, who were active in the early seventeenth century and promoted more secularized and nonmoral views on economy. Joyce Appleby goes so far as to regard Mun as a writer who, by addressing the economy as an abstract system independent of its specific social actors, created a new paradigm for thinking about it. These conceptual shifts and new ideas, evolving since the 1620s, formed the notional infrastructure of the future Financial Revolution.[57] Midcentury thinkers further developed the abstraction and independence of economy as a field, constructing it as analytical and calculative. In parallel, by that time the conservative opposition to taking interest on loans lost its grip in public discourse.[58]

The changes were not limited to the discursive level. Keith Wrightson highlights the mid-seventeenth century as a period of change around which demographic stabilization, falling prices, and increase in real wages combined to shape a new commercial environment, with profound implications for the typical English household that came to depend on the market. The expansion of the market, in turn, diminished the centrality of agriculture.[59] These changes entailed the need to adapt the religious and cultural discourses. The accounts presented in this chapter all took part in this adaptation, and all chronologically followed the climax of these socioeconomic shifts around the midcentury. Most important was the change in the ways the English interpreted Scriptures—the principal means for criticizing and curbing market relations and a fundamental axis in early modern English identity. Appleby argues that, as part of the paradigmatic shift in economic culture, the Bible itself lost its validity as a socioeconomic manual. Conversely, I demonstrated how the tendency toward commercialism reverberated *within* the reading of Scripture itself. Religion was not displaced by new theories, although the attitude to religious foundations certainly did change.[60]

The new reading of usury reflected not only a new economic ideology but also a new stance vis-à-vis the notion of Israel. While early modern English imagined themselves intensively as *Verus Israel*, an association that climaxed during the Civil Wars, this tendency diminished in the latter part of the century. By the beginning of the eighteenth century, the idea of England as the New Israel was no longer considered as adequate nation-building rhetoric.[61] This does not mean that English people stopped relating to themselves as a chosen nation, in biblical terms (as exemplified in Handle's biblical oratories); yet this was no longer as sincere an identification as in the mid-seventeenth century, but more of a national complacence. Protestant England, they believed, was elected by God, but this election only resonated with the historical election of the Jews, rather than embodying concrete identification with the Israelites as a society.[62] The historical contextualizing of the ancient Jews combined with this broader movement and entailed a detachment from and defamiliarization of ancient Jewish society. The English detachment from the biblical Israelites that was well on its way by that time facilitated the cultural acceptance of pro-commercial tendencies, and their permeation even into the English Bible itself. The shutting of the door on biblical economic ethics co-occurred with the opening of a new phase in English economic history. The Financial Revolution, as it came to be known in the recent decades, introduced to England and other countries in Europe a new matrix of politics and economy based on new credit instruments. These flared up public discontent with the ethical, social, political, and economic implications of the new system. The following chapters address this new situation, which, I demonstrate, also had profound consequences for the ways Jews were imagined.

PART II

Finance

Chapter 4

Jews and the Financial Revolution

As money was necessary on many occasions to who had none locked
up, the Jews, who have always despised land property, made a trade
of lending; and this drew an odium upon the practice. I can ascribe
it to no other cause. Our manners are totally changed; and Christians lend money at interest well as Jews. Neither trade, industry or
credit can subsist without it; and as money cannot be lent, without
allowing interest be taken, interest is become the basis of the whole
system of credit.

—James Steuart

This passage, written by the Scottish political economist Sir James Steuart in
1765, demonstrates the sea change that the practice of lending with interest
had undergone in public life, in terms of both its growing economic centrality
and its public reception. According to Steuart, usury was abhorred throughout Christian history not because of any intrinsic quality of the practice or its
economic impact, but merely because of its association with Jews. The recent
shift in the credit system, he goes on to demonstrate, eroded this conception.
Steuart himself was a staunch Jacobite, indicating how the Whig-Tory controversy on the basic question of the place of finance in the national economy
had become blurred by the second half of the century.

Peter Dickson refers to the process described by Steuart as the Financial
Revolution, and since the publication of his 1967 monograph on the subject
it has been thoroughly studied as such by historians, sociologists, and literary
critics.[1] According to sociologist Niklas Luhmann, this process marked the
shifting of weight from the early modern *personal* credit, based on a social

network and personal trust, to an anonymous system of mediated credit on national and international scales, based on confidence in the system itself.[2] In turn, this revolution generated problems different from those that character-ized the personal system. Accordingly, as discussed in the following chapters, the figure of the Jew was reconstructed in keeping with the new concerns.

What was the kernel of this Financial Revolution? Scholars debate over the most revolutionary ingredient in this process. The classical approaches focus on the state's success in raising funds by new instruments, backed by parliamentary authority: the introduction of long-term national debt (Peter Dickson); raising of short-term loans (Dwyryd W. Jones); or improved tax-collection mechanisms (John Brewer). Others add the thriving secondary mar-ket in securities as a decisive factor.[3] Still others stress the constitutional and political shifts that England underwent from 1688 as factors that increased the state's credibility and hence its ability to raise funds.[4] Finally, others empha-sized the development of new conceptions of money and credit.[5] Whichever factor was the most decisive, the combination of these developments was unique to England, soon Britain. Although new political-economic views and some of the financial instruments were developed in the Netherlands in the seventeenth century and preceded parallel developments in England, they did not involve a national debt backed by the state and traded regularly in a secondary market. In the Netherlands, the focus was much more on private rather than public finance.[6] It was precisely this aspect that raised the concerns of English contemporaries, as they quickly became aware that their economy was changing dramatically. The creation of an unprecedented national debt—aimed at maintaining the ever-growing expenditure on warfare—profoundly transformed the financial relations between the state and its subjects.[7] Bonds of government loans became the pivot of the prosperous securities market, attracting growing domestic and foreign investments. The national debt kept expanding. Peter Dickson estimates that from £6.1 million in 1694, lent by five thousand creditors, it swelled to £78 million in 1750, lent by sixty thou-sand. By 1713, the debt was six times higher than the annual revenues (half of them spent on repaying the debt), and by 1742, despite the relative peace, it amounted to eight times the annual revenues.[8] Consequently, more and more people became involved and affected by state finance, becoming financially bound with the government.

Many realized that the debt was an indispensable national economic instrument if England was to attain global supremacy, yet for most contem-poraries this caused profound concerns. It was perceived as courting national disaster, an illusory blessing that would prove to be a curse for both the entire nation and private households. The public debt was seen as disastrous not only because it could not be settled, but also because it transformed social and political relations into creditor-debtor relations. Moreover, it subjugated the power of the state to people's imagination, opinion, and fantasies, under the reign of speculation.[9] What is important here is that excitement from and concern about the new financial opportunities were enmeshed. Some of the most vociferous Tory intellectuals who engaged the new culture of credit were themselves involved in financial investments.[10]

The national debt was part of the broader ramifications of the shifts in the economic system and culture. Joint-stock companies were not an innovation of the 1690s, but from this period onward they proliferated.[11] Whereas before the 1690s there were 15 such companies, owning £0.9 million, in 1695 their number soared to 150, owning £4.3 million. Between 1717 and the South Sea Company crisis of 1720 alone, investment in joint-stock companies soared from £20 to £50 million.[12] The crisis of the South Sea Company Bubble was only a temporary setback. While in 1720 there were around 40,000 shareholders overall, in the 1750s there were 60,000, and in 1800 there were 500,000.[13] These numbers reflect not only an increase in capital invested, but, more important for our purposes, a steady increase in public involvement in the financial market. Initially, financial investment had been restricted to the wealthiest; by the middle of the eighteenth century, broader social sectors took part in it.[14] This point—I shall demonstrate in the following chapters— was central to a shift in the critique of both the financial market and the Jews.

* * *

All these factors coalesced into a transformation that triggered an intense and enduring public debate. The critique of the financial system hinged on several fundamental, interrelated problems: It facilitated radical social mobilization up and down the ladder and consequently shook the social order; it created a dangerous link between men of capital and politicians that corrupted the political system, diverting it from true national interests; it diverted assets from commerce and manufacture to financial speculations; it promoted a profession of trade in stocks, or stockjobbing, which was inherently deceptive; and it allowed and even encouraged investors to benefit from national catastrophes, thus creating a strong domestic sector whose interests could be directed against the nation. All these themes were bound together by the spirit of gaming, conceived by contemporary critics to have cast a spell over all ranks of society, and undermining social ethics. The opening of vast opportunities for speculative investment unleashed the penchant for gambling, which embodied and promoted disorder and irrationality. Security speculators either were gamblers themselves or, worse, exploited others' propensity for gambling.[15]

What characterized the discourse on the new financial market from its very onset was a series of binary representations aiming to distinguish between "good" and "bad" commerce, relating to schemes, persons, and spaces. The task of the observer or participant, as sharply expounded by Daniel Defoe already in 1697, was to distinguish between substantial and invented schemes, mainly by discerning their contrivers. The deceitful trader in finance soon came to be dubbed as the stockjobber, who traded in all kinds of stocks fraudulently, tricking naïve investors. A 1699 dictionary, which declared itself "useful for all sorts of people (especially foreigners) to secure their money and preserve their lives," defined stockjobbing as "a sharp, cunning, cheating Trade of Buying and Selling Shares of Stock" of different companies or the state.[16] Samuel Johnson defined the stockjobber as "a low wretch who gets money by buying and selling shares in the funds." This figure was perhaps the most central in the discourse on finance, epitomizing its worst social effects, and was denounced by both advocates and opponents of the new mechanism. Stockjobbers were depicted as devilish man-eating creatures, having "the Figure of a Man, but the Nature of a Beast."[17]

Another normative distinction was spatial. Late seventeenth- and eighteenth-century economy was linked to the urban geography, and contemporaries differentiated between good and evil urban economic spaces: The Royal Exchange (established in 1571) was conceived as harboring positive commerce, while its adjacent counterpart, Exchange Alley, was the spatial embodiment of stockjobbing. Part of the commercial activity in the Royal Exchange was the transfer of shares, but initially this constituted only a fraction of the transactions, which were carried out without intermediators. With the growing sophistication and volume of the securities market, such transactions became an independent trade.[18] Several unsuccessful attempts were subsequently made to regulate the stock market, including the exclusion of stockjobbers from the Royal Exchange.[19] The separation of stock broking from commodities broking in the Royal Exchange was a fundamental shift in the perception of the two and highlighted their contradiction—the idea of civilized commerce and order against social and moral degeneration. As one writer bluntly described the stockjobbing in Exchange Alley, "[T]he Den from which this Beast of Prey bolts out is Jonathan's Coffee House, or Garraway's, and a Man that goes into either, ought to be as circumspect as if in an Enemy's Country."[20] The map shown in Figure 1 may give some impression of the urban geography of Exchange Alley.[21] With this at hand, one can easily follow Daniel Defoe's guidance of this hazardous region in his *Anatomy of Exchange Alley* (1719):

> The Center of the Jobbing is in the Kingdom of *Exchange Alley*, and its Adjacencies; the Limits, are easily surrounded in about a Minute and a half *viz.* stepping out of *Jonathan's* into the Alley, you turn your Face full *South*; moving on a few Paces, and then turning Due *East*, you advance to *Garraway's*; from thence going out at the other Door, you go on still *East* into *Birchin-Lane*, and then halting a little at the Sword-Blade Bank to do much Mischief in fewest Words, you immediately face to the *North*, enter *Cornhill*, visit two or three petty Provinces there in your way *West*: And thus having Box'd your Compass, and sail'd round the whole Stock-jobbing Globe, you turn into *Jonathan's* again; and so, as most of the great Follies of Life oblige us to do, you end just where you began.[22]

The national debt and stockjobbing were perceived by critics as mutually enforcing. The lion's share of securities traded was made up of various forms of public debt, and in turn, the great injury that was attributed to stockjobbing—other than moral decline—was that it undermined trust in the system and the state's credibility. The baneful traffic of stockjobbing, argued Lord Egmont in a 1763 treatise, is the "offspring of public debts, [and] has been nourished by the distresses of the nation," and their further increase "may be fatal to our credit and commerce."[23] The contemporaneous growth of the national debt and opportunities for investment and speculation resulted in a conspicuous economic injustice: While the nation as a whole—and particularly the landed estate—struggled under the burden of taxation, some individuals amassed riches. Stockjobbers were conceived as playing a pivotal role in economic crises since the mid-1690s and were believed to play that role by various manipulations: of news, of people's innocence, and of business information. These new problems touched on the core questions of the social order and national stability. Consequently, a key term in the discourse, used by all sides, was "national interest." It sought to distinguish between "true" Englishmen and various Others, who benefited from the expanding debt and

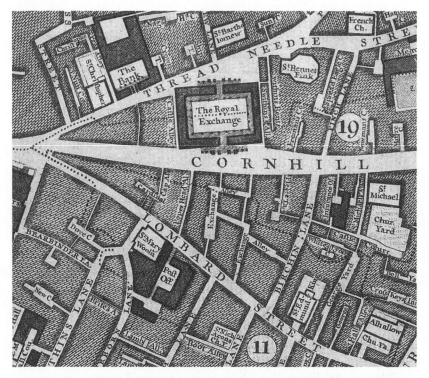

Figure 1. Map of Exchange Alley, between Cornhill and Lombard Street. Detail
from John Rocque's Map of London, 1746 (sheet E-2): *A plan of the cities of
London and Westminster, and borough of Southwark, with the contiguous buildings.*

The Beinecke Rare Book and Manuscript Library, Yale University,
Darlington & Howgego Maps of London.

lacked any concern for national interests. Indeed, a substantial part of the debt
was invested by foreigners, including Jews, who were potentially disloyal and
disinterested in the public good, a fact that exacerbated this tension.[24]

Jews and the English Securities Market

It is hard to assess the involvement of Jews in the nascent financial market
of the turn of the eighteenth century. As with other economic actors, the
term *broker* could refer to a broker of financial securities or a broker of commodities, just as the Royal Exchange traded mainly in commodities but also

in securities. The first known official Jewish broker at the Royal Exchange was Solomon Dormido, who was admitted in 1657 but sworn in only in 1668. After him, we know of thirty-two additional Jewish brokers until the Act of 1697, which was the first to regulate the stock market. The act was designed to curb unauthorized activity, in the wake of the bust of the stock-market boom earlier in the decade. It required brokers to be licensed under oath, pay an annual fee, and carry a medal of identification while working at the exchange. It forbade them to trade on their own account, regulated their commissions, and mandated severe penalties for transgressions. It also limited the number of licensed brokers to one hundred, out of which, as a regulation of the City, no more than twelve could be Jews and no more than twelve could be aliens of other nations. After 1697 Jewish brokers would replace each other after one of them died or retired.[25]

By the early eighteenth century, contemporaries tended to believe that Jewish brokers were increasingly involved in stock dealing. This was at least partly true, for indeed quite a few Jews were engaged in it, albeit mostly on a part-time basis and without increasing their wealth considerably.[26] This was accompanied by a gradual increase in the number of Jewish stockholders and their invested capital. Out of the first 1,272 shareholders of the Bank of England, six or seven were Jewish, contributing an insignificant amount. By the 1710s, however, Jewish investors figured in the top section of stockholders (10 out of the 74 holders of £5,000 and more), a trend that only increased by the middle of the century.[27]

The South Sea Bubble offers a telling perspective on Jews' involvement in the market. As Ann Carlos and her coauthors show, Jews' share in stocks was high: Out of all individuals who made at least one transaction during 1720, 4.3 percent were Jewish, yet they were involved in roughly 20 percent of the total volume of transfers. What is of no less importance is that their involvement intensified after the bubble burst, primarily as buyers of securities, contrary to the common trend. Whether intentionally or not, this helped cushion the fall and limit the scope of the crisis. Consequently, the average loss of a Jewish participant in the market was £780, much more than that of the average investor. Another important point they highlight pertains to the social characteristics of the involvement of Jews in the market. Of the 1,480 transactions in which Jews participated in 1720, in only 166 cases were both buyer and seller Jews.[28]

The year 1720 also saw the emergence of a highly important player in the English financial market, as well as in Anglo-Jewish relations—Samson (sometimes spelled "Sampson") Gideon. Gideon was born in England in 1699 to a Sephardic East Indian merchant. He began his business career in 1719, not as part of the family trade but in the bourgeoning London money market. He dealt in lottery tickets, government securities, and the stocks of the Bank of England, East India Company, and the South Sea Company. Gideon did very well on speculations: He estimated his wealth in 1719 at £1,500, in 1720 at £7,900, and in 1729 at £25,000. In the same year, he was sworn in as a broker in the City—an indication that the lack of such a license had never prevented him or others like him from trading. However, it was in the 1740s when he made his great fortune. The war of the Austrian Succession (1742–1748) and the Jacobite Rising in 1745–1746 placed the government under great financial stress and opened investment opportunities to new social sectors beyond the parliamentary and City elite. Gideon seized his opportunity and entered the first rank of influential financiers.[29] This will prove pivotal, I shall demonstrate, in the shifts of the political-economic meanings attributed to Jews in the eighteenth century.

The involvement of Jews in the financial market was significant, yet nevertheless dispensable. No less important was the role that the figure of the Jew played in the cultural construction of the new system. The anxieties that the new economic situation raised were not only social, as demonstrated earlier, but in a sense also epistemological. As Jean-Christophe Agnew put it, hovering over the new system was the question of "how one's self, one's motives, and one's relations were to be represented in a world where traditional reference points were increasingly subject to the market's overarching rule of full commensurability."[30] The perception of the Jew became a central perspective for contemporaries to engage with their concerns of the emerging modern system of finance on all these levels.

One barometer of eighteenth-century English society which may help us decipher these concerns was the theater—the leading form of entertainment in the period and a landmark in the urban cultural landscape. The experience of contemporary theater expanded beyond the stage itself, encompassing the social, the aesthetic, and the political.[31] It engaged head on with many of the period's social issues. The commercialization of society, culture, and politics was one of the most crucial among them, and its reverberations intensified with the Financial Revolution. The intensive social criticism of the financial market found an immediate and prevalent expression on the stage already in the 1690s, not only reflecting reality but also remodeling it, as Jean-Christophe Agnew suggested.[32] The dramatic medium was another central arena where the place of the Jews in English society was negotiated, both separately and in relation to financial concerns. Accordingly, the theater will be used in the following chapters to sketch a broad view of the English approach to the Jewish-financial nexus throughout the eighteenth century. As I demonstrate, this approach changed significantly around the middle of the century, particularly in the consequential context of the Jewish Naturalization Bill of 1753, to which the following chapter turns.

The 1753 Jewish Naturalization Bill and the Polemic over Public Credit

Doubtless the most resonant event in Anglo-Jewish history in the two hundred years between Jewish readmission and emancipation was the polemic around the 1753 Jewish Naturalization Bill, or the Jew Bill, as it came to be known. The bill, intended to enable the naturalization of a small number of wealthy, foreign-born Jews by a private act of Parliament and without the prerequisite of swearing a Christological oath, sparked an unexpected public clamor. Dozens of newspaper articles, pamphlets, and caricatures were published in the six months between the bill's introduction in the Commons (May 1753) and its repeal (November 1753), and widespread outcry persisted even after. The event's considerable resonance stood in apparent contrast to its minimal social and political implications, and this chapter aims at answering the puzzle of this discrepancy by illuminating a dimension of the polemic that has been somewhat overlooked by historians who have explored it.

A crucial frame for understanding the event is the internal conflict within English society over the place of finance in the social and political matrix in the wake of the Financial Revolution, touched on in the previous chapter. Contemporaries debated whether the post-1688 regime, its fortunes hinging increasingly on public finance, could avoid corruption in both the governors and the governed. The issue entailed conflictual conceptions of the state and its relations with its subjects, along with different concepts of loyalty and liberty. It also contested two notions of the economic man and the relationship of property and personality. Advocates of the new political-economic system praised the mobility of the individual enabled by an increasingly commercial society through interpersonal exchanges. In contrast, adversaries emphasized the independence that could be acquired only by stable property that made its owner independent of the men in government and thus able to resist the corruptive power of patronage, wrought to a great degree by new modes of finance.[1]

This enduring debate acquired new implications in the 1740s and early 1750s, with the escalation of the contest for global dominance among European powers. Imperial expansion, with the belligerent rivalries it entailed, required a corresponding increase of financing, which Britain attained by expanding its national debt and a sophisticated financial system. At the same time, somewhat paradoxically, empire was hailed by nationalistic patriots as an emblem of national virility and a check against the decadence spread by a corrupted ruling elite, whose chief means for maintaining power, it was argued, was the public debt. Moreover, midcentury nationalistic imperialism was characterized by marked xenophobia that coupled the peril of "strangers" with that of administrative corruption.[2] This point of view entailed another paradox, for in contrast to the nationalistic patriotic vision of the empire, foreigners in fact played an important role in the imperial endeavor in the development and maintenance of commercial networks. These tensions were expressed in the question of citizenship, which had an important economic aspect and so became an unsettling matter in the imperial context of the eighteenth century.

This configuration lent Jews—both as an image and as social players—a new relevant significance. By the mid-eighteenth century, as shown here and in the following chapters, they came to epitomize in the public imagery the prevalence of the new forms of finance. Consequently, I suggest, the Jew Bill highlighted anxieties over the role of finance and its ramifications, making the polemic a channel through which existing ideologies found new shapes and vigor. The discussion of Jewish naturalization became—at different levels of explicitness—entwined with the dispute over the place and status of finance in the economic, political, and social system.

The progress of the bill and the polemic has been well documented, and I offer here only a brief outline.[3] As Jewish readmission to England was never formally endorsed, legal lacunae existed around Jews' status, and the intent of the limits posed on them was ambiguous. Jews, because they did not adhere to the Anglican faith, lacked certain civic rights—such as being elected to and sitting in Parliament, holding office in municipal corporations, and entering universities—disabilities shared with Catholics and Dissenters, who were the intended focus of the legislation. Moreover, about half of the Jewish community had been born outside England and hence endured alien disabilities, central among them the duties charged on traders, prohibition of owning land, and exclusion from colonial trade and ship ownership. It was this second set of restrictions that the Jewish petitioners sought to overcome. As the procedure of private denization did not exempt Jews from alien duties, the only remedy for commercial inequality seemed an act of Parliament that would modify the demand for a sacramental test in order for Jews to obtain naturalization.[4]

In January 1753, Sephardi magnates approached the duke of Newcastle, Thomas Pelham, with a request for such a measure. The king's ministry, indebted to Jewish financiers for their financial support during the last Jacobite rebellion, was favorably inclined toward the request. The bill was introduced in the House of Lords on April 3, approved on April 16, and first read in the House of Commons on April 17. In spite of some opposition during its second reading (May 7), it passed and reached its third reading on May 22. At this point an expansive and acerbic public polemic began, yet royal assent was nevertheless given on June 7, shortly before the parliamentary recess. The polemic raged widely throughout that time, most intensively in newspapers and in polemic pamphlets. Magazines and satirical prints played a lesser role, and the issue was also polemicized in nonprint performances, such as public speeches, club debates, and protests. Advocates of the bill gained a much smaller share of the discourse. When Parliament reconvened on November 15, a bill of repeal was hurriedly enacted by the ministry, and public debate soon dwindled.[5]

Scholars have grappled with assessing the episode. Some believe it is best explained in the context of English anti-Judaism, the bill providing an opportunity for the venting of deep-seated Judeophobic feelings.[6] The mainstream explanation, however, promoted primarily by Thomas Perry in his still-valuable monograph, claims that the episode was first and foremost part of a longstanding division between Whig and Tory ideological traditions regarding foreign immigration and its political-economic implications— Whigs encouraging immigration as a demographic measure for fostering English economy, Tories opposing it as an injury to national cohesion and to "true" English prosperity. The question also involved another traditional Whig-Tory conflict, the diminution of church influence, for foreign-born immigrants were unlikely to be conformist in belief. According to this view, the episode was not a contest about Jews (whose involvement was merely incidental) but rather a political conflict, an opportunity for the out-of-power Tories to rally their cause against a powerful ministry in an election year.[7]

Both approaches have weaknesses. Interpreting the episode as mainly an anti-Jewish expression is incompatible with the sudden decline of the discourse once the act was repealed and with the absence of physical violence during the episode. On the other hand, interpreting it as a manifestation of partisan political struggle does not explain why the issue of Jewishness was so powerful a tool on the political scene nor why the most minimal of all naturalization schemes in the eighteenth century evoked the most severe public response.[8] Moreover, many of the opposition texts were without political orientation, sometimes denouncing the politicizing of the discussion per se. Perry's conclusion that the arguments of both sides had merely "incidental pro and anti-Jewish variations" that did not alter the nature of the polemic as a dispute over immigration is an exaggerated simplification that disregards what contemporaries actually said and read. On the contrary, the intensity of the polemic testifies to the cultural, social, and political significance bestowed on the Jews either as symbols or as actual subjects. The downplaying of the Jewish element of the controversy seems somewhat artificial.[9]

Considering these weaknesses, historian Todd Endelman has offered a synthesis of both approaches, suggesting that the clamor may have been triggered for political gains but that the feelings it brought to the surface were traditional derogatory images of the Jew that had become "part of England's cultural heritage."[10] But what was this "cultural heritage," and why did it appeal specifically to mid-eighteenth-century Englishmen? Here we may find useful the framework offered by literary scholar James Shapiro in his influential work on the perception of Jewishness in the consolidation of English identity during early modernity. Shapiro argues that what made the controversy so acute was the vulnerability of Englishness at the time. For adversaries, Jews embodied otherness—racial, religious, social, and hence national; the polemic over their civil status thus became a shibboleth in a struggle of self-definition, a struggle much wider than the specific debate. Other scholars have followed this approach and explained the debate as an attempt to redefine English national identity at a time of crisis, emphasizing how Jewish otherness worked as a marker around which English—or British—identity could crystallize.[11]

Following that lead, this chapter substantiates the somewhat general use of the term "identity" by focusing on the way in which the controversy grappled with political economy. As the political economy was an integral element in the matrix that constituted contemporary English identity, emphasizing it could help us understand some conflicts of English self-conceptions of the time and how notions of Jewishness were at play within them.

The aspect of political economy within the polemic has been generally overlooked because the public controversy is conceived to have been stimulated by religious rhetoric. Perry has shown that what actually triggered the public clamor was a harsh opposition petition submitted to the Commons by the City of London on May 21, the evening before the bill's third reading, imbuing the debate with the language of religion and nationality.[12] The petition proved exceptionally influential and set the tone for the chief part of the oppositional discourse as well as for that of supporters of the bill, who had to reply to the denunciations. Henry Pelham recognized the petition as "the foundation of that seditious spirit afterwards propagated with so much industry through the whole kingdom," by giving "a religious turn to the dispute."[13] Accordingly, the petition divided between the brief early phase of parliamentary discussion that focused on material questions, and the second and more substantial phase, which blended theological, scriptural, and historical ideas with prejudices about the Jews.[14] Yet political-economic concerns in the public phase of the discourse were embedded within the religious language. The following two sections engage the theme of political economy in these two respective phases and the ways in which different perceptions of Jewishness and finance informed them.

The Debate in the House of Commons: Jewish Finance, the National Debt, and English Society

The main discussion in the House of Commons over the bill was held on May 7 and can be schematically analyzed as hinging on two interrelated issues: the effect of "Jewish finance" on the English economy (including its colonial network) and the wide-ranging impact of the national debt.[15] Both sides agreed on the assumption that Jews were mostly employed in commerce and finance, not in manufacture. What they disagreed about was the contribution, or damage, that the naturalization of Jews—conceived to trigger the introduction of Jewish immigrants—would cause. Thus, the bill's supporter Lord Dupplin (Thomas Hay), a pivotal figure in the administrations of Walpole, Pelham, and Newcastle, argued that the Jews, by their extensive global correspondence and their "great command of money," promoted the commerce of every country in which they dwelt.[16] All the bill's supporters argued for the profound contribution Jews had made to both commerce and government finance in England since their readmission to the country.[17] On the other hand, John Barnard, a merchant and former mayor of London and a fierce opponent of the bill, argued that, because Jews were never "bred to be manufacturers or mechanics or indeed to any laborious employment," their integration within English society would not result in a contribution to English commerce but rather a quick takeover of it. Jews were especially diligent in "recommending one another and in playing into the hands of one another," and they would hinder any Christian from gaining profit from either foreign or domestic trade. They would become England's only merchants, leaving "the laborious part of all manufactures and mechanical trades to the poor Christian," of whom they would be masters.[18] It is telling that the point debated was not the Jews' economic propensity but whether boosting the financial sector would enhance English productivity. Proponents of the bill encouraged bringing capital into the system as a means of augmenting commercial and productive capacities, while adversaries implied that the kernel of productivity is labor, and that finance is not included in that category.

Schematically, the conflicting stances promoted contradicting conceptions of economic dynamics. Barnard's view of Jewish monopolism relied on a conception of the economy as a restricted and fixed system that could not be developed beyond given limits set by manufacture, finance, and commercial connections. Once all conditions were fulfilled to the maximum—as he believed was presently the case in England—bringing in additional economic agents would result in reduced profits to the English in favor of foreigners (Jews).[19] In the other camp, MP Nicholas Hardinge, secretary to the treasury and a Cambridge classical scholar, neo-Latin poet, and lawyer, argued that the economic system was open, and that even in well-developed commercial countries such as England (perhaps especially in such countries), "new men will probably make new experiments, and by new experiments, new channels of trade may be discovered, through which new and additional quantities of our manufactures may flow to a foreign market." Here the Jews entered the picture, for no people were supposed "more capable, or more ready than the Jews, to make these new experiments, because of their great propensity to trade, and because of the curse that attends them"—namely that Jews were deprived of a national land.[20] Hardinge and Barnard, as representatives, may have held a similar view of Jewish commercial inclinations, yet its combination with a contrary economic framework yielded contrary judgments.[21]

The other theme, which was debated more expansively, was the national debt and its link with Jews. Begun in the 1690s to support the expanding military expenditure, the debt was consistently growing with the almost constant warfare in which England (later Britain) was engaged. Although it was thought that debt was the only means for financing the military's needs, many believed that Britain would never be able to fully pay it off. The debt became a crucial frontline between the Whig government and the opposition, which saw it as a national disaster and a source of governmental corruption, supplying it with limitless funds. Moreover, it was argued that the government became dependent on its investors' belief (or disbelief) regarding its capacity to pay back its debt, making the fluctuating value of public stock the index of the government's stability or instability. This speculative fantasy transformed government-citizen relations, and by implication those among all citizens, into relations between debtors and creditors.[22] While opposition members perceived the debt as antipatriotic, members in favor of the government saw it as a responsible fiscal method and a true national scheme without which Britain would lose its power.

The opposition's anxiety over the national debt was well articulated by Tory MP Nicholas Fazakerley in his speech in the Commons. Concluding a long historical reflection on the Jews in England, Fazakerley identified the Glorious Revolution as a crucial moment of change. For although the revolution freed the nation from bigotry and tyranny, it instilled a new form of subordination—the raising of governmental funds on interest. This new fiscal measure had been "so favourable for the Jews" but "a most unfortunate custom for the nation," as it resulted in the setting up of stockjobbing—the contemporary term for fraudulent financial schemes. Jews and other foreigners "were invited by act of parliament to practise that trade of usury upon the state," a trade particularly abused by the Jews who "by Edward the 1st's law . . . had been forbid to practise upon the subject."[23] The influence of the debt on the state was seen as destructive. Since its introduction, England has been "like a young extravagant heir, who proportions his expence not to his income, but to his credit, without plaguing himself with the troublesome thought how the money he borrows is to be repaid."[24] Public credit had not only ruined national responsibility but also "encouraged and enabled our ministers to engage us in needless wars upon the continent, or to continue those wars longer than the interest of this nation required."[25]

To this main claim, other arguments were added. William Northey maintained that, as Britain was not in a state of war that demanded a large budget, there was no sense in offering naturalization at that moment. Even in such a case, he added, "we should not, I think, part with our birthright for nothing."

Barnard claimed that Jewish investors would adhere not to the public interest but merely to their own profit, and hence would lend money to the state without the necessity of naturalization.[26] The question of the nature of the loyalty to the state and society would recur throughout much of the debate. However, not only the loyalty of the Jews was in question but also the loyalty and interests of investors in public debt in general, both English and foreign.

The association between the economic nature of the Jews and Britain's destructive debt reached a peak in the third reading of the bill in the Commons on May 22. After the four petitions were presented, the opposition presented a motion to postpone the debate for a month. As this timing would slide into parliamentary recess, it meant the bill would be killed. The only contribution to the discussion that we know of was by opposition member John Perceval, the earl of Egmont. His powerful speech conflated Anglo-Jewish history, economic anti-Jewish views, and criticism of current fiscal policy:

> The trade of the Jews, as it appears by the oldest of our histories,
> and the earliest records both here and in other countries, was
> usury, brokerage, and jobbing, in a higher or a lower degree. By
> this traffic, in former ages, they distressed and ruined the Christian
> subjects in such numbers every where, as to draw down upon them
> from time to time the resentment of all nations, and in this traffic
> they have improved so far in this age, as now to ruin whole king-
> doms instead of individuals, by aiding ministers to beggar the states
> they serve, by which traffic also they have greatly aided to plunge
> this nation into a debt of near eighty millions.[27]

Lord Egmont identified the Jews' economic persona as potentially devastating for the nation. One instance of such an affliction, his speech implied, was the establishment of the national debt through a Jewish conspiracy. Jews could never be incorporated in the nation on an economic basis, for they were not capable of "real" and "honest" commerce. This was proved, he argued, by the history of Jews in England since their readmission, where in spite of their wealth and the greatest commercial opportunities, they did not carry on any substantial trade. All the fortunes made by Jews in England had been acquired by "contracts, subscriptions, commissions, and correspondencies, and all kinds of jobbing with the necessities of the public in the late war." Their proposed naturalization therefore would lead to "no important addition of property to this kingdom; to no possible increase of strength; to no improvement in manufactures; to no extension of commerce."[28]

The supporters of the bill painted a contrary picture of the Jews, the debt, and governmental policy. Robert Nugent, a canny Irish-born politician having lately reconciled with the Pelham ministry, claimed that since the Glorious Revolution the Jews had been extremely useful to the state "by supplying our government with large sums of money for carrying on expensive wars we have been necessarily engaged in."[29] He specifically emphasized Jewish financial aid in preserving the public credit during the Jacobite rebellion of 1745 as an indication of their loyalty and contribution. Advocates of the Jewish cause not only argued for the legitimacy of the Jews' contributions but for the legitimacy of the means itself: the service to the state by maintaining its debt.

Advocates also argued that the Jew Bill would allow the domestic economy to benefit from much of the annual dividends paid on the debt, currently spent abroad, sometimes "among our most avowed enemies." Pelham contended that Britain was losing £1–2 million of dividends annually sent abroad to investors who would prefer to live on its soil.[30] The clearest expression of the issues at stake was given by Nicholas Hardinge, who emphasized not only the Jews' financial and commercial contribution but also the national and constitutional importance of the national debt. For it was the public credit, much advanced by Jews, "to which we in a great measure owe the preservation both of our religion and liberties."[31]

Tellingly, just as some adversaries attributed to Jews the establishment of the national debt, not only their current investment in it, so did proponents of the scheme, including Hardinge. This was an anachronistic projection of the relative prominence of Jewish stockholders of government loans from the early and mid-eighteenth century back to the period of its establishment in the 1690s.[32] It is a handy illustration of the dynamic of the parliamentary debate in its political-economic perspective: Adversaries agreed on the "facts," even the fabricated ones, yet disagreed about their significance. The disagreement derived to a great degree from their wider perception of economic dynamics and the role of finance in the modern political economy of a commercial state. These contrasting perceptions entailed distinct notions of loyalty and productivity, for where one saw a benefit, the other identified deterioration. These lines of engagement in the Commons debates provided the contours for the public polemic that soon spread and took on new life.

Religion and Political Economy
in the Public Opposition Discourse

As noted, the public debate was ignited by the City's petition coinciding with the third reading of the bill. While the religious rhetoric indeed became prevalent from that point onward, political economic concerns were not discarded but rather incorporated. This convergence took several forms. Opposition writers often linked religious decline with economic misconduct and luxury. This well-established theme, commonly employed by critics of both the political system and society at large, was enhanced around mid-century, as Kathleen Wilson aptly illustrates.[33] Yet its use in the context of the Jew Bill was not merely a reiteration.

The notion of religious decline prompted by the material lure of financial economy was promoted by writers across the opposition spectrum and most blatantly expressed by the *London Evening Post* (henceforth *LEP*), the leading organ opposing the bill. "Old England," a frequent letter-writer to the paper, asserted that the bill sought to further subordinate the nation to "the baneful Power of Money," inciting ministers to rely on the power of money for gaining political influence and to bypass the constitutional power of the Commons and the sentiments of the people. The result would be not only the subordination of the English to the Jews and the corruption of the political system but also damage to religion—"Religion, Conscience, Honour, and Publick Good, laugh'd at as Cant and Foible." The letter concluded with a call to fellow "Britons, Christians and Protestants" to wake up, for the Jews were at the gates, "coming for the Keys of your Church doors."[34] Likewise, "Timothy Freeman" stated that Jews would buy with their money the "very souls" of English people.[35] Other writers conflated blasphemy and extortion, depicting advocates of the bill as favoring pecuniary profit even when the implication was the undermining of religion: "Jew-like, we are to mind nothing in this Bill but Trade. Our God and our Religion Are to be quite out of the Question, and Money, ALMIGHTY Money, is to be the Basis of our State."[36] The power of money as opposed to religion was expressed in recurring allegations that Jews intended to overtake Christianity with their money. One writer imagined a dialogue between two Jews, Zimri and Shylock: "Why surely, Friend Shylock, thou can'st guess at the Cause / Ha'n't we bought a whole Nation, Religion and Laws? / A Land overflowing with Milk and with Honey / Where their Christ and their God may be bought with our Money?"[37]

By this view, the prospective Jewish takeover evolved from the spread of luxury and its impact on English society, which had enabled the presenting of the Jew Bill in the first place. The Zimri-Shylock column from *LEP*, for instance, was followed by a comment on a "Deluge of Luxury overspreading all Ranks, Sexes and Ages, [which] raises the Indignation of the Few that remain still on firm Ground." A month later another *LEP* writer, identified as a Dissenter, argued with "a religious horror" that the Jews took advantage of the "Luxury and Corruption of the Times [in order to] purchase to themselves such Privileges as have hitherto been constantly denied to as good Subjects as any in the Nation."[38] "John Christian" related religious decline to a general corruption of manners and claimed that the Jews had an extensive destructive influence on the minds of many by their immoral economic practices.[39] Accordingly, adversaries concluded, the present base economic conduct would provoke godly wrath. The signs were already apparent: An earthquake in Cheshire was attributed to the bill's enactment.[40] Set on this course, English society was doomed to share in the Jewish curse of landlessness; hence it should be every Englishman's wish that godly punishment of the Jews would not be delayed before they obtained too much power. "John Christian" closed his letter, "Let G[ideon]'s Gold, and old sly Shylock's Purse, Instead of Blessing, prove to them a Curse."[41]

The connection between Jews' corrupting economic conduct and their conflict with Christianity was promoted also in opposition caricatures, many of which have already been studied, and to some I will turn later.[42] Here I want to dwell on another form that was extensively used by the opposition—pamphleteering. Reverend William Romaine, the most prominent clerical writer against the Jew Bill, summarized Anglo-Jewish history: what a "prevailing Engine the Jews Money was, and how successful they have been in trusting their Cause to its Influence." That money, he argued, explained not only the introduction of Jews into England by both William the Conqueror and Oliver Cromwell but the whole course of Jewish history, enduring "by the self same Money-Engine—preferred by too many, who call themselves Christians, even to Christ himself and Christianity."[43] The claim that Jews did not endeavor to convert others, Romaine said, did not take into account that Jews' first priority was making money, which had become their worshipped idol. Economic conduct was profoundly interwoven in the religious life of the Jews and hence would similarly affect England at both economic and religious levels.[44]

The conflation of the religious and the economic was reinforced by frequent use of biblical style, images, and history. An illustrative example is a piece published in *Read's Weekly Journal*, under the title "The 1753rd Chapter of the JEWS," which recounted the history of the Jews in England in a pseudobiblical manner. The Jews were depicted as hard-hearted vagabonds, worshipping the Devil in the form of money. They found England suitable for their purposes, as its people were "given to foolish Bargaining." "Peradventure," the Jews understood, "they will want our Silver and Go'd; then shall we have their Lands, and become their Lords to rule over them." Consequently, they "trafficked greatly, and supplied the Wants of the Extravagant and Proud, and increased in Riches and Power." At that point a leader was erected among the Jews—Shylock—who promised them to accomplish the overtaking of England, and the Jews deposited their wealth in his hands for that end. The story stopped there, to be continued (though it never was), implying the unclear future of the Anglo-Jewish conflict.[45]

A recurrent motif was the association of the Jewish cause with the Golden Calf. "Britannicus" asserted that courting the Jews for their riches was worship of the Golden Calf, and "Civis Londinesis" stated that there were few people who had "not yet fallen down and worshipped the GOLDEN IMAGE," set in place by the Pelham faction.[46] In another mock-biblical account, the *LEP* stated that only a few people "had not kissed the Golden Calf, nor bowed their Knees to the Idol of the Times."[47] *The Connoisseur*, a satirical London weekly produced by George Colman and Bonnell Thornton and inaugurated just as the Jew Bill was repealed, expressed much concern in its first issues regarding the bill and the Jews. In a letter allegedly written by a Jewish man of taste buying pieces of art on a trip to the Continent, the writer recounted his acquisition of a picture titled *The Elevation of the Golden Calf*, which he intended to set up in the Royal Exchange "as a typical representation of myself, to be worshipp'd by all Brokers, Insurers, Scriveners and the whole fraternity of Stock-jobbers."[48]

Perhaps the most pervasive religious motif in the opposition discourse was that of circumcision. The opposition propagated the threat that the Jew Bill would result in the Jews taking over England and forcing the circumcision of all males. In one sarcastic remark, the bill was referred to as "the Law in favour of the Circumcision."[49] One could dismiss this obsession as whimsical, as Perry argues; yet broadening the perspective to the long-term historical occurrence of the theme reveals an early modern English preoccupation.[50] That this motif was employed for political aims by opposition polemicists does not exclude its prevalent cultural significance. Consequently, several scholars have explored its meaning in the polemic, emphasizing the

conflation of masculinity, dignity, and power as the fundamentals of a consolidating British identity against which Jewish identity was posed as a foil.[51]
Following this approach, I argue that an important aspect of the cultural work
done by that concept was achieved by an association between circumcision
and finance, which was part of the more general conflation of religion and
economy. Circumcision was a striking image to depict the danger of the Jew
Bill, I suggest, because the eighteenth-century image of the man of finance
was of a feminized economic creature controlled by his passions and fantasies—very different from the image of the conquering man of finance of the
modern era.[52] The circumcised Jew epitomized not only physical unmanliness
but also economic effeminacy. What lent it its force was the co-occurrence
of the polemic within a tense nationalistic atmosphere in which perceived
threats to the nation—political, military, and economic—were often imagined as both the result and the reflection of "feminization."[53] While the
fear of *physical* circumcision by the Jews was apparently absurd, its symbolic
aspect—*economic* circumcision—could be seen as an imaginary manifestation
of existing socioeconomic anxieties. The long-lived prejudice against Jewish
circumcision intersected with an uneasy and highly gendered social discourse
on socioeconomic matters, producing accordingly effective propaganda.

Opposition texts frequently depicted circumcision as a Jewish demand
in exchange for financial support. "Timothy Freeman" in the *LEP* remarked
that "for Money shal circumshise us, if they plese,"[54] and MPs supporting
the bill were mocked as being on their way to circumcision by seeking Jewish financial support.[55] This was a current trope also in visual materials, as
illustrated in Figure 2, a broadside featuring two prints and two texts.[56] On
the right-hand side, the print *The Circumcised Gentiles* presents a British
politician driving a Jew on a donkey and behind him a bishop. On the ground
there is a New Testament, and the bishop is holding a Talmud. The politician
carries a moneybag of £100,000 and in the same hand a circumcision salve.
He declares that he does not know "how it fares with your Brother behind but
this I am sure of that if Circumcision agrees as ill with him as it does with me
he wont keep his SEAT long."[57] In another print, *The Grand Conference or the
Jew Predominant*, Thomas Pelham, sitting at the center of the table, urges his
brother Henry Pelham to receive a bribe of £200,000 from Samson Gideon
for advancing Jewish Naturalization, declaring "It comes seasonably to me at
this Juncture Circumcision or any thing."[58]

Coin clipping, a crime Jews were traditionally accused of, was also associated with circumcision, and opposition polemists made keen use of it. Thus,

Figure 2. *The Jews Triumph, and England's Fears, set forth;*
The Circumcised Gentiles; Or, A Journey to Jerusalem.

Catalogue of Political and Personal Satires, Department of Prints
and Drawings, British Museum (3206).

in the satirical song "The Pork of Old Engand," Jews of the day were compared to their medieval ancestors: "In brave Edward's days they were caught in
a gin, / For clipping our coin, now to add sin to sin, / As they've got all our
pelf, they'd be clipping our skin. / Those foes to the pork of Old England."[59]
The writer creates an imagined continuity between past and present: Having already commandeered all English money, Jews were turning to clipping
other objects instead.

Notably, circumcision played a part in the polemic in the frequent use
of the biblical story of Dinah and Shechem (Genesis 34) as epitomizing the
threat to English society. The most elaborate adaptation of the story is found
in an *LEP* column, "The 34th Chapter of Genesis," which conflated the
biblical story with current events. English girls triggered the affair when they
visited Jewish girls in their synagogue. There they were seen by the "Sons
of Gid[eon], of Shylock, of Mend[ez], Fran[co], and Salv[ador]," who lay

with them by force and defiled them. Consequently, the Jewish financiers, the boys' fathers, approached "the Pelh[ami]tes," and asked them for "your Virgins for Wives" in exchange for "so many Bank Notes and Gifts." Up to this point, the British were equated with the biblical Jews, and the Jews took the role of the Canaanites. The roles inverted at the point when the Jewish magnates demanded the British to be circumcised in order to marry Jewish girls. If not, they threatened to withdraw their money from the funds and be gone. The Pelhamites ordered all subjects "to be circumcised, to depart the Land, or to be deliver'd over as a Prey to the Israelites." Gideon and Shylock gathered the Jews at the Exchange and announced the agreement. And on the third day, "whilst [the Britons'] Private Parts were sore," the Jews "took their Swords, and slew every Male of the Britons," including the Pelhamites.[60]

The opposition's conflation of religion and the economy paralleled the broad theological division of Judaism and Christianity, with the conflict between the apparently corrupting contemporary, speculation-based economy and the traditional, stable commercial economy. This pattern is illustrated in a letter by "Britannicus," a writer previously mentioned, who was a leading voice in the *LEP* in the 1750s and has been identified by Bob Harris as Paul Whitehead, a satirist and poet strongly connected to opposition politicians. Presuming that states should adopt religious structures compatible with their political-economic structures, "Britannicus" maintained ironically that only Judaism could fit England as a religion. As "Gold is the sole Mover of our grand political Machine," with no regard to the future of society nor tradition, "would not therefore the Naturalization of the Hebrew Race greatly strengthen and confirm our political System?" While the present economic-political conduct was perfectly in accord with Jewish views, gold being "all that the Jews expect or desire of God," as evident in the Old Testament, "the Christian Religion is very inconvenient for a commercial People; it so cramps Men in Pursuit of their worldly Interests, and raises within their Breasts that frightful Chimera call'd Conscience." Appealing for replacing the national religion, "Britannicus" assured his audience that the shift would not be very noticeable, as "every Man, who calls himself a Christian, but acts only upon the Principles of worldly Interest, is indeed, tho' uncircumcised, already a Jew."[61] "Honestus," in *Read's Weekly Journal*, contended that commerce depended on Scripture, which regulated all personal and social practices. As Scripture itself highlighted the unbridgeable breach between Jews and Christians, both in conduct and beliefs, it strictly forbade communication between Jews and Christians in matters of commerce and commercial norms.

An anonymous pamphleteer argued that the basic notion behind the bill contradicted the political economy of Christianity; hence in no way could it be seen as a measure for promoting the conversion of Jews to Christianity, as proponents of the bill repeatedly claimed. The essential idea of Christianity is the denial of the material world, and in contrast the Jews and their supporters are ardent in their desires for material gains.[62]

Another anonymous column in the *LEP* claimed, again ironically, that naturalizing rich Jews could do England no harm. The bill "cannot hurt Trade in general, because the Jews are not general Traders; and what they do in the City is not Trade, nor any thing like it." Rich Jews were "entirely in the Money Way, concerned in the Stocks, as State-Brokers and Jobbers," an economic arena that excluded Christians, who had "some strange scruples about the Lawfulness of this Possession." This incommensurability of Jewish and Christian trade, the writer comically argued, made the Christian trade immune to Jewish damage. The rich Jews traded only in stockjobbing, and stockjobbing was the plundering of the public; but because a Christian could not plunder the public, consequently he could not trade in stocks. The piece was whimsical, yet to achieve its point it both conveyed and assumed that the audience would conceive a distinction between Jewish and Christian economies, equating trade in credit with Jews.[63]

The conflation of economy and religion, as exemplified in these excerpts, sought to depict Judaism and Christianity as not only distinct religions but also as two contradicting economic ethics. This important and powerful thrust of the oppositional discourse was not pursued by all opposition writers, however. Some, with whom I do not deal here, did not focus on economic matters at all but only on religious issues. Still others who did focus on the economic aspect expressed a profoundly different attitude to the relation between economy and the Jews, and between economy and religion.

It would be wrong to depict the two camps solely in binary terms of liberalism and tolerance versus conservatism, stagnation, and narrow-mindedness. Certainly, the prevailing tone in opposition propaganda was vehemently prejudicial, relying heavily on traditional anti-Jewish libels. However, few opposition voices expressed a complex set of socioeconomic assumptions and perceptions of Jewishness. Although all connected the Jews intrinsically to the question of the financial system's functioning, some expressed qualified approval of the system and only denounced Jews' influence on it.

A central point of division regarding Jewish economic behavior was the question of its historicity. Was the Jewish propensity to finance, and the

Jewish economic nature in general, innate or changeable? While adversaries commonly depicted an essential link between Jews and finance, and the new financial system as Jewish in nature, advocates argued that it was through external circumstances that Jews came to occupy typical trades in what I designated earlier as the circumstantial explanation of Jewish economy.[64] This dimension of the polemic was part of a broader context of changing conceptions in the eighteenth century of difference and a developing preoccupation with classification. Are there innate differences between peoples or races, and what elements constitute them? With the decline of the explanatory force of Scriptures from the latter part of the seventeenth century in engaging with these questions, secular racial explanations took their place. The Jew Bill polemic was an effective platform for developing images of both bodily traits and inherent social features of Jewishness.[65]

Tellingly, some opponents employed the pro-Jewish circumstantial reasoning to attack the bill. For if the socioeconomic limits on Jews were removed, they claimed, Jewish economic uniqueness would diminish, and hence their expected contribution hailed by advocates would never materialize.[66] Moreover, some opposition writers accepted, at least outwardly, the importance of the national debt for consolidating British power, and they used the advocates' own arguments to illustrate the bill's futility. A writer in Read's Weekly Journal, for example, argued that Jews must be excluded from investing in land (as the bill allowed), so that "upon any Emergency" their money would be liquid for backing the state.[67] In contrast, other opposition writers disputed there could be any favorable outcome of an influx of foreign (Jewish) capital. A letter to the Public Advertiser in mid-November argued that the whole polemic had been conducted wrongly; had the opponents focused seriously on economic questions, they would have easily brought about the repeal of the bill. Enticing rich Jews to settle in England with their capital would create an external and artificial injection of money into the market. Far from enhancing the economy, it would harm it, causing a general rise in prices. Money by itself, detached from production, could not extend the commerce of any state nor weaken its rivals, as envisioned by the traditional mercantilist theories on which advocates of the bill relied. Moreover, an injection of money would encourage both the government and individuals to run further into debt, unbalancing the system. Rich immigrants were merely consumers with no productive benefit, and governmental policy should prioritize industrious working people.[68]

A similar emphasis was offered by Jonas Hanway, a merchant and philanthropist and a leading adversary pamphleteer who sought to differentiate between industrious and idle financial activities. It was not the system of public finance itself that was to blame, Hanway argued, in contrast to other opponents to the bill, but the manner in which Jews employed it for gain—"the injurious practice of jobbing in stocks, and the supplying national demands by our submitting to the means of extortion." As public credit was meant to strengthen the state at moments of hardship, support of the debt should depend on "our own merchants and money-holders," who should take it as their national responsibility. Jews, as outsiders to the nation, could not be counted on in such moments, as was evident during the suppression of the Jacobite rebellion in 1745, when the intervention of English merchants prevented the execution of a "Jewish project" that "must have involved this nation much deeper in debt."[69] Here again the notion of loyalty was central in the conception of the public credit system. Reliance on the debt was not an antipatriotic scheme, yet in order to secure its legitimate use, one had to ensure that only truly loyal citizens took part in it. Jews, though basically not disloyal, lacked a genuine commitment to society and state; this lack rendered their involvement in public credit suspicious and imperiling to national liberty, for they inclined to private interests rather than to communal ones. This difference in inclination had the power to "raise or depress us as a free nation."[70]

According to Hanway, the essential reason for the rejection of the Jew Bill lay in the Jews' incapacity to integrate into the English patriarchal social system, for they could never adopt the required social responsibility. Integration was a precondition for being a trustworthy investor in public finance and evidently also for holding land. Consequently, Jews' liberties should be restricted to the commercial sphere.[71] In this vein, Hanway tendentiously interpreted the opposition posture, that "so far from depressing the Jews, their opponents never meant to deprive them of any weight in their commercial capacity; but rather to keep from them every temptation which might divert them from so useful a pursuit."[72]

The distinction between Jewish productive commercialism and Jewish stockjobbing was reiterated in the *LEP* the following year, several months after the general elections, triggered by news that Prussia was encouraging immigration of traders of all nations and religions. It was assumed that such news might reignite the push for Jewish naturalization. The writer warned that one should attend to differences in the constitution of the two countries: Jews' usefulness in Prussia relied on the government of a "Philosopher" who would "take care that they shall never have there no Stock-Jobbing, no Funds, no publick Debts, to exercise the Industry of the Children of Israel; so that their Talents must be turned to Commerce." Echoing Barnard's arguments in the Commons, the writer argued that "where Trade is but in its Infancy, [Jews] may be made very useful under a wise Governor." However, as people in general were not as wise as their governors, the English "might in less than Half a Century be jostled or wheedled out of Religion, Liberty and Property, by the Introduction of a Swarm of rich Hebrews."[73]

The emphasis on industriousness articulated by adversaries to the bill was not far from the same emphasis made by the most important political-economic defender of the bill, the Reverend Josiah Tucker. Tucker perceived naturalization schemes in general and Jewish naturalization in particular as efficient means for engaging monopolies and privileges, which he saw as remains of the tyrannic "Gothic" past. These obstacles hindered economic growth, which could be sustained only by free competition that would boost industriousness. Yet Tucker differed from adversaries such as Hanway in his notion of industry in two important aspects, as Jonathan Karp has demonstrated. First, Tucker regarded population increase as a substantial and crucial factor; and second, he regarded the Jews as adaptive people, not inherently inclined to unproductive financial schemes.[74]

The Jew Bill in the Context of Eighteenth-Century Naturalization Debates

To return to the basic question regarding the episode of the Jew Bill, how unique was it in its wider political context? Was it only another Whig attempt in a string of naturalization bills? An apt example of partisan propaganda? Does it deserve an examination as a distinct event? The common assessment, promoted by Perry, is that the polemic was simply a handy topic for rallying both parliamentary and public opposition against a Whig ministry in view of upcoming general elections. Such an understanding emphasizes the correlation of the Jew Bill with preceding naturalization bills, the last of which were proposed, in vain, in 1746, 1747–48, and 1751.[75] The Jew Bill, it was noted, was advocated by the same figures who promoted these earlier bills, and mostly it was opposed by similar parliamentarians—notably, apart from John Barnard, who supported Protestant naturalization.

The Jew Bill, however, differed in significant points from the other bills of this type. It was the only bill designated solely for non-Christians; it was a bill with little practical significance; and it generated an unprecedented public clamor, undoubtedly one of the most forceful instances of mobilization of public opinion in the first half of the eighteenth century. Other naturalization bills also received fierce parliamentary and public opposition, yet the rhetoric that characterized the Jew Bill polemic was profoundly different. While opposition to previous naturalization schemes relied on political-economic arguments, antagonism to the Jew Bill hinged on religious reasoning, at times—as demonstrated—conflating the two into a political-economic perspective of religious identity and difference.[76] These distinctions lent the discussion a social and cultural vigor that did not derive from the partisan interests themselves and had independent life and influence. Another reason why the controversy resonated so strongly in the public sphere, I suggest, was the interrelation of the subject matter and concerns about public finance. Jews were good tools for thinking about economic matters, and in this particular case they emblematized the question of public finance. Unlike previous general naturalization attempts, the Jew Bill was aimed exclusively at wealthy Jews, and it was acknowledged that it arose solely as a return of favor for Jewish magnates who had backed the government financially during the Jacobite rebellion. The recurrent argument for the measure was that it would provide capital for public funds. Consequently, the Jew Bill proved a timely circumstance that intersected central axes that preoccupied mid-eighteenth-century English society: the scope of religious toleration, economic improvement, the valuation of the post–financial-revolution market and its social effects, and the nature of citizenship. All these issues intensified in the interwar period between the War of Austrian Succession and the Seven Years' War.[77]

The Jew Bill's relationship with public finance introduced a new element into the series of controversies around naturalization bills, and focused a spotlight on the nature of the new financial culture and its instruments. These questions were important to the way that Jews themselves were perceived, the polemic firmly linking them with the undecided social status of finance. The polemic was interwoven with common questions that had preoccupied the public in previous debates, but this time they were reshaped to reflect concerns around finance.

The first concern was that of economic productivity. While earlier naturalization debates considered the demographic and occupational aspects of this question broadly, the current debate focused the discussion on the economic productivity of trade in credit. This question hovered above the polemic and over the assessment of the productivity of the Jews and their potential contribution to English commerce. A writer in the *Westminster*

Journal claimed that the Jewish money the bill would bring into England would improve nothing, for "money, or credit, circulating through a nation, from hand to hand, without producing labour and industry in the inhabitants, is direct gaming; and what else can be expected from the Jews, upon their naturalization."[78] Another *LEP* column, following a discussion of the Jew Bill, stated that "Men may be very *active* and *busy*, without being at all *industrious*; that the *Labour* of the *Hands* or *Brain* must be well directed to merit this Appellation; and that *Dealing* of *Cards*, or *Shuffling* of *Stocks* from *Morning* to *Night*, tho' it may be a *gainful*, is not an *industrious*, Employment" (italics in original).[79] Some adversaries emphasized the futility of trade in finance and claimed that Jews were preoccupied with such enterprise. "Britannicus" in the *LEP* maintained that a Jewish economic contribution would be negligible, for Jews' commercial capability "is chiefly in the Stocks, and their arts of Merchandize are exerted principally in Exchange-Alley." Britannicus portrayed Jewish society as having a common economic characteristic: While the poor among them might cheat the public peddling with counterfeit commodities, the wealthy grew rich not by trade in real commodities but by "State Jobbs, Lotteries, and other iniquitous Arts of Exchange-Alley," itself forms of counterfeit commerce.[80] Similarly, another writer argued that Jews "deal largely in the Mysteries and Iniquities of Stock-Jobbing, and get vast Estates by plundering the Publick."[81] Their professionalization in the dodgy arena of stock trade substituted for their total lack of productive abilities, or "real commerce," as Lord Egmont phrased it in the third reading of the bill, for Jews could neither toil the land nor engage in manufacture. As we have seen, these were recurrent themes in all opposition media: parliamentary polemic, the press, and pamphleteering.[82] Advocates of the bill, on the other hand, emphasized the contribution of the public debt to national power and hence also to the growth of national economy, and the contribution made by Jews to the public fund. Yet the advocates, too, established a borderline between a productive trade in credit and a harmful one, castigating the practice of speculative stockjobbing. Consequently, they sought to exonerate the Jews from this association repeatedly made by opponents.[83]

A second central theme in naturalization debates was political liberty. During the eighteenth century the notion of liberty came to be profoundly related with commerce. Polemicists argued as to whether liberty was a precondition for free and thriving commerce or vice versa, yet all accepted the pivotal role of both in the growth and wellbeing of societies. By mid-century the ideology of liberty reached an apotheosis, becoming the fulcrum of English identification both by English people and foreigners.[84] Predictably, it was a prevalent theme in the Jew Bill polemic, as it had been around previous naturalization schemes. The bill was repeatedly depicted by the opposition as a scheme that would lead to the enslavement of the English by the Jews, and to the disintegration of all social and political institutions. This aspect has been extensively referred to in all accounts of the episode, and there is no need for reiteration here. Advocates of the bill replied with the same coin. The central obstruction of commerce, they argued, was superstitious intolerance; hence it was also a major impediment in the progress of liberty. In response to the opposition, they had to prove that Jews were capable of the civil qualities of liberty and so had to exonerate them from accusations of antinational and antisocial economic conduct. Jewish economic conduct, they often claimed, was not essentialist: Jews were not bound to specific economic activities and were susceptible to the adoption of the manners characterizing their host countries. In England these would include the "Love of Liberty and their Country."[85] But the form of liberty promoted by advocates was inherently different from that employed by opponents. While opponents insisted on the intrinsic relation between English liberty and Christianity—a confessional liberty, as Justin Champion calls it—advocates of the bill promoted a notion of civil, nonconfessional, liberty.[86] What mattered was not the denomination of a group but the civil implications of its doctrines; to a great degree, advocates argued, Judaism was closer to Protestantism and enhanced loyalty to the state more than Catholicism and Dissent. Consequently, the attack on the Jews was an attack on English liberty that would encroach eventually on Christians' liberties.[87]

However, for opponents of the bill it was not only Jews' religion that made them illegitimate as free citizens. As discussed earlier, most opponents claimed that public credit endangered political liberty by placing unlimited power in the hands of the government and disintegrating social institutions. Jews, they argued, gained from this system of credit, enhanced it, and had an interest in its endurance. As with the Jews of old, who were employed by kings for financial backing while bypassing Parliament, thus forming a unit against the people—as elaborated by antiquarians who were commonly referred to by opponents[88]—the employment of public credit by contemporary Jews had the same anticivil and corruptive effect.

Eighteenth-century naturalization bills were as a rule unsuccessful, and so the fate of the 1753 Jew Bill was not exceptional.[89] There was one piece of legislation, however, that stood apart in this series of attempts and can serve as a foil for the 1753 polemic. The Plantation Act of 1740 allowed foreigners who had resided for seven years in the American colonies to naturalize without a parliamentary bill, and it exempted Quakers and Jews from Christian oaths. This measure was designed to enhance colonial trade in the Americas, most importantly against the nation's prospering Dutch rivals (who had already taken similar measures of naturalization in their colonies). Why did such a bill pass without agitation, in spite of the provisions it offered Jews, while the 1753 bill aroused unprecedented clamor? The difference, I suggest, resulted in part from the inner conflict embedded in a national empire relying on commerce. Distribution of citizenship enhanced commercial networks essential for imperial expansion, yet it also entailed sharing national identity. Jews, like other marginalized sectors with commercial influence, posed a dilemma: By the mid-eighteenth century it was commonly acknowledged that Jews loomed large in the global commercial matrix of Britain and were valuable in its expansion,[90] yet they were perceived as essentially alien. The option for naturalizing Jews in the colonies allowed legislators to potentially benefit from their commercial advantage while keeping the tension around questions of national identity far away; in contrast, it is plausible that the failure of the 1753 attempt to allow naturalization in the motherland owed much to its bringing the problem of national identity into the metropole.[91] However, as this chapter has sought to demonstrate, the 1753 polemic had another important feature that discussions on colonial naturalization in 1740 did not involve: concern over public credit. This issue related to the metropole rather to the colonies. But also, the 1740 legislation took place at an early stage of the consolidation of the association of Jews with public credit, while the events of 1753 occurred in a changed setting.

* * *

The previous section illustrated that the 1753 polemic over Jewish naturalization differed from preceding naturalization proposals in that it introduced distinct political economic questions, namely, concerns about the post–Financial Revolution system. However, arguing for this distinctiveness again brings the problem of uniqueness to the fore: If the polemic hinged on the question of finance, in what sense was it different from earlier controversies over similar concerns characteristic of the eighteenth century? The question intensifies when one examines the rhetorical moves of the 1753 opposition in comparison with the social critique raised during the 1720 South Sea Bubble crisis, for example. Finance as opposed to the Christian spirit, the role of

Providence, and the relations among political, social, and religious corruption generated by financial inclinations, among other motifs, were all employed in both cases.[92] Was the economic anti-Jewish rhetoric of 1753 merely a reiteration of existing forms of social critique? This question is consequential for understanding the "Jewishness" of the polemic, still a point of debate among historians. If the issue of the new forms of finance was one of the reasons that the apparently minor question of Jewish naturalization evolved into such a vigorous polemic, as I have been suggesting, then whether the Jews have been merely incidental in a largely reiterated dispute becomes a substantial question. The following chapter engages with this question, winding it up together with the current discussion, by offering a broader contextualization of the history of finance in eighteenth-century English culture.

Chapter 6

Jews, Finance, and Gender
on the Stage and Beyond

War, war, loss of credit; fall of stocks; debt upon debt; tax upon tax
. . . other people's loss is my gain—so lies my account.

—Richard Cumberland

Cumberland put those words in the mouth of Issachar, a crafty Jewish broker who exploits falling English aristocrats in the play *The Note of Hand*
(1774). In retrospect, it appears emblematic of the prejudicial association of
Jews and crafty finance—commonly conceived as located on a continuous line
of economic anti-Jewish sentiments, in the spirit of Marx's "On the Jewish
Question," stretching from medieval usury to Bernie Madoff.[1] I attempt to
show here, however, that the association of Jews and modern finance was far
from a linear, natural, or unavoidable process. Remarkably, during the time
the financial developments and their impact on English society and politics
were the most contested—that is, circa 1690s–1720s, when the role played by
Jews in the market was already conspicuous (as demonstrated earlier)—references to Jews as financial suspects were sporadic, failing to coalesce into a
full-blown image. It was only around the middle of the century that the idea
of an inherent link between Jews and finance became resonant. This chapter
engages this puzzle, focusing on the theatrical discourse. Together with chapters 5 and 7, it illuminates the midcentury as the setting for the maturation of
this notion. In his important work on the theatrical representations of Jews
in eighteenth-century England, Michael Ragussis demonstrated how instrumental they were in engaging with the challenge of consolidating a shared

British identity.[2] While I draw on his work, my aim here is more specific: I wish to illustrate this in relation to political-economic concerns of the time, and in turn, how these concerns integrated with the broader issue of identity.

By the eighteenth century, the dramatic figure of the Jew already had a notorious pedigree. The first early modern English play to exhibit a Jewish character was probably *The Jew*, from the latter third of the sixteenth century, now lost. The play was referred to as "representing the greedinesse of worldly chusers, and bloody mindes of Usurers."[3] Alongside the character of Barabas in *The Jew of Malta* by Christopher Marlowe, and of course, William Shakespeare's Shylock, the three pieces each featured a Jew as the epitome of usury.[4] After these plays, however, for almost an entire century, the Jew was hardly noticeable onstage. (A qualification is needed here, as I exclude from the discussion figures and themes pertaining to *ancient* Jewry.)[5] There is no way to determine whether the dwindling of the figure in seventeenth-century English drama was related to changing attitudes to usury. What is certain, however, is that changing attitudes to finance were an essential backdrop for the Jew's reemergence on the eighteenth-century stage.

The Jew reappeared as a central character in 1701, in a reproduction of Shakespeare's play by George Granville—a Tory aristocrat and politician and later first Baron Lansdowne—titled *The Jew of Venice*. More than a reproduction, it was a freehand adaptation, profoundly changing the play's trajectory and, with it, Shylock's character and particularly its economic dimension. *The Jew of Venice* was fairly popular, being performed forty-two times between its first enactment in Lincoln's Inn Fields in 1701 until 1754.[6] Dimming much of the original complexity of the characters, Granville rendered his Shylock a comic greedy villain, whimsical and one-dimensional, in contrast to Shakespeare's complex and grave figure. This was embodied in the choice of the actor—Thomas Dogget, the most renowned comic actor of the time.[7] In contrast to the deep sentiments of revenge of the original figure, what motivates Granville's Shylock is simple greed. For example, his attitude to his daughter's flight is much lighter, simply adjoined to his loss of money. Granville also adds a new scene where Shylock is dining and being entertained at the table with the Venetian men and raises his own toast for his "Mistress that outshines 'em all. . . . O may her Charms encrease and multiply; My Money is my Mistress! Here's [a toast] to Interest upon Interest." Money as his central motivation is again apparent when Antonio and Bassanio part, and he mutters that "These two Christian Fools put me in mind of my Money: just so loath am I to part with that."[8]

Granville not only enhanced Shylock's greediness but also hinted at a
link with contemporary concerns with the credit market, which were much
different from those of Shakespeare's time. In the prologue, written by Granville's relative, the poet Bevill Higgons, Shakespeare's ghost states: "Today
we punish a stock-jobbing Jew, / A Piece of Justice, terrible and strange; /
Which, if persued, would make a thin Exchange."[9] Alluding to the City's
1697 regulation that restricted the number of Jewish brokers in the Royal
Exchange to twelve, this passage places the figure of the Jew in the context
of the social concerns with recent financial innovations, concerns that were
typically expressed by Tories of Granville's profile. (It should be noted that,
like many other critics of the financial market, Granville held £20,000 in
South Sea Company stocks when the bubble burst in 1720.)[10] Dogget's performance plausibly enhanced this association: He often played characters of
stockjobbers, and also played the clownish Jewish villain Sancho in Dryden's
Love Triumphant a few years earlier (more on that play shortly). Thus, he
conveniently merged the two in his Shylock, embodying, as Abba Rubin puts
it, "the rumored greed and wealth of the Jews on the stock exchange."[11]

This connotation was developed in another piece of the time, *Hampstead
Heath* (1706), by Thomas Baker, a playwright who often engaged with the
social anxieties accompanying the Financial Revolution. The play features a
fake Jewish fop whom one of the characters impersonates to delude a lady
courted by his patron. No less than a "real" Jewish character, this interplay is
valuable in presenting a stereotype of the Jew. After the fake Jew manages to
draw the lady into a (fake) marriage, he informs her that the next day her entire
estate will have to be sold, for "the Jews turn all into ready Money; we follow
Stocks, Brokerage, and insure Ships, prove very rich, or very Beggars, as the
Wind blows."[12] In contrast to the stable landed model, this new type of economic person aspires to liquidate assets and substitute production with finance.
This presents the Jew as the epitome of the Financial Revolution social type.

Perhaps surprisingly, despite the visibility of Jews in the London stock
market at the time, the association as seen in these two instances was exceptional and did not strike a chord in the popular culture of the first decades of
the century. Apart from these two references and some marginal ones, I did
not find any other theatrical association of Jews with the financial market.[13]
This is remarkable, because the period between 1695 and 1720 is characterized by fierce and extensive theatrical engagement with such concerns.[14] This
apparent disinterest is even more conspicuous in pieces that engaged with the
stormy events of the South Sea Bubble. As noted, during this period Jews

participated significantly in stock trading: between three to five times more than their share in the market participants and far more than their share in London's population. The figure of the Jew, however, had only a secondary role in contemporaries' perception of the events: It did not bear any economic uniqueness but rather served as an example of the general social pervasiveness of the market. In *Exchange-Alley: or, the stock-jobber turn'd gentleman* from 1720, the stockjobber sings about the illusion of making a fortune in the funds, mentioning Jews only to emphasize the all-embracing character of immoral conduct: "The Turk, and the Jew, And Priests not a few / The Country, the Town, and the C[our]t; / Here Ladies and Peers, And some without Ears / To Cheat, and be Cheated resort."[15]

It is in this sense of the social scope of the financial misconduct that most references to Jews are to be interpreted. This is most clearly expressed in the common phrase, "Jews and Gentiles," for example, in renowned satirist Edward Ward's *South Sea Ballad*: "Here stars and garters do appear, Among our lords the rabble; / To buy and sell, to see and hear, The Jews and Gentiles squabble." Similarly, in the *South Sea; or the Biters Bit* from 1720, a rustic who comes to London to buy shares hears about stockjobbers for the first time and wonders about their religion. He is answered: "Religion! why, they don't mind Religion in Change-Alley. But Turks, Jews, Atheists, and Infidels, mingle there as if they were a-kin to one another."[16] A visual parallel of this tendency can be seen in William Hogarth's famous 1721 print (Figure 3), *The South Sea Scheme*, which depicts in the bottom left side a Jewish high priest, an Anglican priest, and a Catholic monk playing dice.

Rather than capitalizing on a particular Jewish essence of economic corruption, this trope relied on the similarity of Jewish and English economic vice. Although this could be alternatively interpreted as suggesting that society as a whole was becoming corrupted along Jewish standards, the Jewish figures in all these cases were never depicted as leading the way but rather as part of a list of other shady characters. Thus they were used to show that religion as an institution was losing its power as a moral check on society. In no case did I find the English depicted as "Judaizing," as frequently seen in earlier periods of tension regarding commercialization—most commonly in late sixteenth-century debates over usury (see earlier, in the introduction). At times the figure of the Jew was equated with corruption, but not specifically one pertaining to finance. Moreover, it was used to emphasize the financial corruption prevalent among the *English*. For instance, Thomas Gordon, one of the harshest social critics during the South Sea crisis, scolded

Figure 3. William Hogarth, *The South Sea Scheme* (1721).

Courtesy of the Lewis Walpole Library, Yale University.

contemporaries that "there's as much Honesty in a Stockjobber, as Sincerity in a Jew, or Chastity in a Bawd," using the Jew as a sign of deceit and not as an image of stockjobbing. Likewise, in *The Chimera*, which engaged with the culture of stockjobbing, one figure remarked that "there's more Honesty in a Jew, than a Stock-jobber!," distinguishing between the two.[17] Had the Jew been identified with stockjobbing, this phrase would not work. Jewishness reflected greed in general, but was not associated specifically with the concern over destructive financial activities. Similarly, other texts, sermons among them, used the Jews to highlight the greedy conduct of investors or company directors (which was said to be worse), but this was a historical or traditional point of comparison, not a contemporary one. It is noteworthy that Thomas Gordon and John Trenchard, writers of the highly renowned and popular *Cato's Letters* (1720–1723)—one of the sharpest vehicles to indicate and attack the political-financial corruption that led to the crisis—did not relate to Jews in any of their essays on the subject.

This tendency is fleshed out when compared with another major financial center affected by the crisis: Amsterdam. While the relative scope of transactions by Jews in the Amsterdam Bourse was about half of that in London (10 percent vs. 20 percent), the Jew was perceived in Dutch popular culture as an emblem and scapegoat of the crisis, much different from his cultural role in England.[18]

It is not that English society and culture were lacking in anti-Jewish sentiments. The venomous "A Historical and Law Treatise against Jews and Judaism" was printed eight times between 1703 and 1753, but nevertheless, in itself demonstrates that relative disinterest. Although it did protest against the situation in which Jews held shares of joint stock companies and the public debt, it did not accuse them of financial manipulation, but rather of infringing their legal status—holding shares implied a partnership, allegedly forbidden to them.[19] The reluctance of associating Jews with the evils of finance implies, I suggest, that during the early eighteenth century, the notion that Jews were intrinsically connected with the financial market and manipulated it had little resonance in English society.

The 1701 *Jew of Venice* reinforces that explanation. Despite apparently "ideal" conditions—Jewish prominence in the financial market, anti-Jewish sentiments, financial crisis and social anxiety, and intense articulation of these concerns in popular print and especially onstage—Granville's construction of a stockjobbing Jew was exceptional and seemingly did not resonate much. It was also depreciated by Shakespeare's first eighteenth-century editor Nicholas Rowe, who argued that his rendering of Shylock as a comic figure—achieved by these very attributes of a stockjobber—was inadequate to the play, which required a more tragic performance.[20] To rephrase my earlier argument, economic attributes seem not to have been central in constituting the Jew's otherness at the beginning of the eighteenth century.

Instead, at the center of the Jew's otherness in popular print and on the stage was a concern with him being a *sexual* rather than an *economic* villain. This was embodied in the character of the "Beau Jew" that emerged at the turn of the century. The Beau Jew was also associated with money, but not as an end in itself; what defined him was the attempt to acquire an Englishwoman. The first dramatic Beau Jew was also the first Jewish figure to appear after the long silence of the seventeenth century—in John Dryden's last (and unsuccessful) play, *Love Triumphant* (1694). A much more elaborate figure is found in Thomas Baker's *Hampstead Heath*, mentioned earlier. Here, the lead character chooses the figure of a fake Jew in order to manipulate a

Figure 4. William Hogarth, *A Harlot's Progress*, plate 2 (1732).

Courtesy of The Lewis Walpole Library, Yale University.

lady because, he claims, recently these Jewish Beaus "disperse themselves in all publick Places," and through "Treats, Balls, and raffling away a world o' Money, were the Ladies only Favourites." As long as he maintains extravagance, he is assured, he would be preferred by the ladies despite his religion: "I design to treat 'em, play with 'em, shatter about my Guineas like Barley Corns among the Fowl, and ingross the whole Sex." He spectacularly succeeds with the lady, who covets his money and marries him, not knowing the marriage is fictitious. Eventually, she realizes she has been exploited and seeks rescue by the English protagonist, whom she finally marries.[21] Other early eighteenth-century Beau Jews are Beau Mordecai in Theophilus Cibber's dramatization of *The Harlot's Progress* (1733); the protagonist of the anonymous ballad opera *The Jew Decoy'd* (1733);[22] and Charles Macklin's renowned *Love à la Mode* (1759). Rather than misers amassing money, they were extravagant squanderers, attempting to buy entrance into high society by enticing

Englishwomen. Underlying this deception was an inherent contradiction: The Beau Jew commonly articulated his hatred of English society, yet still strived for mobility within it through the Englishwoman.[23]

This trend of representation is aptly visually illustrated in plate 2 of William Hogarth's 1732 engraving series, *The Harlot's Progress* (Figure 4). The country girl is kept as a mistress by a wealthy Jewish colonial merchant, who apparently lives according to the fashionable upscale norms of the higher class. These markers of wealth include a fancy mahogany table and furniture, a porcelain tea set, a West Indian serving boy, a monkey, and the Englishwoman herself. However, the print indicates that this is a deceptive imitation, by both the woman and the Jew, as all the pretenses crumble in the scene. The Jew is cuckolded by the girl with the aid of the servant; the fashionable table turns upside down; the monkey (another signifier of imitation) runs away; and the tea set breaks. Even the astonished alien servant boy realizes that there is nothing behind the veneer of respectability.

* * *

Toward the middle of the eighteenth century, the balance of economic and gender concerns that constituted the image of the Jew shifted. Increasingly, the core identifying mark of the Jew became his active and unruly participation in the financial system, rather than the threat he posed to the Englishwoman. As somewhat of a counterpart to the milieu of Granville's *Jew of Venice*, which opened the eighteenth-century, this new phase was marked by another production of the *Merchant of Venice*. On February 14, 1741, in London's Drury Lane Theatre, actor and dramatist Charles Macklin revived Shakespeare's original text after four decades in which only Granville's adaptation had been staged. Macklin featured a profoundly different Shylock: a grave figure with emotional depth, motivated by deep-seated revenge and hatred. This play made Macklin's fame. He kept it going for 176 performances over 48 years. Its critical and popular success was astounding: "Never was Performer's triumph more complete," ensuring him "immortal fame as an actor." Most renowned was the couplet often attributed to Alexander Pope, after having seen the first performance: "This is the Jew that Shakespeare drew."[24] Macklin undertook the new production against the cautions of his friends. He made serious preparations for the role, reading about Venetian Jews' apparel and Jewish history, and making daily visits to the Royal Exchange and its adjacent coffeehouses to acquaint himself with the deportment of Jews. Thus he promoted a new style of "scientific" acting that became the hallmark of his career and transformed English drama.

Following eighteenth-century observations, scholars recognized the 1741 production as a trigger for expansive anti-Jewish sentiments. Apparently, it did provoke a significant shift in public attitudes to the Jews, by offering an effective imaginary vocabulary for approaching them, as Frank Felsenstein illustrates.[25] Before going into the details of this vocabulary, I would like to dwell on a preliminary question raised by this change. Prima facie, Granville's production was anti-Jewish enough; why did it not evoke similar public responses to Macklin's? What was it in the 1741 production that made it so effective, or what was lacking in the earlier version? Searching digital databases yields hardly any occurrences of the name "Shylock" before Macklin's production, outside concrete references to the play. The few references found did not identify the name specifically with Jews but with general immoral behavior.[26] This is remarkable considering that Granville sought to temporalize Shylock in the mold of the stockjobber, at a time of surging public criticism against stockjobbing. In contrast, after Macklin's production, the name "Shylock" gradually came to overlap with "stockjobber, adding to it an anti-Jewish dimension and a deeper sense of cruelty. Increasingly, it came to stand for Jewish financial fraudulence. Note that Macklin returned to Shakespeare's original text, which—unlike Granville's—made no hint to eighteenth-century concerns with finance.

For example, a compendium of scandalous chronicles printed in 1742 describes "Abrahamites"—among them Moses, Aaron, and Shylock—who "swarm all Day at the *Bourse*, like Bees, trying every Art, and making use of every Chicanery to get Money." Adding Shylock to a Jewish trinity of leaders demonstrates how financial craftiness came to be associated with Jewishness and perhaps also Jewish religiosity. A column in the *Westminster Journal* depicted a fictional Jewish fraudster named Shylock, who manipulated the fall of stocks by false news, pleasing himself with the thought "that he was only getting so much of his own, as a Son of Abraham, whose Seed were to inherit the Earth." And in a satirical report of underground London after the 1750 earthquakes, the Jews—a Shylock and a Tubal among them—anxiously await their messiah in Exchange Alley, as they conceive the rising stocks (in contrast to the fall of London) as a sign of his coming. The eschaton their messiah heralds is not a religious but rather a financial one: He has enough money to bribe all British politicians, and eventually "Stockjobbing will gain universal Empire."[27] This pattern intensified during the polemic over the 1753

Jew Bill, as demonstrated in the previous chapter. By the end of the century, the name "Shylock" as connoting Jewish economic manipulation had permeated into popular language so deeply that, as aptly demonstrated by Michael Ragussis, public discussion on the social characteristics of Jews and the possibility or impossibility of their emancipation revolved around this figure. Moreover, this stereotyping process was countered by new revisionist theatrical figures of Jews that sought to promote toleration.[28]

Thus the seeds of using the name "Shylock" as it came to be known in Western heritage were sown in 1741. This does not imply that Macklin's influence was deliberate. His dramatic innovation was inspired by dramatic vision and career ambitions. Note that his new production was also part of a wider emerging trend of Shakespeare revivals that culminated in 1740–41.[29] Moreover, throughout his extensive biographical and autobiographical documentation, there is no hint of anti-Jewish tendencies. Finally, and ironically, Macklin emphasized in Shylock different dimensions than those that came to be associated with the figure and with Jews in general. The new popular stereotype was cast not in the grave and dreadful mold of his Shylock but rather in that of Granville's greedy Jew.

This model was quickly adopted in a series of dramatic pieces. Macklin himself soon produced a Jewish stockjobber figure in *Miss Lucy in Town* (1742), an afterpiece by Henry Fielding that featured a simpleminded newlywed girl from the country who mistakes a London brothel for a hotel. Her eagerness to comply with the decrees of fashion makes her an easy prey for the madam and clients, among them Zorobabel the Jew, played by Macklin. Coming from Exchange Alley, Zorobabel finds out the girl has been promised to another and rebukes the madam for affronting Jews in general—her crucial financial support. When the girl flinches from Zorobabel's sexual advances, the madam advises her to comply, for "this Gentleman [will] make you a fine Lady: 'Tis he, and some more of his acquaintance, that make half the fine Ladies in Town."[30] The association of Jewish wealth with Englishwomen is a trope that recurs throughout the play. Accordingly, Michael Ragussis demonstrates how this figure articulates the Jewish sexual danger to Englishness—Zorobabel being a typical Beau Jew.[31] However, this is a partial explanation of the character, for the Jewish sexual threat is coupled with an economic one. Zorobabel's possessions have been deceitfully acquired from English people: "the Money of Christian Men pays for the Beauty of Christian Women—A good Exchange!" he exclaims. The girl's husband, who returns to meet his wife, is also aware of that. Recalling that Zorobabel has defrauded him, he kicks the Jew off the stage, rebuking him as a "low, pitiful, stock-jobbing Pickpocket."[32] Zorobabel is thus not simply a Beau Jew of the kind we have seen before, but the effective conflation of that figure with the stockjobber Jew in one character.

This conflation was articulated in another piece by Macklin, this time as a writer. Premiered in 1759, *Love à la Mode* was one of the greatest theatrical hits of the century, featuring four suitors of an English girl who tests them by pretending to have lost her inheritance. One of them is the foppish Mordecai, an Italian Beau Jew. Mordecai is rebuked for trying to pass as a gentleman and win her heart, but also for peddling lottery tickets in Exchange Alley.[33] It is this entwined threat—contrasted with the soldierly morals of the Irish suitor who eventually wins the girl's heart—that matured to become a staple figure of the Jew in mid-eighteenth-century England.

* * *

Another aspect that became immanent with the Jews-economy nexus around midcentury was political corruption. It was increasingly implied that British politics was affected by an intricate and crafty union of Jewish men of finance and politicians who served each other's needs, the potent Jew pulling the politician's strings. This compound climaxed during the public controversy over the Jewish Naturalization Bill in 1753. Note, however, that the association of Jews with the perils posed by the financial system to politics developed before the Jew Bill episode. Here I want to linger on the resonance of this image in the theatrical medium, apart from its relation to the legal controversy.

The new mindset is aptly expressed in a short dramatic sketch, *The Temple of Laverna*, published in the *Gray's Inn Journal* in 1752. The play attacks the close opportunistic relationship between Jewish finance, in the figure of Exchange Alley stockjobbers, and government ministers (one can see a visual counterpart to the play in Figure 4, cited earlier). The revered magnate in this group is called Caiphas (after the name of the high priest at the time of Jesus's crucifixion) and is cast in the figure of Samson Gideon. Having just returned to the alley after being "closeted with the Great Man"—a reference to an eminent minister, probably Henry Pelham—discussing affairs "of the greatest importance to our nation," Caiphas is praised by Jewish brokers for his political power, as ministers dare not refuse his demands. He is "the axis upon the wheel [of finance] turns," and thanks to that Great Britain is "obliged to solicit the assistance of our [Jewish] nation."[34]

The piece takes the common critique of the corruptive effect of the public debt-based financial system and projects it on the Jews, seen as a threat to England's core identity. When a Frenchman is shown "the great scene of stockjobbing," he is told that the ministers are unable to carry out any plan without Caiphas's consent. Expressing his astonishment, he is sarcastically told that one should not compare "enslaved" France to the "free people" of England. The sarcasm is accentuated when Caiphas promises a clergyman to arrange a church sinecure for him. In this light, Jewish finance is perceived not only as an economic threat, but also as an identity-political one. The Jewish-Christian conflict is constructed first by the characters' names— Caiphas, Judas, Moses, and Aaron—but also by their very discussion: The Jewish stockjobbers conceive their negotiation with the ministry as part of a historical struggle against Christianity, not as a mere attempt at profiteering. When Caiphas returns from his convention with the ministers, his fellows ask him: "Shall we have a fixed place of residence at last? Have we baffled the prophecies of the *Gallileans* [Christians]?"[35]

The theme of the Jewish stockjobber as a threat to the British political system recurred in relation to specific historical settings. The general elections in April–May 1754 are a case in point. For instance, *The Gray's Inn Journal* satirically described a meeting of Jewish stockjobbers in Jonathan's Coffeehouse, where they resolved to support MPs who backed the Jew Bill. The note was signed by several notable Jewish stockjobbers, among them Malchizidek Mammon and the Shakespearean-inspired figures of Joseph Shylock, Lancelot Gobo, and Jeremiah Tubal.[36]

The prohibitively expensive and at first abortive Seven Years' War provides another such case. *The Taxes* (1757), by clergyman Phanuel Bacon, deplored the proliferation of taxes due to the burgeoning national debt. The nation is led by the courageous Lord Worthy, who reforms the corrupt management of the debt and prevents parasites from profiting from it. Informed about his plan, a group of stockjobbers—among them Sampson—undertake to curtail the reform. They join forces with Old Politick, a savvy man of intrigues, but their attempt is rejected by the public and fails. Eventually, the nation restores internal unity, liberty, and its international supremacy, with the last speaker expressing his assurance of the audience's support, "unless you have some excisemen, some jews, or stock-jobbers, amongst you." The link between finance and political corruption, and its disintegrative influence on society, is marked by the central role attributed to Jews: Whereas all characters are given abstract names related to their role (Transfer, Gripe, Old

Politick), the Jewish stockjobber is a concrete character clearly associated with a specific social group.[37]

* * *

By the last third of the century, the stage Jew has become a stock character of the conniver financier. This is indicated as the term "Jew" comes to denote financial scheming even when not personated as a character. Earlier in the century the term was used to emphasize the universality of market vices, but it now acquired an economic sense distinct to Jews as financial manipulators.[38] This inclination was the basis of the construction of stage figures of Jews in the 1770s, a decade that produced a series of plays featuring Jewish men of finance. Two plays by Richard Cumberland are apt examples. In both *The Fashionable Lover* (1772) and *The Note of Hand* (1774), a crafty Jewish broker is used to exploit decent English families or falling aristocrats. In the former, Napthali (sic) the Jew manages to take over assets of extravagant aristocrats by manipulating the legal interest on loans given to them. In *The Note of Hand*, the Jew Issachar is employed to gather financial information. Both gain great profits from national disasters and lack any moral check. Napthali welcomes disasters, for they offer new options for profit: "war is a var coot [good] thing; and then the plague; a blessed circumstance, tank [thank] Heaven; a blessed circumstance, coot 7 per cent." Similarly, Issachar's motto is "War, war, loss of credit; fall of stocks; debt upon debt; tax upon tax . . . other people's loss is my gain—so lies my account."[39]

A similar model drives Samuel Foote's *The Nabob* (1772), Eglantine Wallace's *The Ton, or, Follies of Fashion* (1788), and Thomas Holcroft's *Duplicity* (1781). In all, the main villains are Englishmen who seek social mobility and reject or misunderstand the moral obligations of polite society. To achieve their goal, they associate with crafty Jewish brokers, who practice financial manipulations and dupe their competitors. While the villainy of the English is at the fore, it is a Jew who pulls the strings. Without the Jew who masters the tricky world of finance, the English villain is impotent.[40] This idea is accentuated in an exceptional theatrical Jewish character in Richard Sheridan's successful *School for Scandal* (1777). Here the Jew is an honest man tasked with tutoring an Englishman in the intricate system of knavery finance. The Jew maintains the knowledge of the intricate system that no Englishman could master without his guidance. The student is assured that, as his Jewish tutor is so immersed in the art, he will become "a complete rogue before [he has] turned the corner." This model highlights the threat of the Jew to English society as the contaminating agent of the modern financial plague. As Michael Ragussis suggests in his analysis of *The Fashionable Lover*, this trajectory displays English society in an internal conflict between "Judaizing" and authentic forces.[41]

Was this prejudicial pattern of representation connected to social life? One figure that certainly inspired this image was John ("Jew") King, né Jacob Rey (c. 1753–1824), a notorious moneylender, radical political pamphleteer, and later also Jewish apologist. Born to a humble street peddler, Rey persistently upscaled his social and financial standing. He Anglicized his name to John King, gained experience as an attorney's clerk, and embarked on a moneylender career. This position boosted his wealth quickly and allowed him entrance to high society. Unlike financiers such as Samson Gideon and Joseph Salvador, who contracted loans for the government, King aimed at personal moneylending. Indeed, aristocrats with a penchant for gambling and living beyond their means were his loyal clients, Charles James Fox being the most renowned. Public concern with gambling aristocrats and politicians entangled by Jewish creditors was aptly illustrated in contemporary caricatures.[42]

King's financial undertakings attracted strong resentment, mostly, as expected, from his debtors. Yet tellingly, as Todd Endelman reveals, his Jewishness did not play a role in the attacks on his character.[43] This indicates a gap between social reality and popular culture: While real life offered triggers and catalysts to popular culture, the latter soon embarked on an independent route. It also indicates that different cultural discursive currents were concerned with different issues. We will see this pattern again in Chapter 9, regarding the debate over Jewish emancipation.

The theatrical Jew was used onstage not only as the engine behind English social climbers' unsavory success but also as such an aspirant in his own right. Such are the Jews in Thomas Lewis O'Beirne's *The Generous Imposter* (1781) and Miles Peter Andrews's *Dissipation* (1781).[44] A more elaborate example is *The South Briton* (1773), which confronts an Englishman, a Scotsman, and an Irishman struggling with their mutual prejudices. Eventually they confirm their dependence on each other and the unity of the three nations, which make up the common empire. As shown by Ragussis, the Scotsman and Irishman are replaced by the character of the Jew as an archetypical Other.[45] Yet I argue that, more than merely religious and ethnic otherness, economic conduct makes the Jew. Issacher (sic) is a financier who assists the English as a broker. He maintains an elegant appearance and seeks to enter high society, as he proclaims to his wife: "Have I not now de government contract, don't ministers, ambassadors, and secretaries employ me to do deir stocks, and why shou'd not de Portuguese Jew raise his manners with his fortune, as well as de English christian?"[46]

His deceit is exposed when his wife rebukes him for taking advantage of a relative's bankruptcy and reveals that his financial rise in England was a fraud. In contrast to the characters of the three nations who transcend their particular interests for the common good, the Jew symbolizes unbridled self-interest that does not leave room for any social solidarity—not even in the family. This is a preface to the subsequent discovery of Issacher's scheme to take over a young woman's inheritance and deceive his English employer. When he is threatened by a lawsuit, he evokes the influence of his money in the corridors of power: "to my friend at Gray's Inn, dere be de turn in de law for both side of de question, and we who have money need never fear it's engines working for us." Once again, as apparent in *The Temple of Laverna* and *The Taxes*, the Jew's success depends mainly on the corrupt government mechanisms, to the detriment of English society.[47]

The conflation of the gender and economic aspects of the Jewish threat that was taking shape around the middle of the eighteenth century remained highly effective in its latter part. The aspirant Jewish financier was often portrayed as using an Englishwoman to improve his position. An example is *The Young Quaker* (1783) by John O'Keefe. Shadrach is a man of finance and the main rogue of the play, who maneuvers the protagonists by loan contracts and craftily seduces a chaste English girl called Dinah. Capitalizing on the biblical narrative of Dinah and Shechem (Genesis 34–35, a common theme during the Jew Bill polemic, as I discuss in the previous chapter), the play renders the Jewish threat as the ultimate peril for English social morality and order. Perhaps the best-known character of that type was Isaac Mendoza, the moneylender in Sheridan's *The Duenna* (1775)—the second most successful opera in eighteenth-century London. Like Shadrach, Mendoza endeavors to rise up the social ladder by acquiring an Englishwoman with his money. He is duped and marries the old Duenna instead, while the English heroine marries her true love.[48]

Here too John King's figure could plausibly inspire the images propagated in popular drama. He was a social climber and attracted criticism for that. Indeed, he was known to have intimate relations with Englishwomen, among them celebrity actress Mary Robinson and the Countess of Lanesborough. His longstanding relations with the latter were likely genuine; at

the same time, they certainly opened crucial social doors for him.[49] Note
that King became a public figure only in the late 1770s, while the patterns of
representations of Jews demonstrated here emerged before that. For our purposes, he is important as a typical rather than idiosyncratic model, although
he was undoubtedly distinct in other aspects. Samson Gideon was an earlier
example of a socially aspirant Jew who sought an entrance ticket to high
society by financial means, married a Christian woman, and yet did not totally
sever his relations with the Jewish community.

By the latter part of the eighteenth century, the image of the Jew as a
conniver became deeply entrenched in English popular culture. The beau
from the early century became a stockjobber. A late adaptation of Macklin's
Love à la Mode (1759) highlights this shift in the balance of representations.
Neither's the Man, by Margaret Holford (1798), maintained Macklin's basic
plot of a suitors' competition, but changed the figure of the Jew. While
Macklin's Mordecai is primarily a Jewish Beau tainted by financial connivance,
Holford's Mordecai is stripped of his foppish attributes—that now charac-
terize his rival—and in their stead becomes a purely scheming stockjobber.
Throughout the turns of the plot, Mordecai appears as a miser who only
seeks to increase his worth. He is depicted as a "frightful old Jew with his
shent per shent conshols" and with "monshtroush possessions in de shtocks."
Lacking any self-consciousness, he blames others for avarice.[50]

The other suitor and the guardian himself also attempt to use the girl
for their benefit. She is aware of that but pretends to partake in their greed,
assuring the guardian that she would prove a proper mate to Mordecai as she
"did not neglect to exshact mosht exhorbitant interesht for [her] monish"
that she had allegedly lent to the poor.[51] Before announcing her decision, she
compares the supposed virtues of her suitors, describing the Jew thus:

> With beard so well cut, and so spruce, see the Jew,
> With an eye like a gem, and complexion so wan . . .
> Though shtocks are advanshing, and dividends due,
> Sho fond . . . of his gold too . . . and doubt, if you can,
> With monish sho plenty, that he is the man.

The description is sarcastic, the Jew having previously been described as ugly
and swarthy. After describing the Lord with similar sarcasm, she concludes:
"The Beau or the Broker . . . which, which is the man?" This binary phrase
deprives the Jew, now purely a financier, of the dandiness that characterized

him since the early eighteenth century. The Jew seeks to marry the English girl with his money and for further gain, but also conceives her as a financial investment in her own right. After she dismisses both, Mordecai complains that "dish ish de lasht time I shall consharn myself about shtock, of vitch a voman ish de proprietor." The pervasiveness of finance in the stock Jewish character now becomes total.[52]

* * *

Beginning in the 1780s, the pervasiveness of the Jew-finance nexus is evidenced by a new philo-Jewish dramatic wave. This trend will open the discussion in Chapter 9 on the debate over Jewish emancipation and will be analyzed there from a broad perspective; here I wish to dwell on its discursive composition and implied meanings. In 1781 Gotthold Ephraim Lessing's *Nathan the Wise* was published in English, translated by the German scholar Rudolph Eric Raspe. As Raspe suggested in his introduction, it was hoped the book would "counteract the poison which barbarous ages have left in the minds of fanatics, and Shakespeare and political factions may, some time or other, stir up again and put into fermentation." Soon a debate over what one could call a theatrical emancipation of the Jews was invoked in the literary sphere, where the characters of Shylock, Nathan, and others were pitted against one another in an ongoing public controversy over the social characteristics of the Jews.[53]

An important milestone in this development was advanced by Richard Cumberland. In a series of essays published in his periodical *The Observer*, he used the Jewish pseudonym Abraham Abrahams to promote an alternative representation of the Jew. First introduced in issue number 64, Abrahams sends a letter to Cumberland pointing to the social harm caused by the prejudicial rendering of Jews in English drama and calls on him to undertake a reparative theatrical project. Numbers 119–22 offer a sketch for such a model. Abrahams is brought to life, and he entertains a company of acquaintances with a story of helping a young girl and her mother, who have been molested by a cruel creditor. The story conveys a message of tolerance toward the Jew, which culminates in a scene in which the characters visit the theater itself—thus resolving the dramatic tension created in the first presentation of Abrahams in number 64—where the narrative onstage resonates with Abrahams' own story and brings to light his moral character.[54] What is all the more remarkable is the framing of these essays in the broader design of *The Observer*. The essays about Abrahams follow a series of theological polemical essays (numbers 113–18), which open with theological history and turn to refute attacks against Christianity by Jewish polemists—aliens "who assault our religion" and "undermine the strong foundation of our belief" while "living under the protection of our laws."[55] Thus, Cumberland maintains a vindictive theological position against the Jews while at the same time promoting their civil inclusion.

Almost a decade later, Cumberland produced a play to answer the call for a new representation of the Jew. *The Jew* was performed at Drury Lane in May 1794, and featured a benevolent Jewish stockbroker and moneylender, Sheva, who secretly intervenes to financially help a young couple and their friend against the father of bridegroom, a rich and prejudicial English merchant. Eventually, Sheva's philanthropy is discovered, a revelation that counters the characters' prevailing prejudices. The play prompted a public discussion that took the artistic representation of Jews as a springboard to question the place of Jews in English society and the place of tolerance and benevolence toward the alien within English identity itself. The play won great success: It was performed throughout England and restaged in 1815, 1818, and 1821; it was published in seven editions and translated into various languages.[56] *The Jew* also triggered a line of similarly philo-Jewish theatrical and, subsequently, literary works. Thomas Dibdin produced two such plays: *The Jew and the Doctor* (1798), in which a benevolent Jew raises a Christian orphan and returns her to her father; and *School for Prejudices* (1800), which also featured a Jewish moneylender and the society's attitudes toward him. And Cumberland himself produced another play in that line, *The Jew of Mogadore* (1808).[57]

What is common to these philo-Jewish dramas is the immersion of the Jewish protagonist in the world of finance. He is always a broker, and his benevolence is imbued with a financial obsession. This differs from Lessing's *Nathan the Wise*, which undoubtedly influenced the English playwrights. Lessing's Nathan has some obscure business of collecting debts, but this is a minor aspect of his character, as well as of his economic character. He is depicted as a rich man, more of a merchant than a moneylender. In contrast, the English version of the benevolent Jew is profoundly of a man of finance, rendering him incurably socially detached. Sheva remains a miser despite his generosity, dislocated from reality and social life.

This distinctive trait is emphasized in the dialogues between Abednego the Jew and Emily the Christian orphan in Dibdin's *The Jew and the Doctor*, when Abednego repeatedly digresses to petty financial relations in the middle of tender moments, reciting his motto, "I always minds de main chance" as pertaining to any aspect of his life.[58] *The Critical Review* apprehended that point and commented that "the character of the Jew is well designed, and affords an humorous exhibition of a mind generous, where large sums are concerned, yet parsimoniously scrupulous in the minuter details of gain."[59] Similarly, in *The School for Prejudice* by the same playwright, a Jewish broker finds £10,000 in an article he purchases from a widow and returns them to her, refusing any compensation. When his benevolence is discovered and he gains the appreciation of the other characters who have previously denigrated him, he insists on parting immediately, telling the widow, "If dere is any ting vat you vou'd say to me apout business . . . I vill talk to you; but I can't afford my time for noting."[60] In all these versions, no matter how benevolent the Jews are, they cannot participate in basic social relationships as their entire being is immersed in money.

Similar figures of benevolent Jews emerged in other forms of popular culture and were confined to the same characteristics. The humorous compilation *Laugh when you can* (1795?) introduced a song titled "The Benevolent Jew." Its gist is presented in a short prologue that the Jew recites. He is a stockjobber in Exchange Alley, and the song recounts his life from childhood to his current condition. Recounting his daily financial successes, he admits that he lives "by taking advantage of de folies of mankind." Yet he has a strict moral code in his dealing, and that is never to take advantage "of a fellow-creature in distress." He grew up as an oppressed orphan and sold petty products for his living. His diligence and honesty made him prosper—and he committed to be just: "'Gainst the distress'd and truly needy, I ne'er will shut my door—But both my hand and heart be ready For to relieve the poor."[61] Here again, perhaps with greater clarity, the benevolent Jew cannot be separated from financial craftiness. He is exceptional in his charity to the oppressed, but when it comes to ordinary social and exchange relations, he represents and promotes a devious and degenerate system. Thus his patriotic proclamation that ends the song cannot be taken at face value. The Jew claims that in England, all subjects "are good and kind, This is the place for me: So long may GEORGE o'er England reign, The Land of Liberty!" But the kindness of people is the source of his profit, and the constitutional liberty is what enables it.

These examples, and others like them, exhibit a similar paradox—overcoming prejudicial attitudes to the Jews while at the same time enforcing existing pejorative images. How should this seemingly Janus-faced philosemitism be interpreted? Analyzing the dramatic work of *The Jew*, Jean Marsden argued that Sheva must be represented with a sharp Jewish otherness in order to be identified in the end as part of the social whole.[62] This might be true if we were to account for *The Jew* on its own. Yet the plethora of philo-Jewish representations that nonetheless build on and enhance the stereotype of the Jew as immersed in finance—and commonly as a manipulator at that—suggests that this was not a carefully calculated move, but rather an instinctive, entrenched connotation.

* * *

The association of the Jew with manipulative finance, or stockjobbing, in the eighteenth century, is a narrative more of gradual change than of an abrupt revolution. My aim was to demonstrate not when this association first occurred, but when it gained cultural currency; a question not of "beginnings" but rather of resonance and effectiveness. The depiction of Jews as crafty men of finance had already existed early in the century but became a common and expected way of representing the Jew only from around midcentury, with the Jew gradually becoming an epitome of the vices and perils of the new financial system. Note, however, that even at this later stage not all plays and texts that related to the social problems of finance identified them with Jews. The image of the Jew was a component—a compelling one—in a complex matrix through which contemporaries negotiated with their changing economic reality.[63]

A popular medium in the eighteenth century, the theater was especially effective in promoting social ideas and images. Theatrical Jewish characters reverberated beyond the stage. Shylock, of course, is a leading example, but minor characters were adapted across genres as well. Zorobabel from *Miss Lucy in Town* was adopted as a Jewish nickname in opposition discourse during the Jew Bill polemic, as well as in popular printed texts on economic questions.[64] Shadrach, as I illustrate in Chapter 7, went back and forth among theater, print, and other forms of public discourse. Neither was drama the only medium where such ideas developed. As the following chapters demonstrate, there were extensive links between different media, genres, and cases pertaining to the question of Jews and finance.

The account in this chapter pushes a new question at our door. What was it around the mid-eighteenth century that lent force to the association of Jews and finance in public imagery? Textual and theatrical developments such as the new production of the *Merchant of Venice* by Macklin are unlikely to have driven a major shift in public opinion merely by themselves. It is usually their give and take with political and social circumstances that amplify their resonance. The intense public polemic over the 1753 Jewish Naturalization Bill was indeed one such juncture, which shaped the developing economic conception of the Jews. It did not create it from scratch. An enduring heated controversy over public finance and national debt (that was often integrated with the persistent debate over luxury and its social impact), the growing Jewish presence in the financial market, and a textual and theatrical language—as shown in this chapter—created an atmosphere susceptible for a negative association of Jews and finance. When the controversy over the Jew Bill took England by surprise, it was ripe for use.

Chapter 7

Finance and the Eschaton

It is said to be founded in revelation that all the Jews must be
converted to christianity before the end of human things; if this be
true, the end is yet far off, and the world is in a state of retrogres-
sion. For my own part, I am inclined to think from a view of the
times, and from a desire of supporting the authority of scripture,
that there is a mistake in the text, and that on the contrary all the
Christians must become Jews; by which construction the progres-
sion towards that solemn event is visible and rapid.

—Thomas Erskine

Referring to the vices of modern financial culture in his 1776 treatise quoted
in the epigraph to this chapter, Thomas Erskine (later to become an MP and
Lord Chancellor) sarcastically expressed his fear of the Judaization of English
society.[1] This was not exceptional. From around the middle of the century,
the flaws of the prevailing financial order were increasingly Judaized in the
public discourse. Jews became the perfect scapegoats: religious and ethnic
aliens, with extranational interests and networks, ignorant of English social
norms and manners, and aspiring for mobilization and paradoxically also for
the dissolution of the social order. Thus the image of the Jewish stockjobber
delineated in the previous two chapters became a handy tool for differentiat-
ing between less and more acceptable aspects of the emerging market.

The critique of the post–Financial Revolution social order from the
middle of the century was different in its tenor toward Jews from that of earlier
critiques against finance. Just as Jews were increasingly linked with finance in
drama, as shown in the previous chapter, they came to emblematize the vices of

this order in other media of social critique. A treatise from 1755, for instance, deplored the chaotic and manipulative trade in securities in Exchange Alley as "conspiring to pick the pocket of every body not in the secret. Those who are, can make stocks rise and fall at pleasure, and pocket the difference. . . . It must be allowed, that our native sharpers come in but for a small share in the profits of the *Alley*. The *Jews* are the great ingrossers of it . . . . yet there are some men absurd enough to fancy, that we are extremely beholden to the *Jews* for condescending to set up their trade amongst us" (italics in original).[2]

Jews were repeatedly depicted as the manipulative masters of the mysterious financial market. One critical treatise of that time portrayed Exchange Alley as a place where the Jews are the most ingenious schemers—"they can without the least embarrassment run through all the mazes of this labyrinth, yet will puzzle the steps of others who imagined themselves guided by an equally unerring clue of thread."[3] The London weekly *Connoisseur* characterized a person immersed in the world of business as one who "understands the rise and fall of Stocks better than any Jew."[4] The association between Jews and finance grew stronger later in the century. During a parliamentary discussion, MP Thomas Townshend exclaimed "with great indignation" that the "vile scene of stock-jobbing" by the Jews of the Alley must be stopped.[5] Jews became completely conflated with finance: Every Jew was associated with finance and every stockjobber was a Jew, or at least associated with Jews.

Why did the association of Jews and finance become effective only from around the midcentury, despite the heated debate on finance taking place already from the 1690s? It is futile to attempt to account for the reason why something did *not* take place. What I attempt to show, instead, is what made the midcentury especially prone to the emergence of that discourse. This cannot be explained by mere increase in the activity and visibility of Jews in the London financial market, as this was significant already at the beginning of the century. The share of transactions by Jews during the 1720 South Sea Bubble in London was about double their share in the Amsterdam Bourse, and, in contrast, Dutch popular culture expansively correlated Jews with the crisis. Presumably, the English ground was ripe for depicting the Jews as epitomizing modern financial vices already early in the eighteenth century, a period that melded social anxiety regarding the market, financial crisis, highly visible involvement of Jews, prevailing anti-Jewish sentiments, and a cultural-religious heritage that associated Jews with immoral economic practices.

The anomaly that the Jewish trope struck little chord in English public discourse during the height of the Financial Revolution and its accompanying

debates intensifies when we examine the social features of the critique that
was pointed at Jews at the time. It did relate to their financial activities and
their harm to society, but was circumscribed to the limited circle of their economic competitors. After the Act of 1697 set a limit of one hundred licensed
brokers in the Royal Exchange, there were calls among City authorities to ban
Jews from brokerage altogether. (Eventually a limit of twelve Jewish brokers
was set.) And after the general limit was removed in 1708, the limit on the
Jewish brokers remained in force until 1830. At least one petition against Jewish brokers was submitted to the mayor and Court of Aldermen, which Tovey
D'Blossiers in his *Anglia Judaica* ascribes to the year of the South Sea Bubble.[6]

What I sought to demonstrate in this part of the book so far is that
the middle decades of the century provided a new setting that enabled the
development in the public mind of a linkage between Jews and finance,
which was missing in earlier stages. The new setting was constituted of both
concrete social elements and fictional elements, and critical shifts in them
occurred with temporal proximity. Macklin's new characterization of Shylock (expanded in the previous chapter), though not aiming to change views
regarding the Jews, reverberated forcefully and made Shylock a handy trope
in social discourse. The midcentury also saw the rise of Samson Gideon to
financial and political prominence, which also resonated powerfully in popular print. The War of the Austrian Succession (1742–1748), conjoined by
the Jacobite Rising in 1745–1746, placed the state in need of vast amounts
of credit. Thus the opportunity to obtain government loan contracts dispersed more broadly, beyond the circle of privileged MPs and City merchants. Gideon offered the government a list of Jewish subscribers of a total
of £600,000, which was accepted in 1742, with similar lists accepted in the
following years. In the midst of the Jacobite Rising in 1745, he collaborated
with other financiers who succeeded in restoring credit. These activities made
him a prominent financial adviser of the government and enriched him: His
wealth increased from £44,650 in 1740 to £350,000 in 1759.

Gideon was not the first prominent Jewish financier who helped the
British government. Sir Solomon de Medina (c. 1650–1720), who settled in
England in 1670, served the state as a contractor in the Nine Years' War,
providing both short-term loans and grain shipping to forces on the Conti-
nent. He was an army contractor during the subsequent War of the Spanish
Succession, providing the Duke of Marlborough with funds and supplies. In
June 1700, he was knighted by King William III in recognition of his ser-
vices. Gideon's activity differed significantly from Medina's, however, above

all due to the different financial systems in which they operated. Medina operated as a contractor in a "traditional" way, providing funds and supplies to the English forces. Gideon operated at the center of a new system of public finance that hinged on a national debt and its apportioning into tradable shares, which involved the broader political nation and broad sectors from the middle class upward. By lending to the government, Gideon and others bolstered this system, a process that had profound social and political effects that were not known in the pre–Financial Revolution context. This aspect made Gideon different also from contemporary court Jews on the Continent, who were financial managers to single rulers where a system of public credit was less developed. This made him a novel historical type, and it is for this reason, I argue, that he attracted so much public attention. For contemporaries, he epitomized both the vices of the age and an alien identity, a volatile compound especially when combined with power.

Publications such as *The Art of Stock-Jobbing, a Poem. By a Gideonite*, from 1746, bolstered his notoriety by describing his destructive effects on the nation. Another treatise, from 1748, *A Winter Evening's Conversation in a Club of Jews, Dutcmen* [sic], *French Refugees, and English Stock-jobbers*, used his figure to expose the perilous flaws of the new system and its corruption. The pamphlet allegedly exposes the behind-the-scenes dealings of the 1748 loan subscription, which offered, so argues the writer, very generous terms for the investors and brokers at the public's expense. Gideon (here named "Gibeon") is depicted as manipulating both the ministry and the masses, using his connections and exploiting politicians' greed. He is posed against Sir John Barnard, the glorified conservative spokesman and fierce opponent of stockjobbing, and later a leading opposition figure during the Jew Bill controversy, who, as Gibeon mentions, "is Fool enough to think of nothing but the publick Advantage."[7]

It is perhaps no coincidence that the first criticism by a Jew on the Jewish inclination to financial trade also appeared at the same period, although it is speculative to explain it as relying on the growing English denunciation of Jews and finance. In 1746 the German-born Jewish doctor Meyer Loew Schomberg composed a Hebrew manuscript, plausibly in preparation for print, in which he harshly attacked the Sephardi community of London. Schomberg's goal, probably part of a personal feud, is not clear, and many of his arguments are out of line. Despite being himself a deist by that time (his children left the Jewish fold, and he asked to be buried in a Christian graveyard), he attacked his foes with religious moral language, accusing them of abandoning the Ten Commandments and deifying gold and money. Of

interest in this somewhat corny accusation are its details: Schomberg criticized the Jews for being preoccupied with stock trading, with which they are
obsessed even on the Sabbath.[8] In language not dissimilar to that of the new
English denunciations of the Jews, he describes their addiction to commercial
news, which transforms their minds with a manic depression.

This context explains both why the public clamor over the 1753 Jew Bill
was so potent and its long-lasting impression. Although the bill itself was
neutral on the question of finance, its process was connected to the inten-
sification of Jewish investment in public debt. It was initiated by prominent
Jewish financiers, first among them Joseph Salvador, who advanced it as a
repayment for the Jewish financial devotion to the state during the wars of the
1740s. As soon as it turned into a subject of public debate, opposition latched
on to the image of the financial Jew. It was the figure of Samson Gideon,
however, rather than Salvador, that epitomized the threat in opposition discourse, as illustrated in the abundance of prints and satires that focused on
his character. This was ironic, for Gideon himself adamantly opposed the bill,
which eventually made him cut his ties with the Jewish community, a fact
that obviously did not hinder the opposition discourse.

Linking the intensifying anti-Jewish economic sentiments to the figure of
Gideon requires some clarification. His role as a powerful financier with extensive political connections does not fit the character of the Jewish stockjobber
that flourished in his wake, that of a basically low-class figure. Indeed, one can
discern a move from associating stockjobbing Jews with corrupt politics in the
1740s and 1750s, to their association with lowlife greed and craftiness, especially
from the 1770s. This pattern corresponds to Gideon's activity: from its peak
in the 1740s, to his retreat from high finance from the late 1750s, to his death
in 1762. However, these apparent two phases are not unconnected. A basic
component in the depiction of Gideon was his portrayal as a leader of Jewish
finance, strongly connected vertically to a system of Jewish economy rather than
horizontally to his English peers. This implied conceiving of Jewish finance as a
single whole, where high financiers and low stockjobbers play side by side. Both
Gideon and a lowlife Jew in the Alley were on the same range.

This trope is evident in many of the sources (some of which were examined earlier, in Chapter 5), which pose Gideon, or a fictional equivalent, as a
central figure amid a Jewish collective, often as their leader who takes care of
their interests against an "English system." The powerful Jew does not stand
alone but is the leader of a gang of Jewish stockjobbers who all cooperate in
pursuit of shared purposes that are harmful to the nation. The great Jewish

magnate and the petty Jewish stockjobber range along the same spectrum: promoting the same schemes and embodying the same threats.[9] This conflict is epitomized in a phrase by a Jewish character in the 1748 *Winter Evening's Conversation*, discounting the scrupulous protests of an English banker against harming public credit: "Country! what is Country, or any Country to me, but according to what I get by it? O my Country! the Language of Patriots, that is the Language of Simpletons, if they are really serious; *Religion* and *Patriotism* are two excellent *Cloaks* for *Ambition* and *Self-interest*, but no wise Man ever made Use of either for any other Purpose" (italics in original).[10]

James Gillray's and Isaac Cruikshank's political caricatures (Figure 5 and Figure 6) aptly express the concern of the destructive influence of Jews on national interest via the national debt.

A noble Lord, on an approaching Peace, too busy to attend to the Expenditure of a Million of the Public Money ——

Figure 5. James Gillray, *A noble lord, on an approaching Peace, too busy to attend the Expenditure of a Million of the Public Money* (1787). Prime Minister Shelburne is attacked for the peace preliminaries of 1783, presumably accused of timing them for purposes of speculation. On the left, three Jewish-looking brokers hand him debt arrangements.

General Collection, Beinecke Rare Book and Manuscript Library, Yale University.

Figure 6. Isaac Cruikshank, *The Political Pawn Brokers* (1793). A satire on
the loan of £4.5 million proposed by William Pitt in 1793, which was much
criticized for its disadvantageous terms. On the left, Baron Grenville, secretary
of state for foreign affairs, bargains with three Jewish pawnbrokers.

Courtesy of the Lewis Walpole Library, Yale University.

* * *

The surge of theatrical and other popular printed pieces around the 1770s,
which criticized the detrimental effects of finance on contemporary society
using the character of the Jew, coincided with specific changes in the economic arena. Following a speculation boom in the second half of the 1760s,
Britain—and the rest of Europe and North America with it—experienced
severe credit crises. The value of the East India Company's shares crashed in
1769, followed by a crisis in 1772–1773 that originated in the failure of a London bank. All these incited a long-lasting parliamentary and public discussion
on public credit. During the crises of 1772–1773, 1778, and 1784, Jewish and
Dutch investors were held to blame.[11]

The change in the economic dimension of the representation of the
Jew correlated with another process. With the advancement of the Financial Revolution, the mastery of finance became increasingly challenging. This
enhanced the growth of a sector of brokers who became the focal points
of the social critique of the time and the subjects of repeated attempts at

regulation, which mostly proved toothless. However, by the 1760s stock broking was becoming more institutionalized, a shift that stemmed from the brokers' desire to improve their reputation by self-regulation and exclusion of disreputable associates. In 1761 a group of 150 brokers sought to create an exclusive association, with an annual fee and code of conduct. After this initiative failed, in 1773 another group of associates subscribed to the purchase of a new building in Sweetings Alley, to be called the "Stock Exchange." A significant part of the stock trade was concentrated there, but it remained dispersed in various other places as well.[12]

These processes of professionalization, institutionalization, and growing respectability were concurrent and plausibly related to a gradual decrease in public antipathy to the financial market and to the notion of a perpetual public debt. By the middle of the century, broad social sectors were invested in the public debt (as shown earlier, in Chapter 4), and the degree of respectability associated with it grew. The popular guides to the financial market, which flourished from the middle of the century, reflect growing public interest.[13]

Thus we can see two contradictory trajectories, both shifting around the middle of the century. Public critique of the national debt and of the bourgeoning financial market seems to have declined from its peak at the beginning of the century and around 1720. At the same time, the association of Jews with modern financial vices shifted from a sporadic association to a point where their linkage with the new system became commonplace. The gentrification of financial activity around the middle of the century was part of the acknowledgment that the new financial system was here to stay, with its benefits and perils. While in the early eighteenth century the new system of financial trade was conceived as simply unethical and as a threat, from about the middle of the century it became an unavoidable reality, and thus the need to differentiate between acceptable and unacceptable conduct became crucial.[14] There was no more point in rejecting the system altogether, as aptly done by Daniel Defoe and others early in the century.

The question remains whether all these distinct changes—the groundbreaking new Shylock, the rise of Jewish financiers, the Jew Bill controversy, the economic crisis of the 1770s, and the institutionalization and gentrification of stockbroking—had a causal relation with the changing representation of the Jew in popular culture. Such a relation cannot be definitively proven; however, I suggest that the accumulated whole was a critical mass that made the second half of the century very different from the first. It is hard to imagine that the dramatic changes, some of which were explicitly linked to contemporary Jews, did not influence their imagery in English society.

The image of the Jewish stockjobber thus became a handy tool of social critique. Epitomizing the evils of the system, it allowed the whitewashing of the new prevailing norms of English society. Consequently, I argue that the economic anti-Jewish ideology of the eighteenth century was not antimodernist but rather the opposite. Here I disagree with Todd Endelman and others, who characterize the new hostility toward Jewish financiers as the expression of reactionary ideology.[15] True enough, in several instances the critique of Jewish stockjobbing was raised by antimodernists—perhaps the most renowned example is William Cobbett at the beginning of the nineteenth century (as will be elaborated in Chapter 9). Yet in its founding period this notion was inspired by forward-looking interests and needs. The modeling of Jewish stockjobbing derived from the acceptance of the new system, not from its rejection. Such broadening acceptance required specific "bad guys" who were not required previously—at least rhetorically—when it was opposed altogether.

This is demonstrated by the different attitude toward Jews in the raging public criticism in 1720 and in 1753. Despite the many common tropes and rhetoric moves in the two episodes, there was also an essential difference in the perception of the dangers of finance: The 1720 discourse depicted the social perils of finance as evolving from within society itself, while the 1753 discourse ascribed them to an exterior factor—the Jews, as contradicting the very nature of Englishness. The events of the 1753 Jew Bill polemic, as it were, bolstered and consolidated the new association of Jews and the defects of the financial system to be further employed throughout the century. From this perspective, the argument often made that the 1753 polemic had no historical impact is misleading.[16] While it did not trigger any change in the formal status of the Jews, it marked a new representation of their relationship with English society.

Every Man His Own Broker

The use of the Jew as part of the English way of coping with the new financial system and its integration into a normative social-economic framework is epitomized in the first guidebook to the stock exchange, published in 1761: *Every Man his Own Broker, or, A Guide to Exchange Alley*. Written by the publicist

Thomas Mortimer (1730–1810), it won great success: it saw a fourth edition before the end of the year, with fourteen editions by 1807, and was translated into German, Dutch, French, and Italian.[17] Mortimer acknowledged the importance of the securities market for the economy and for enhancing state power. For him, it was an effective means for a free government, enabling it to raise vast funds efficiently and swiftly, in contrast to rival despotic regimes that devastated their subjects. This was a virtue that should make "the breast of every Englishman . . . glow with rapture and admiration." At the same time, he castigated the way corrupt brokers transacted a great part of this trade. The prevalence of stockjobbing tainted the entire system with fraud and deception: He himself lost a fortune in the mid-1750s under the misdirection of a broker. These were two sides of the same coin, for, according to Mortimer, like other abuses "the iniquitous art of STOCK-JOBBING has sprung . . . out of the best of blessing, LIBERTY." He argued that minimizing iniquities while retaining the benefits of the system would not be achieved by regulations (as consistently attempted) but by circumventing the brokers, by a do-it-yourself approach to investments.[18]

Despite its critique of the current abuses of the market, Mortimer's was a classic modernist attempt. This backdrop explains a lot of the cultural work for which he used the image of the Jew, which he developed in the preface. The first two editions were published anonymously, for fear of harsh treatment by the "gentlemen of the Alley." This anonymity allowed him broader literary freedom in accounting for his life and persona in the latter part of the preface of the two first editions. In a whimsical yet symbolic account, he presented himself as the offspring of two contradictions: chaste Lady Credit and a seductive Jew "of the tribe of Gideon."[19] Although "she had long resisted many base attempts to seduce her," Lady Credit, the emblem of English economic morality and prowess, finally fell prey to the delusions of the Jew who promised her a son who would "raise her to the highest pinnacle of worldly power." This well-nurtured son, the author himself, named by his father "Israel Jobber," intentionally became a stockjobber and instead of supporting his mother undermined her consistently: "filling my own pockets with the profits I pretended I was gaining for her; and to procure which, I always made use of her name." Eventually, having been wrecked by her son, the mother chastises and urges him to leave his father's base conduct.[20]

Mortimer's molding of the image of credit is telling, for it relied on an available set of images yet gave it a new twist. The feminine personification of public credit was a common stock in early eighteenth-century literature, of which Defoe's rendering of Lady Credit in his *Review* (1706) and Joseph Addison's in the *Spectator* (1711) are perhaps the best known.[21] The classical interpretation of this literary phenomenon by John Pocock and others who followed him stressed the seductive power of the financial market, embodied in the female stereotype of Lady Credit, on the rational capacities of men, enticing them into the senseless investment of themselves and their money, thus symbolically effeminizing them. As femininity symbolized the changeable, unpredictable, imaginative, and irrational, it was handily used by contemporaries to represent the profound shifts their society was undergoing.[22] However, credit was conceived also as a passive persona, whose fate and virtue depended on male economic agents. Lady Credit could be both chaste and perverted, being involved in a mutual pseudosexual relationship with her suitors, depending on their own virtue.[23] This construct was built on an entrenched eighteenth-century tendency to integrate practices related to the market and to sex in a shared semantic field, using concepts such as commerce, intercourse, and conversation to describe both.[24]

Mortimer's imaginative account played on this sensibility, portraying the Jew as defiling chaste Credit. The Jew is the only base suitor who manages to seduce Credit, and "during his criminal intercourse with her," robs her and leaves her penniless on his death. Credit becomes dependent on her son, the product of the intercourse between Jewishness and the English market, whose conduct would determine her virtue and vitality. The son (the author) manifests a self-contradictory character, deriving from his hybrid descent. After his father's death, he takes his place in cheating for personal gain under the banner of public credit. However, his mother's plea affects him immediately, and he resolves to alter his ways. This calls for a profound conversion. Credit directs him to leave the Alley and publish a treatise against "the diabolic art of stockjobbing," but also, that he "may for ever forget [his] unhappy descent and calling on the father's side, agree to be baptized by the name of PHILNATHROPOS" (the author's pseudonym in the first edition). The author is thereupon baptized, and his "first act of rational Christianity" is writing the treatise "for the service of the public."[25]

Mortimer's use of Jewishness is ambiguous. Mother Credit admits that her son, having been educated by his Jewish father, has great financial talents. It is implied that otherwise he would not have become so well informed as to be able to write the treatise. Yet to become a Dr. Jekyll he has to erase all Jewish traits and convert, consequently defining his past Jewish self as a financial

Mr. Hyde. This impression endures also in the third and following editions. Disclaiming "all alliance with the Jewish race," the author explains that the "fabulous account" of his origin was aimed "to give the public some account of the birth and progress of modern Stock-jobbing."[26] Jewishness maintains its centrality in Mortimer's new life story after discarding the original fictional account: His premature aspiration in the market ("in the warmth of youth, led on by its constant companion, vanity and self conceit") was to "gain—the riches—the credit—the importance, nay, even the name of a second * * * *." From the seventh edition, the asterisks are replaced by the initials S—G—, standing for Samson Gideon. The secrets of success in the Alley, Mortimer admits, are "uncommon subtilty and a total disregard for the real welfare of [the] country." Jews are the perfect model for quick success in stockjobbing, many of them from "pitiful beginnings . . . soon acquired sufficient to make their names singularly famous, and to enable them to purchase every advantage of Dignity, Ease, and Elegance." At the same time, Jews are also the perfect "tutors" in the Alley. One of them, Aaron, was for many years "high priest" of the Alley, he notes.[27]

Mortimer's work is an example of linking Jews to the detriments of the financial market while maintaining the system's integrity. Clearly, it did not seek to minimize public financial activity but rather to open it to broader sectors. Together with an instructive map of the financial market, the work offered its broad readership an interpretive cultural framework of it in which Jews had a profound role. Note that an effective rhetorical means Mortimer employed was associating Jewish depraved finance with Jewish depraved sexuality. Apparently, this move had a strong resonance. As illustrated in Chapter 6, this linkage was fostered in theatrical pieces of the period. While early in the eighteenth century the theatrical Jew figured mainly as a suitor (the Beau Jew), from around midcentury this feature was combined with financial depravity. Such linkage is constitutive of pieces such as *Miss Lucy in Town* (1742), *Love à la Mode* (1759), *The Duenna* (1775), *The Young Quaker* (1783), and *Neither's the Man* (1798), all discussed earlier. It was also a key element in the opposition discourse during the raging public polemic over the Jewish Naturalization Bill, as elaborated in Chapter 5.

The specter of Jewishness posed both financial and sexual perils to the English nation and identity. Combined, the effect multiplied. Linking economy with sexuality and gender, or specifically with Jewish sexuality, was not an eighteenth-century innovation; it had a substantial pedigree in European imagery. Moreover, as several scholars have emphasized, the eighteenth-century public discourse on the ethics of finance was highly gendered, designated by Emma J. Clery as the "feminization debate."[28] For writers like Mortimer, who capitalized on these discourses, the figure of the Jew proved especially effective, for it had the potential to combine both gender and economic concerns. Accordingly, it could be employed as a new framework for making cultural sense of a new economic setting.

It is no coincidence, I propose, that Mortimer's work was published in the mid-eighteenth century and offered this model of Jewishness. Both the target audience and the image itself ripened by that time. Once the financial market won public approval, there emerged a growing need to formulate a counter-image, to explain its deficiencies, at least symbolically. By that time, the Jew was a handy notion for that.

Shadrach: A Second Shylock

The ways and reasons certain images come to resonate with and become entrenched in public imagination while others do not are a mystery. Shylock seems in retrospect a predictable and understandable case, yet, as I sought to illustrate, it took almost 150 years for it to catch on. Having become established, however, the powerful figure of Shylock eclipsed other figurative means that were meaningful and useful for eighteenth-century contemporaries and resonated their grappling with their shifting economy. We find a hint for one in a 1798 children's book called *Youth's Miscellany* by William Fordyce Mavor, a prolific writer and educator. At the start of its fifth chapter, "Shadrach, the Jew," he writes:

> YOU have seen a venerable Jew, with a long beard, either named, or nick-named, Shadrach. Never shall I forget his graceful form, his mild deportment, and the philanthropy of his heart. He used to travel the country with a few trinkets and watches; and, contrary to the usual reception of his sect, where he had once dealt he was sure to deal again.
>
> It is generally said, that the Hebrews are selfish and unprincipled. Alas! We make them so. We allow them scarcely the feelings or the sentiments of human beings: by degrees they yield to the destiny they cannot avoid, and become roguish because no one will give them credit for honesty.[29]

Mavor presents here his version of a trope not uncommon at the turn of the century—the (financial-) benevolent Jew, a trope discussed earlier, in Chapter 6, and on which I will dwell again in Chapter 9. Putting the stereotypical qualities of the Jew aside for the moment, what is of interest here is his name. *Shadrach* was the Chaldean name given to Hananiah, one of the three fellows of Daniel in Babylon (the other two being Meshach and Abednego). According to the author, this was a nickname popularly associated with Jews, imbued with a specific charge of economic craftiness. Its first mention that I found is in Charles Macklin's *Love à la Mode* (1759), where Mordecai is twice nicknamed "little" or "old" Shadrach.[30] From the 1780s, the name *Shadrach* for a crafty Jew appears regularly in popular print, especially in drama. Actor Robert Baddeley, who played various Jewish characters, presented crafty figures of Shadrach in two unpublished interludes: *Moses and Shadrac; or a Specimen of Jewish Education* (1780), and *A Specimen of Jewish Courtship* (1787). In the former, Moses is the father of young Shadrac and teaches him the art of financial connivance, "the instructions which have been handed down by tradision [sic] in our family from father to son." In the latter, the two characters are merged into one figure of a financial manipulator—Shadrach Moses.[31] Perhaps the most renowned use of the figure of a Jewish stockjobber named Shadrach is that of the main rogue in the *Young Quaker* (1783)—a crafty man of finance who tries to seduce the chaste English girl Dinah. The name was also used marginally in many other plays.[32] An illustration of its resonance can be seen in a prologue presented on the opening of the theater at Salisbury in November 1790 which featured three stereotypical figures—a Frenchman, an Irishman, and a Jew—where the Jew made this indicative short speech:

I hate all promises except—"To pay
To Shadrach Sion, or order, such a day,
So much monies, value recheiv'd—d'ye see—
No oder promises will do for me!"[33]

The use of the name *Shadrach* to connote a crafty Jew was not limited to drama. In Joseph Moder's *The Adventures of Timothy Twig* (1794), the protagonist is turned by his pals to drinking and gambling and borrows money from Shadrach the Jew. And in a print from 1800, we find a caricature of Jewish diamond merchant Lyon de Symons figured as "Shadrach Lyon."[34]

The figure continued to be used in the nineteenth century. Remarkably, some English versions of translated plays added a Shadrach to the original. In

Richard Brinsley Peake's *The Bottle Imp* (1828), based on a German folktale, a new character of a Jewish peddler named Shadrach was added. In a revised adaptation of the French play *A House to Be Sold* (1802), two deceivers sell a house they do not own to a Jew named Meshec (sic)—the biblical companion of Shadrach.[35] Another playwright who featured a biblical companion of Shadrach, this time Abednego, was Thomas Dibdin in *The Jew and the Doctor* (1798), discussed earlier. Abednego (who has a Jewish associate named Shadrach), is a figure of a benevolent Jew, yet as I illustrated earlier, he is obsessed with finance.[36]

The name *Shadrach* and its semantic field was thus a common way to conceive of Jews, especially for denoting pejorative economic behavior. However, it was not a name given to real Jews, in contrast to its use—though not very common—by Englishmen. Presumably, Shadrach is part of the eighteenth-century trend in English drama and popular print of using biblical or pseudobiblical names for fictional Jewish characters. The fact that the name was not Hebrew but Chaldean might have been overlooked by its users. It is not implausible that the name *Shadrach* was picked up inadvertently and then caught on. Yet I want to speculate here that, rather than accidental, it was a highly meaningful choice, and that this is why it became broadly used.

After its casual use by Macklin (1759) mentioned earlier, the first elaborate use of the name appears in Mortimer's *Every Man His Own Broker* (1761), on which the previous section of this chapter centered. In his preface Mortimer states that the goal of his book is to teach the English people how to master dealing with stocks without getting lost or duped. In the idiom of Exchange Alley, this is called "thrusting hands into the fire," but Mortimer reiterates it with some nuance: "in other words, teaching grown people to walk thro' the fiery furnace of J[onathan]'s Coffee house unhurt; a task extremely difficult for a Christian author to perform, and equally hard for a Christian people to attain. Shadrach, Meshach, and Abednego, have indeed granted policies of insurance to all their descendants, and there fore it is rare to see a Jew so much as singe his beard, in this mansion of Belzebub; while poor Christians very often consume bills, bonds and jewels, in a few days, betwixt the hours of one and three, when its heat is most intense."[37]

Mortimer provides here a possible explanation for the resonance of the name *Shadrach* in the context of contemporary engagement with the expanding financial market. I propose that the resonance of *Shadrach* in this period's drama and popular print extended beyond the witty resemblance with Exchange Alley parlance. It relied on the eschatological mindset that pertained to the reading of the book of Daniel, a biblical text with great centrality for eighteenth-century English society.

The book of Daniel has always been a linchpin of Christian millennial thought. In early modern England, it was particularly current and was often attached to the English sense of nationality. It was especially resonant during tense political periods, such as the late sixteenth century, the mid-seventeenth century, and the mid- and late eighteenth century. Daniel's prophecy on the four succeeding empires, by now having fallen, and the fifth everlasting empire that would outstand them all, was an effective and appealing lens for the profound geopolitical changes occurring in a period of nascent imperialism. It was also extensively used in English religious thought on the place of the Jews in theological geopolitics, specifically concerning England's role in the world.[38]

What I suggest here is that the apocalyptic imagery of the book of Daniel (as part of the broader Christian eschatological canon) was also deployed as a framework to engage the new and profoundly unsettling financial system. Critics depicted the prospects of a finance-oriented English economy and politics as a dystopia, a reverse eschaton. One can see the currency of such language especially around the South Sea Bubble episode.[39] This framework was especially effective for thinking about the Jews and their role in this system from around the midcentury. Jews, so it was often presented, undermine the English economic-political system to promote their own subverted eschatological prospect. Many of the sources examined in the previous two chapters convey this mindset: The threat crafty Jewish financiers and jobbers pose to English society is not merely economic but embedded in a religious-eschatological danger. Gideon was commonly depicted as a Jewish messiah, leading to the undermining of England, on whose ruins, so goes the satirical *Adventures Underground* (1750), "Stockjobbing will gain universal Empire."[40]

During the Jew Bill polemic, the eschatological-financial trope gained prominence, as apparent in many of the texts examined in Chapter 5. This anti-Christian, anti-English, Jewish-financial inverted eschaton was often associated with the figure of Shylock, as aptly exemplified in a column titled "The Prophecies of Shylock," which exclaimed: "Therefore, thus saith the Lord, I will destroy them in mine anger, and give you their land for a possession. I will establish you as their rulers, and strengthen you by the word of my power."[41] It was also effective in visual takes on the event. The double broadside *The Jews Triumph, and England's Fears, set forth* and *The Circumcised Gentiles; Or, A Journey to Jerusalem* (see Figure 2) assembles several pieces—both textual and visual—in this vein.[42]

The *Merchant of Venice* and Shylock were profoundly connected with the book of Daniel, as the play's climax—the trial in act 4—unfolds. Thomas Luxon sophisticatedly demonstrated how Portia, renamed Balthasar—Daniel's Chaldean name (according to the Vulgate spelling)—hinges the trial on a complex Jewish-Christian polemic on law and grace reflected in contrasting interpretations of the book of Daniel. While Shylock hails Portia as "a Daniel," a wise judge who comes to enforce the absolute power of the law of the contract, he tragically refuses to recognize that this Daniel applies a very different conception of law, and misses every opportunity to secure his case. Invoking the book of Daniel to make a moral sense of commercialized society, then, was not something new to the eighteenth century.[43]

Attention to the centrality of Daniel in the Shakespearean play helps us solve a puzzle regarding its eighteenth-century rendition. When Macklin prepared himself for his role as Shylock, he sought to have the character be as realistic as possible and took pains to study real Jews in London. He paid daily visits to the coffeehouses of Exchange Alley, conversing with the Jews there, and also delved into Josephus's history of the Jews. In his diary we find these notes: "Jewes their history. an instance of human incertainty—from the Creation to the Flood—in Egypt leaving it—robbing their masters, mutinying—Jericho—wilderness—murder of the Innocents—captivity—lion's den—Shadrack, Meshack, Abednego, Babel. go thro the history of it—act the great characters."[44]

Once the centrality of Daniel in the play is clarified, Macklin's focus on the biblical story of Daniel and his three friends makes perfect sense. Note also that Macklin was the first to use the name *Shadrach* for a Jewish figure, in *Love à la Mode*, several years after his new rendering of Shylock.

The meaning of the book of Daniel was not fixed, and in eighteenth-century England, it had distinct nuances. As part of its eschatological impact, it reverberated in the enduring and boiling public discourse on finance and its relationship with the English state and society. This was the bedrock, plausibly owing much to the Shakespearean tone, on which the image of Shadrach as a representative of Jewish manipulative finance evolved. The figure of Shadrach, I suggest, epitomized a linkage between perverted millennialism (the unchristian interpretation of Daniel) and perverted finance (the unchristian way of managing credit). This linkage drives many of the writings on the subject, some of which have been explored earlier, in chapters 5 and 6. Aptly, one finds Shadrac the Jewish boy in the prelude *Moses and Shadrac*, instructed by his father that should they have "all de Monies in dish

Countrey" they would then be able to "buy all de Lands, and give our wandering People a Shettled Habitation."[45] As many scholars have demonstrated, the question of Jewish restoration was a prominent hinge of substantial aspects of the discourse on English and British nationalities from the seventeenth to the nineteenth century.[46] The critique of the financial system of the second half of the eighteenth century capitalized on the eschatological language of Jewish restoration, inverting it to signify a dystopia based on mismanaged finance.

PART III

Reform

Chapter 8

Economic Crime and Criminal Economy

The previous chapters demonstrated the ways ideas about Jews were infused in the public engagement with the pressing economic concerns of the time through their growing association with financial manipulations. Jews also became linked with contemporary economic concerns through another process: their involvement or, more important, the public *perceptions* of their involvement, in crimes against property. This chapter probes the characteristics of Jewish crime in the eighteenth century—mainly trade in stolen goods—the public reaction to it, and its public representation.

From the middle of the eighteenth century, critics increasingly referred to Jewish crime in terms of an organized network and conceived it as a counter-economic system. The distinct threat of Jewish crime was seen not in the attack of individual Jews on individual English people, but rather in maintaining an autonomous and competing system—Jewish versus English commerce. As we shall see, during the second half of the century, the concept of "system" became the key motif for interpreting Jewish crime. This was correlated with the emergence of the figure of the Jewish stockjobber, which, as demonstrated in the previous chapters, was also often conceived as part of an organized system. However, by the early nineteenth century, these two anti-Jewish notions took a different turn, as I elaborate on in this chapter and the next.

The main thrust of this chapter can be illustrated through an image that will serve as a synecdoche for the subsequent analysis, a 1777 mezzotint print entitled *Jews receiving Stolen Goods* (Figure 7). The scene depicts four Jews around a desk who receive loot from a highwayman, including watches, seals, and notes. The group is framed by an elaborately decorated fashionable screen in the background and a pet dog in the foreground. Together with

Figure 7. *Jews receiving Stolen Goods.* A highwayman tries to sell
stolen articles to a group of Jewish receivers. Mezzotint, 1777.

Courtesy of the Wellcome Collection, London.

the dignified attire of the Jewish man in the center, who receives the loot,
and the one behind him, they are indicative of wealth and genteel aspirations
and signify the Jewish ambition to integrate into polite English society.[1] Yet
each of the urbane elements is out of place: The screen conceals the crimes
taking place behind it; the dog appears to be a mongrel version of the voguish
spaniel, and clearly does not display the affectionate relations typical of a well-
bred pet; the stolen seal connotes a stolen identity; and the two outwardly
dignified Jews are naturally affiliated with two low-class men, making for a

Figure 8. Detail of *Jews receiving Stolen Goods* (1777).
Courtesy of the Wellcome Collection, London.

coordinated unit, or "system." The context of the print thus provides a stark interpretation of the Jewish attempt to integrate in polite English society. What appears to be a straightforward appropriation of genteel mannerisms is meant to conceal the Jews' real endeavor: exploiting English society and undermining its foundations. The print suggests that Jewish integration in the English middle and upper class is a pretense that subverts the natural order and disguises a growing danger.

Within this general framework, we see at the center of the piece an interplay of pointing and gesturing hands (Figure 8). Two hands point upward and two point downward; one of the hands of the man at the center is open, showing coins, and the other is concealed. The design conveys a religious overtone, which transcends the matter-of-factness of the economic transaction and involves the very essence of the Jews' identity. The hand gestures express a tension between the mundane and the spiritual. This is stressed by the white attire and wig of the Jew at the center and his grave expression, which lends the scene a somewhat solemn atmosphere. Yet the spirit of the image belies its content, which apparently has nothing to do with solemnity. The viewer is thus torn between the two contradictory thrusts of the image, a tension that is epitomized in the figure of the dignified gentleman at the center, who is at the same time the mover and shaker of the entire criminal cabal. The coins in his hand and on the table allude to Judas Iscariot, the figure that captures most poignantly the perception of the Jews in Christian eyes as both solemn and corruptive.[2] As we will see in the following discussion, these are the fundamental ingredients in the shifting discourse on Jewish crime in the eighteenth century.

Throughout the eighteenth century, the Jewish population in England (concentrated almost exclusively in London) steadily increased. In 1695 it was estimated at 900, or 0.16 percent out of an approximate total of 575,000 Londoners; in midcentury, about 8,000 out of 675,000 (1.18 percent); and at the turn of the century, about 15,000 out of 900,000–1,000,000 (1.55 percent).[3] This rapid growth of the Jewish population entailed decisive changes in its social characteristics. The initial Jewish community, many of whom were traders, was of Sephardic descent. By the 1720s Jews of Ashkenazi descent outnumbered the Sephardim. Many of the Ashkenazim were of low social strata and lacked professional skills. They employed themselves in petty itinerate trade, such as in selling used clothes or trinkets. By the middle of the century, poor Ashkenazim comprised the majority of the Jewish population in England. Moreover, the ratio of the poor in the Sephardi community was also increasing rapidly. By the beginning of the eighteenth century, an estimated quarter of Sephardi households were supported by community charity.[4] The authorities of the Jewish communities sought to limit the pour of impoverished immigrants from the Continent. They forbade immigrants without a profession to arrive in England and even paid some to leave the country, though with little success.[5]

Accordingly, it is not surprising that Jews became increasingly involved in criminal activities, as part of the upsurging crime against property that England, and especially London, experienced in the eighteenth century. Such involvement is well documented in the most conclusive source for studying historical crime in London: the proceedings of the Old Bailey, London's central court. Based on these records, Todd Endelman found that the 1730s saw the first cases of convicted Jews, whose numbers steadily increased, most remarkably during the 1760s, when the number of Jews sentenced to death or transportation doubled compared to the 1750s. The 1770s saw an ongoing increase in the number of Jewish convicts, which then gradually ebbed before rising again in the 1810s and 1820s.[6] Comparing Endelman's figures with the total number of convicts at the Old Bailey indicates that, during the 1760s, when the number of Jews sentenced to death and transportation doubled, the general number increased by about a third. Likewise, the rise in Jewish convicts in the 1770s was matched by a much slower increase in the general figures.[7]

Note, however, that the Old Baily records dramatically underrepresent the experience of crime in eighteenth-century London. Only a very small portion of criminal transgressions—whether by Jews or non-Jews—arrived at court. Patrick Colquhoun, a Scottish merchant, prominent public figure, and eminent magistrate in the late century, estimated that no more than 1 percent of the cases did.[8] On top of that, when examining the specific phenomenon of Jewish crime, we see that most defendants can be identified as Jewish only by their names, which leaves out many cases. (The judiciary was not interested in the Jewishness of suspects as such, unless it arose in testimony or had specific significance in the trial.) Moreover, Jews who prosecuted other Jews often sought remedy from community authorities rather than civil courts. While the real figures of Jewish crime are unknown but certainly higher than those presented here and by Endelman, those we have indicate that Jewish involvement in crime was noticeable, as expressed not only in the popular press (see the pages that follow) but also in visual culture (see Figure 9). Given the social structure of Anglo-Jewish communities, this is not very surprising. Indeed, Jews were mostly convicted of transgressions that were characteristic of the poor in general—pickpocketing and little burglaries—and, like other defendants, many claimed they acted out of economic distress.[9]

* * *

Jews were commonly criticized as the dominant traders in stolen goods. Receiving stolen goods was pervasive in eighteenth-century England, yet it was very tricky to convict a suspect thereof because one had to prove that the articles had been bought with awareness of their stolen status. Furthermore, unless the thief was tried and convicted as well, receiving stolen goods could be prosecuted only as a misdemeanor.[10] Indeed, as we shall see, many Jews accused of receiving and trading in such goods were acquitted. This makes the estimation of Jews' involvement in such practices even more problematic than in other types of crime, for we learn about it from testimonies and other accounts where the receiver is commonly absent and is not the focus of investigation. Consequently, it also eludes our crime estimates.

A FLEET of TRANSPORTS under CONVOY.

Figure 9. Robert Dighton, *A Fleet of Transports under Convoy*
(1781). A man leads prisoners sentenced to transportation;
the two bearded convicts at the center of the image are Jews.
The background is part of the façade of Newgate Prison.

Courtesy of the Lewis Walpole Library, Yale University.

Many Jews of the lower orders traded in used articles, which lent them
an advantage as mediators between thieves and consumers and presumably
tempted some to take the extra step. In the Old Bailey records, we find several instances of Jewish receivers of stolen goods in the late 1740s: Samuel
Cordosa became a known fence in the 1740s, and he was mentioned as a
receiver by several defendants and a constable from 1748 to 1751, as well as by

magistrate Henry Fielding, one of the founders of the first police force in London (and a prolific writer whom we met in Chapter 6 as the author of the play *Miss Lucy in Town*); Moses Newnez Cordoso, Manasseh Alexander, and Abraham Jacobs are recorded as receivers in 1747; and Samuel Levi is recorded in 1744 and 1745.[11] Much earlier, we also find a woman, Zipporah Cowen, cited as a receiver in 1727. All were acquitted. Levi Chitty, according to the testimony of the convict John Lancaster before the execution of the latter in 1748, was an eminent receiver who encouraged thieves to supply him with valuable goods, remarking "I deal in every Thing: I melt down all Plate that comes to my Hands, and send it to Holland."[12] As many cases demonstrate, the close contact of Jews with Dutch counterparts and the open route they had from London to the Netherlands made it an effective channel for transporting stolen goods.[13]

The practice became much more frequent and significant from the 1760s, in parallel with the rise in harsh sentences of Jews, as seen in Endelman's data.[14] Some of the Jews involved in the practice were depicted as particularly notorious. Abraham Terachina, active in the 1760s, was mentioned in the *Old Bailey Proceedings* as "a notorious receiver of stolen goods." Israel Cowen was tried and sent to a house of correction in 1765 but then returned to business.[15] As a receiver of stolen goods, Cowen employed also Morea Abrahams, Lazarus Abraham, and Hyam Jacobs; Jacobs inculpated Cowan after being taken before magistrate John Fielding (half-brother of Henry Fielding).[16] In June 1767, Cowen was sentenced to transportation.[17] Such cases were abundant well into the nineteenth century, as could be seen not only in trials of Jewish defendants but also (and even more so) in the investigations of other defendants who were associated with anonymous Jewish receivers.

Cases of Jewish fences loomed large in the press as well. In January 1764, Philips Abrahams, aka Scampy, was apprehended by John Fielding, and tried for the fourth time. According to the *Public Advertiser*, he was "for many Years reckoned the most notorious Receiver of Stolen Goods, or Fence to common Thieves in the Kingdom."[18] Indeed, in preceding years, several indicted thieves had mentioned Abrahams as their fence. Scampy was part of a gang of pickpockets composed of Jews and Englishmen, and at his trial, according to the *London Chronicle*, he "impeached several great Jews, who make no small figure in trade, for furnishing him with money, and assisting him in conveying his stolen goods out of the kingdom." Despite his notoriety as a receiver of stolen goods, he was eventually indicted for theft and sentenced to transportation.[19]

* * *

While Jews took part in the London underworld from the beginning of the
century, it was only in its second half that Jewish crime began to be regarded
as a problem. The significant rise in the number of Jewish convicts could
explain that. However, the *qualitative* nature of the public discourse about
Jewish crime had a separate life, and it developed somewhat independent of
the changes on the ground and in the courts. Jews were seen less as the direct
perpetrators of criminal activity and more as its facilitators. Contemporaries
saw the commerce in stolen goods as the infrastructure on which all sorts of
theft and embezzlement prospered, and as an intermediary link between the
criminal and normative economic world. Henry Fielding devoted a chapter
to the commerce in stolen goods in his *Enquiry into the Causes of the Late
Increase of Robbers* (1751), where he referred to the considerable involvement
of Jews in it: "Among the Jews who live in a certain Place in the City, there
have been, and still are, some notable Dealers in this Way, who in an almost
public Manner have carried on a Trade for many Years with Rotterdam, where
they have their Warehouses and Factors, and wither they export their Goods
with prodigious profit, and as prodigious Impunity."[20]

Fielding's rhetoric here is worth noting. The Jewish trade in stolen
goods not only is fully organized but also neatly corresponds to the normative structure of connected dealers, agents, and stations. It is thus conceived
as a counter-economic system. While Fielding describes this Jewish intrigue
as taking place "for many Years," this is the first reference to the problem
that I have found.[21] Following his example, this conceptualization continued
to underpin the public discourse about Jewish crime well into the nineteenth
century.

As the dominance of Jews in commerce in stolen goods increased from
the 1750s, this type of crime came to be interpreted as a Jewish problem.
One indicator of the perceived gravity of the problem was the response of
the Jewish leadership: On several occasions from the 1760s onward, Jewish
leaders sought to repress Jewish crime by gathering information on Jewish
criminals and passing it on to the authorities; setting up thieves by pretending to be Jewish receivers; publicly denouncing criminals; and even seeking to
check the flow of Jewish immigration from the Continent.[22] Naphtali Myers,
the warden of the Ashkenazi synagogue, joined the efforts of John Fielding
and earned—both in private correspondence and in the pages of contemporary newspapers—"respectful Compliments" for his assistance to the civil

authorities in detecting Jewish receivers of stolen goods and for his declared intention to continue his assistance "till the Evil itself be suppressed."[23]

The effectiveness of these steps notwithstanding, public reaction to the notion of Jewish crime was often harsh, at times sensational. In 1765, Rosa Samuel and her daughter Abigail were tried for receiving stolen goods. They were both acquitted in a seemingly unremarkable trial, but an article in the *London Chronicle* depicted them as leaders of "numerous gang . . . that have long infested this city and suburbs," led by the Samuels and one "Gambo a noted Jew." The writer expected "some considerable discoveries" after the reexamination of the women, but a thorough search has revealed nothing of the kind.[24] Similarly, in a letter to Prime Minister Lord North published in the *Morning Post* in 1775, the writer proposed a poll tax on every Jew as payback for their destructive conduct in England, claiming that 90 percent of the burglaries were their responsibility: "A housebreaker the moment he hath got his booty of plate or other valueables goes to the Jews," who swiftly melt it in a furnace readymade for the job. Another letter, in the *Public Advertiser* from November 1777, remarked that low-class Jews were the most notorious receivers of stolen goods and thereby the most effective facilitators of felonies.[25]

William Jackson's *New and Complete Newgate Calendar* (1795)—one of the numerous publications that surveyed criminal cases—highlighted Jewish crime as an organized economic system operating beneath the normative one. Out of twenty-four mentions of Jews in the book, twenty-two related to commerce in stolen goods. (The other two related to murders committed by Jews.) Moreover, the references to Jews were generic. Few Jews were mentioned by names but were instead referred to as a collective that dealt in stolen goods: "The Jews are the most notorious receivers of stolen plate, and consequently the greatest encouragers of housebreakers in this kingdom. If we had a law to make the receiving of stolen goods a capital offence, the property of honest housekeepers would be much more secure than at present."[26]

Other writers sought to offer a more analytical view of crime and proposals for legal, administrative, and social reforms. In the last decades of the century, there was increasing engagement with Jewish crime in publications of reformative nature that shared the apprehension of Jewish crime as a dangerous counter-economic system. The notable surgeon and philanthropist William Blizard, who established the London Hospital medical school, described a tour he made with a Jewish gentleman in Duke's Place, and he described the problem of Jewish crime:

There was hardly a robbery, to any considerable amount, in which
many of these persons were not, either directly or remotely, concerned. That some of them had crucibles and furnaces always ready
for melting down gold and silver; others were employed in different
parts of the kingdom, in disposing of stolen property; while yet
others were sent to Holland, and various foreign parts, to get rid of
articles which cannot be safely or advantageously exposed and sold
in this country . . . The neighborhood of Houndsditch was the
principal seat of these gentry. Put all these circumstances together
and we have the great lines of a dreadful *system* of depredation,
against which we have no *system* of defense and security.[27]

The reader has surely noticed my frequent use of the term *system*. The
commentators presented hitherto did not directly use this term to convey
their criticism of Jews; yet, I argue, the concept of a system was integral
to their writings. In Blizard's critique, and in others that followed, terms
from the semantic family of *system* were used to articulate the perceived problem of Jewish crime. "System" was a prevalent concept in eighteenth-century
thought.[28] It was also prevalent in contemporary English discourse, as indicated by the OED, which offers the pertinent definitions of "a group or set
of related or associated things perceived or thought of as a unity or complex
whole," and "a set of persons working together as parts of an interconnecting
network," both of which (along with others) were in common use. In the
mid-seventeenth century, Thomas Hobbes defined a system in the *Leviathan*
as "any numbers of men joyned in one Interest, or one Businesse."[29] Thus
while Blizard dedicated little volume in his book to Jewish crime, it was presented nonetheless as a fundamental or systemic part of the criminal activity,
well organized and orchestrated, that mirrored the normative English economic system.

Barrister Richard King offered a radically more Judeophobic account
grounded in the same "systemic" outlook. Concluding his *Frauds of London
Detected* with a chapter dedicated to Jewish crime, he writes:

The many notorious depredations and outrages committed by Jews,
are very alarming in a Christian country such as Great Britain is,
remarkable for laws and liberty. . . . The many horrid and shocking murders and burglaries they have committed, and for which
some have justly suffered, though others have escaped, call for the

interference of the legislative power, and the maturest wisdom, in adjusting a code of laws particularly to affect this numerous race of unbelievers, who took upon it as virtue to destroy, cheat and gull the christian world. Through the lenity of our laws, and the impartiality of our judgments, the Israelites elude the justice their notorious crimes demand.[30]

The "horrid and shocking murders and burglaries" probably refer to the murder committed in Chelsea in June 1771 by a gang of Jews who were tried and executed the same year. Yet while the impression of the murder was certainly effective in describing the danger posed by the Jews, the focus of King's allegation is essentially economic. This economic conspiracy (with the aid of English lawyers) threatens the essence of England's civil infrastructure—laws and liberty. King proposes a "retaliation," which is essentially economic in the form of both collective taxation and fines and severe exemplary punishment of Jewish felons. Punishment would deter many Jews from breaking the law, while extensive taxation would make them useful. Should Jewish influence be curbed, King speculates in a semi-utopian tone, "Bulls and Bears would scarcely be found in the Alley, or want of credit and charity on the Exchange." Besides, taxing the Jews is of great utility to the state, "as it might be applied towards discharging the national debt, which they, from time to time, have considerably helped to increase." For King, this is the only means for employing the Jews for the benefit of the state: "[F]or to make them honest is morally impossible; but to make their money serviceable to us, is beyond a doubt, therefore I am for the *lex talionis* being put in force without further delay, and that the Jews should assist in supporting the state in a more ample manner than heretofore" (italics in original).[31]

King's account is remarkable for its fusion of traditional anti-Jewish tropes—such as the description of Jewish activity as diabolical and as a danger to Christianity, and the image of locusts that raid the country and starve English children—with the interests of the modern state, and specifically with contemporary concerns over public credit. The questions he raises, whether it is possible to make the Jews moral so that they could operate within the state and what the limits of membership in civil society are, were becoming crucial concerns in the last third of the century, as shall be soon elaborated. King's answer is as clear-cut as it is reactionary: The Jews are inherently incapable of being members of the state. His choice to conclude the book with a chapter on Jewish crime emphasizes the extreme nature of the phenomenon—the most dangerous threat to the state, touching on all other forms of crime inflicting London.

The most effective writer on urban as well as specifically Jewish crime was Patrick Colquhoun, mentioned earlier—an ambitious magistrate in Shoreditch, London. In this post, he analyzed metropolitan crime and proposed a scheme to prevent it—an extensive system of regulations governing social features and behaviors he found likely to lead to crime. He published his analysis in 1796 under the title *A Treatise on the Police of the Metropolis*. The book was novel in its use of statistics and could be considered the first modern survey of crime in London. It was also a great success: In ten years, seven editions were published; it was translated into French, and by 1800 it had sold 7,500 copies.[32]

The Jews received special attention from Colquhoun, more than did other minorities, and he associated them in particular with two fundamental depravities: commerce in stolen goods and counterfeit money. Elaborating on points raised by the previous commentators, he analyzed Jewish crime as the infrastructure of a counter-economic system. Neglecting incidents of active theft by Jews, he spotlighted on their trade in stolen goods. The "Class of Cheats of the Society of Jews," to use a subtitle in the book, found in every corner of the metropolis, actively encouraged pilfering and were ready to buy any stolen article. Colquhoun estimated that more than 1,500 destitute Jews were occupied in such activities in the metropolis (about 10 percent of the London Jewish population). Eventually, the plunder from both petty pilfering (estimated at £710,000 per annum) and large-scale robberies (£280,000) found its way through connected Jewish dealers from London to the provinces or to the Continent.[33]

Alongside this system, and often symbiotically with it, is another Jewish network, which Colquhoun describes as producing and circulating counterfeit money. He depicts an elaborate organized system of Jewish boys who daily purchase counterfeit shillings, paying for them in counterfeit half-pence, and then passing them for refurbishing before recirculation.[34] The two networks constitute the essence of Jewish crime. Notably, he depicts both as "systems." While he uses the term frequently in relation to institutional systems (such as policing, jurisdiction, and punishment), he also uses it in three instances regarding criminal networks: trade in stolen goods, trade in counterfeit money, and gambling, with the former two being controlled by Jews. Jewish criminality, then, is distinct in its expansive organization ("extensive connections").[35]

In an effective passage Colquhoun, seemingly unaware of its Judeophobic spirit, depicts Jewish society as a unitary entity, informed by a shared code, which coordinates the activities not only of the Jewish underworld but of Jewish society as a whole: "Educated in idleness, from their earliest infancy, they acquire every debauched and vicious principle which can fit them for the most complicated arts of fraud and deception. . . . From the orange boy, and the retailer of seals, razors, glass, and other wares, in the public streets, to the shop-keeper, dealer in wearing apparel, or in silver and gold, the same principles of action universally prevail."[36]

Beyond the structural feature, the circulation of stolen goods and of counterfeit money share fundamental defining elements, as both erode the effectiveness of normative commercial life. Counterfeit coins—as well as notes and bonds whose fabrication lagged behind that of coins but significantly increased from the turn of the nineteenth century—undermine the general trust in interpersonal transactions based on medium of exchange. Receiving and trading in stolen goods facilitate expanding depredations on private property. In a chapter dedicated to the latter, Colquhoun remarks that, undoubtedly, they cause the greatest damage, "inasmuch as without the aid they afford, in purchasing and concealing every species of property stolen or fraudulently obtained, Thieves, Robbers, and Swindlers, as has already been frequently observed, must quit the trade, as unproductive and hazardous in the extreme. . . . Deprive a thief of a sale and ready market for his goods, and he is undone."[37]

The shadow economic systems of commerce in stolen goods and in counterfeit money are integrated in the normative economy. Through the intermediacy of the Jews, the illicit goods are "laundered" and find an outlet, like counterfeit money, in ordinary transactions and usage. Moreover, the Jews assist in supplying the rapidly growing demand for consumer goods and money. They are the counterpart—destructive but inseparable—of commercial culture.

The ultimate intention of Colquhoun's work was public reform, not mere critique. While his grand objective was the establishment of an organized metropolitan police force, he paid specific attention to means that could assist in diminishing Jewish crime. An examination of the seven editions of the book published between 1796 and 1806 reveals the development of his approach. In the second edition (1796), he adds that it is "to be wished that the leading and respectable characters of the Jewish persuasion may adopt some means of employing in useful and productive labour the numerous young persons of their society, who are at present rearing up in idleness, profligacy, and crimes. . . . The system which unhappily prevails in the education and habits of this numerous class of people is hostile to every thing tending to the interest of the state, or the preservation of morals."[38]

In the sixth edition, published in 1800, Colquhoun further accentuates the role of Jewish crime in the metropole. What is of interest here is his developed articulation of the problem. In a new chapter titled "On the Origins of Criminal Offences," he extensively discusses what he considers to be an inherent Jewish social problem with substantial impact on urban crime. The Jewish lower masses are hindered from integrating in productive labor and from acquiring professional skills because they are alienated from general society due to their exclusive customs (particularly dietary restrictions and the observance of the Sabbath), and because the Jewish community does not provide any alternative occupational training. Isolated from the labor market and lacking professional training, they are thus led into crime, and their increase "constitutes one of the chief sources of depravity which prevails in the metropolis."[39]

Colquhoun's agenda was strikingly utilitarian and did not involve any essentialist condemnation of the Jews' social nature. Their criminal tendency, in his words, was "generated in a greater degree by their peculiar situation in respect to Society, than by any actual disposition on their parts to pursue these nefarious practices."[40] Jewish crime had its idiosyncrasies, as described earlier, but Colquhoun saw the Jews' social problems as shared with the rest of the laboring classes. In his view all "have retrograded in morals in the course of the last thirty years," and society as a whole suffered from disorganization in the wake of the French Revolution and the war.[41] What was needed was not more effective punishment but the treatment of the social causes of the problem. The only way out of the vicious circle of unemployment and crime among the Jewish poor, he eventually suggested, required mobilizing the upper Jewish class to support an internal social reform that would facilitate the training of unskilled Jews and "render them useful instead of being too generally noxious members of the Body Politic."[42]

What is remarkable here is the difference between Colquhoun's rhetoric of Jewish crime—its analysis in terms of system—and his reformative proposal, which distinguishes between the middle-upper and lower Jewish classes, focusing on the deficiencies of the latter. This conflict, I suggest, is emblematic of the inner contradictions of both the anti- and pro-Jewish discourses of the period and beyond. To better understand Colquhoun's views, a brief comparison with continental reformers is in order.

From the last third of the eighteenth century, European social critics became increasingly preoccupied with what they saw as defective relations of the Jews with the general society and state. Colquhoun's conceptualization of the Jewish social problem came more than a decade after the renowned works of the Prussian magistrate Christian Wilhelm von Dohm and the French (later revolutionary) Abbé Henri Grégoire. Dohm and Grégoire saw the social ailment of the Jews as contingent on historical circumstances—referred to in chapters 3 and 5 as the circumstantial explanation of Jewish economy—and hence also improvable. In the same vein, they explained Jews' involvement in crime as deriving from their enduring constrained conditions and not from their nature. Accordingly, they sought to remedy it through occupational reform, by training Jews in productive labor.[43] Although I did not find direct traces of these writings in Colquhoun's works, it is difficult to believe he was unaware of them.[44]

Yet while Colquhoun shares the historical approach to analysis and the general view of the solution with his continental counterparts, he diverges from their definition of the Jewish social problem. For Grégoire and Dohm, the constitutive element of Jewish depravity is their "abnormal commercialism," the result of longstanding immersion in financial occupations. Dohm states that the Jews are inclined "toward usury and fraud in commerce," with a devastating influence on their "moral and political character." Grégoire considers usury as a perpetual vice by which the Jews have "debased themselves," corrupting their "national manners"; they "worship no other idol but money, and are infested with no other leprosy but usury." These traits affect not only the masses but also the higher social strata, also targeted for reform. Consequently, both Grégoire and Dohm argue that the state should draw the Jews away from commerce and financial occupations as much as possible and encourage their manual labor.[45] Markedly, French Jewish apologists such as Isaïah Berr Bing of Metz and later the Assembly of Jewish Notables have adopted the critical rhetoric of the Jews' unnatural commercialism.[46]

For Colquhoun, by contrast, Jewish commercialism was part of the solution, not the problem. This approach seemingly evolved from his favorable attitude to the modern financial system, which he saw as an indispensable factor in England's economic and political might and stability. In his view, later articulated in his *Treatise on the Wealth, Power and Resources of the British Empire, in every Quarter of the World* (1814), the national debt was the source of no less than civil liberty and secured society and politics against perilous populist agitations; before the establishment of the debt, English people were in a state of "abject dependence" and "experienced every species of oppression."[47] This might explain the discrepancy between his broad use of the notion of "system" regarding the Jewish population as a unified whole and his focus on reforming the Jewish lower stratum. As we shall see in the following chapter, in the early nineteenth century, Colquhoun's approach became the mainstream sentiment in English public discourse, while the perception of a comprehensive Jewish destructive economic system was limited to radical critics.

Colquhoun's observations affected Jewish community leaders and led Joshua van Oven—a community activist and a surgeon who had trained under William Blizard—to organize a group of Jewish magnates to fight Jewish crime (more on van Oven in Chapter 9). The two met in 1800 and then corresponded on the improvement of the Jewish poor. Van Oven proposed a scheme that closely matched Colquhoun's: mobilizing a group of Jewish notables with the ambitious prospect of establishing a Jewish authoritative body that will attend to London's Jewish poor. A draft bill that would grant it the necessary powers was sent to the Parliament and read in the Commons in 1802, but to no avail.[48]

Obviously, all these good intentions had little impact on Jewish involvement in crime. In fact, Jewish criminal activity kept increasing during the early nineteenth century, as documented by Endelman. Isaac "Ikey" Solomons, for one, the notorious trader in stolen goods and notes (active primarily in the 1810s–1820s), became a contemporary celebrity.[49] What van Oven's failed move did achieve, I propose, was placing the socioeconomic condition of the Jews on the public and parliamentary agendas. As the new century progressed, this issue became integral to the expanding discourse on Jewish integration and emancipation, to which the following chapter turns.

Chapter 9

Jews and English Civil Society

Between Cumberland's *The Jew*
and the Campaign for Emancipation

One of the curious features of early modern Anglo-Jewish history is the conspicuous discrepancy between the English cultural preoccupation with Jewish matters and their absence from legislation. With the exception of the 1740 Plantation Act that facilitated naturalization in the colonies and the failed 1753 Jewish Naturalization Bill (see Chapter 5), from the Middle Ages to the 1830s no laws or statutes were passed to regulate the Jews' presence and integration in England. The unofficial nature of their place within the English polity could serve as a weapon against them, as apparent in the opposition discourse in 1753, yet it appears they mostly benefited from staying away from public scrutiny and keeping a low profile that facilitated quiet normalization. The Jews' undecided status also facilitated intense social interactions with English people, encouraging them to acculturate. As Todd Endelman and others have shown, during the eighteenth century, more and more Jews became practically assimilated.[1]

From the 1790s, however, the question of the Jews' status within English civil society began drawing increasing attention. English society was swept by a reformative agenda, and the formal relationship with the Jews came to be reimagined and contested. This chapter explores this emergent reflective discourse, demonstrating that the controversy over the Jews' status at the turn of the century not only was decisive regarding church-state relations, as usually argued,[2] but also resonated with contemporary deliberations on the moral, social, and political implications of the financial system during and shortly after the costly revolutionary wars.

English attitudes to the bourgeoning financial network often interlaced with views on the Jews' civil status. The economic nature of the Jews was an important hinge of the pre-parliamentary debate over their status, and just as opponents attacked it as flawed and debased, so too were advocates of civil integration pressed to deny, justify, or apologize for it. However, and this is my second argument, when the discourse entered Parliament and was formalized in the 1830s, the tie between Jews and finance was undone. Despite some initial attempts by opponents of Jewish emancipation in Parliament to build up opposition to the Jewish case using financial concerns, it was a failed move. The linkage between Jews and finance lost the cultural force it had had for several decades.

Accordingly, my chronological framework here differs from other discussions on the emancipation of the Jews in England. It does not follow David Sorkin's expansive framework, which construed emancipation in its broadest sense and opens the Anglo-Jewish discussion in the 1650s; nor does it follow studies that restrict it to the narrow political sense and usually take 1830–1858 as their scope. Instead, it begins with the inception of the public discussion in the 1790s and ends when this discourse entered the parliamentary arena in the early 1830s. The Jewish Disabilities Bill was debated fourteen times between 1830 and 1858, when Jews won the right to be elected to Parliament. Despite its prolonged history, the debates on the bill soon became static and hardly shifted in content after the mid-1830s. For this reason, I will end my discussion there.[3]

Scholars often stress the low prominence of the debates about Jewish civil status in England. Evidently, the Jewish minority since the resettlement attracted less animosity than others. Jews did not suffer significant violent harassment, and apart from 1753, public resistance to their social inclusion was less marked in the public agenda compared to that toward other minorities.[4] Their entrance into the struggle for political emancipation was likewise belated. Only after the emancipation of Dissenters and Catholics was granted (in 1828 and 1829, respectively) did the advocates of Jewish political rights embark on their campaign (1830). This backdrop is important for characterizing the process of political emancipation, but it does not help us understand the public discourse that preceded and facilitated it.

A crucial setting for analyzing the development of the public discourse on Jewish integration is the debate about the place and nature of public credit in England. The controversies over public credit that characterized the first half of the eighteenth century took a new shape at the turn of the century.

The revolutionary wars entailed an alarming boost of public expenditure. From £241.6 million in 1794, British public debt soared to £840.1 million in 1822, before gradually declining. Banknotes were overprinted double the value held in bullion, and some country banks were already facing bank runs. With the rumors of a French landing in 1797, Parliament enacted the Bank Restriction Act, which removed the requirement of the Bank of England to convert banknotes into gold. This started the Restriction Period, which lasted until 1821, when convertibility was restored. It was precisely in this period that the discussion about the civil acceptance of the Jews took shape.

From Stage to Print: The Debate over Jewish Integration

A central venue for the emerging discourse on Jewish sociocultural inclusion was the theater. To retrace some of the points made in Chapter 6, the prototype of this development, which embodied the idea of religious tolerance, was Gotthold Ephraim Lessing's *Nathan the Wise*, first performed in Berlin in 1783. The play was translated into English in 1781 and 1805, though never performed in England until the twentieth century. Both translators mentioned in their prefaces, perhaps naively, the play's benevolent impact on the German public and sought to promote similar sentiments in England to advance the civil acceptance of the Jews.[5] Soon after the first translation was published, a debate over what one might call the theatrical emancipation of the Jews broke out. Richard Cumberland—who had capitalized on the figure of the Jewish stockjobber in *The Fashionable Lover* (1772) and *The Note of Hand* (1774)— became the central figure in this development. His series of essays published in *The Observer* in 1785 led the discussion about the social acceptance of Jews. However, as demonstrated in Chapter 6, the paper's pro-Jewish attitude was conflicted and contradictory. Alongside the benevolent Jewish protagonist in the essays, Jews as a whole were revealed as a fifth column. This tension took a new turn in Cumberland's project of Jewish theatrical emancipation, the influential play *The Jew* (1794). Crucial in it was the entanglement of Jewish benevolence and financial obsession. Despite his extreme generosity— or perhaps just because of its unnaturalness—its Jewish protagonist, Sheva, remains a miser cut out from social life. This tension became the DNA of a series of pro-Jewish theatrical pieces.

As several scholars have demonstrated, *The Jew* invoked a public discussion that took the representation of Jews as a springboard for questioning their place in English society and the place of tolerance and benevolence toward the alien within English identity. Sheva was pitted against Shylock, inciting a vigorous public debate over the "true nature" of the Jews which endured (though its hinge changed) throughout the nineteenth century, as Michael Ragussis aptly demonstrated.[6] The essence of this "nature" was economic. Some writers took a conflictual stance, and while they rejected Cumberland's endorsement of the Jewish character, they complacently aspired for the liberalism toward the Jews that he championed. As one writer put it in the *Monthly Visitor* in 1797, Cumberland should be praised "for striving to free an oppressed people from the taunts and insults of the ignorant and malevolent. . . . For though he has failed in endeavouring to present us with a copy of nature, he has done more; he has kindled into a flame the latent sparks of philanthropy, [and] roused the dormant feelings of humanity."[7]

The benevolent Jew epitomized by Sheva is discrepant with the Jews' social reality (a failed "copy of nature"). Still, it is the Jew whom English people should imagine, being a liberal nation. It is therefore unclear whether the acceptance of the Jews depends on their own virtue or that of English society. What makes Sheva's figure unconvincing is his exaggerated virtuousness. However, the economic lens employed here reveals another dimension of his defect: Sheva, as well as other figures modeled on him, is simultaneously altruistic and obsessively absorbed in financial matters—an unsettling element in the discourse on the Jews' cultural acceptance.

In a 1796 equivocal apology for Shylock, Richard Hole exhibits a similar propensity. Shylock's conduct, he argues, should not be evaluated according to charitable Christian standards but according to Jewish socioreligious ones. Unlike Christians, Jews do not consider usury evil, and, "having been long debarred from every other mode of improving their temporal property, usury has been their hereditary profession from the capture of Jerusalem to the present time." Accordingly, although Shylock's self-defense may appear unconvincing to Christians, for Jews, "to whom Stock is *terra firma*, and quarterly interest and dividends ("a breed from barren metal") its living produce, [it would] be unanswerable."[8]

Drama triggered the growing engagement with the acceptance of the Jews, but the discourse soon extended beyond it. Established by the radical bookseller Richard Philips and edited by the medical doctor and dissenter John Aikin, the *Monthly Magazine* was designed to propagate "those liberal principles respecting some of the most important concerns of mankind." Despite its radicalism, the magazine was arguably the most popular of the time.[9] From its first number through to the third, it published a sequential historical account of the Jews in England up to the present (1796), thereby seeking to illuminate their "true nature." Strikingly, the writer started his account of Anglo-Jewish history as early as the time of Nehemiah, revealing again the importance of ancient Jewish history for current discussions of socioeconomic questions, a pattern we have seen in action and discussed in Part I of this book. Under Nehemiah's leadership, following the Babylonian exile, the Jews acquired distinguished commercial talents and developed a deep sense of religious tolerance. These developments provided the basic setting for the history of Jewish-Christian relations: According to this account, the Jews arrived in pagan England and facilitated its Christianization through their synagogues. During the medieval period they supported England's commerce almost exclusively, as they were the only bankers (designated by the masses as usurers) and international traders. Persecutions were the outcome of prejudices, mostly against Jewish commercial success. Eventually, the long period of persecutions degenerated the Jews' social characteristics, and they lost the "virtues of their early character." The "undistinguishing contempt of men, who ought to treat them as equals" dwindled the number of respectable characters among them, and occasioned their employment in disreputable practices, in turn boosting the prejudices against them. Being frequently dislocated, thus "never expecting to see the same customer twice," they developed exploitative habits and were consequently "sunk into a degree of ignorance, which increased to themselves and others the difficulty of bettering their condition."[10]

The notional focus of the account in the *Monthly Magazine* is the strong connection among commercialism, religious tolerance, and social progress. This idea taps into the eighteenth-century *doux commerce* tradition, extensively analyzed by Albert Hirschman.[11] What is remarkable here is the prominent role attributed to Jews in the narrative of the process of civilization. Not dissimilar to Montesquieu's equally exceptional remark that it was through the Jewish invention of bills of exchange in the Middle Ages that European civilization gradually overcame "barbarism" and despotism,[12] the *Monthly Magazine* shifted the focus to *ancient* rather than modern Jewish history, tying both together and linking current political-economic developments with biblical history.

The *Monthly Magazine* was not the only voice calling for the Jews' civil enhancement, though certainly it was an early one. In June 1816 Samuel Taylor

Coleridge published an enthusiastic piece in *The Courier* titled "Treatment of the Jews," where he defended the Jews against enduring prejudices related to their debased economic conduct, which he explained as resulting from their ongoing treatment by their Christian environment: "If they have been hard and gripping in their dealings, may it not have been occasioned by the treatment they have received? To treat men as if they were incapable of virtue is to make them so."[13] Gaining increasing prominence, this rationale integrated utilitarian and moral approaches, as it held English society morally responsible for the depraved social condition of the Jews throughout its history, a condition which in turn undermined the English national interest.

While this budding public discussion did not concretely address the option of full political emancipation, that prospect of emancipation had already been in the air since the 1790s. The writer in the *Monthly Magazine* concludes with the changes in public opinion that are underway—expressed in the works of Lessing, Christian Wilhelm von Dohm, Abbé Henri Grégoire, and, in England, Richard Cumberland himself—and derives practical observations: "There can scarcely remain any apprehension among thinking men, that the slightest popular odium would now be incurred by the legislature, if it repealed every law which incroaches upon the political equality of this and other sects. It may not, however, have been amiss to bring within a small compass, such particulars of the fortunes of this people in our island, and such notices of the writings in their behalf, as may be likeliest to invite attention whenever a reformed and reforming legislature shall consider of their condition."[14]

This last remark is telling, for it reveals that the significance of the Jews' cultural acceptance toward the turn of the century was not confined to the realm of representations but also resonated politically. A similar interconnection is evident in the writings of the eminent literary critic William Hazlitt, whose critique was central in the public acceptance of a new and sympathetic interpretation of Shylock, as first performed by Edmund Kean in 1814. Hazlitt's endeavor against public anti-Jewish prejudices, as expressed in his interpretive critique of the figure of Shylock, dovetails with his fight against anti-Jewish prejudice in the early stage of the parliamentary emancipation campaign.[15] By that time there was a concrete model of emancipation that aroused much interest in England—in France, where Jews became emancipated in 1791 (the same year Grégoire's treatise was published in English). As shown in what follows, not only advocates but also opponents of Jewish integration saw the potential political ramifications of the evolving discourse.

Pre-parliamentary Opposition to Jewish Emancipation

The notion that Jewish emancipation was in the air long before the parliamentary campaign is also supported by the fact that opposition thereto also
preceded it considerably. The ideas of social integration that emanated from
The Jew and from the discourse it inspired, and the unfolding of emancipation on the Continent, were seen as indications for a coming change in
England and incited a denouncing reaction from adversaries to the Jewish
cause. Arguments about the Jews' economic nature were the kernel of this
pre-parliamentary opposition. The most significant and vociferous member
of this opposition was William Cobbett, one of the most prolific and popular
writers of the early nineteenth century. He wrote and published on a broad
range of topics but was, particularly, the most effective political journalist of
his day, his affordable *Political Register* (1802–1836) reaching a weekly circulation of up to 70,000 copies in the late 1810s.[16]

Cobbett spent most of the 1790s in Philadelphia as an anti-Jacobin pamphleteer. He returned to England in 1800 and became the protégé of William
Windham, an enthusiastic adherent of Edmund Burke, with whom he joined
forces around a bellicose form of patriotism. In 1802 Cobbett launched the
Political Register with Windham's financial support.[17] Yet in a few years, Cobbett's patriotism completely transformed. His opposition to the government
shifted from denouncing its policy for not being belligerent enough to a
radical, comprehensive criticism of the system of government. Until his death
in 1835, he staunchly advocated a reformist agenda, focused on the growing
national debt and the defects of the electoral system, which he saw as the
kernel of corruption.

In 1810 Cobbett was convicted on a charge of seditious libel and was sentenced to two years in prison. There, he devoted himself to the study of economics. He continued to publish the *Political Register* and at the same time
embarked on a new project—a series of public letters dedicated to exposing
"the whole science and mystery of Paper Money."[18] In 1815 the letters were
published under the title *Paper against Gold and Glory against Prosperity*. By
1817, he announced that 150,000 copies had been sold.

Cobbett's enduring, vehement criticism resonated the pattern of a
century-old Tory tradition of critique against the financial system (see chapters
5–7), which contrasted it with the country ideal of the aristocratic landowner.
Yet he radicalized and transformed the country ideology. For him it was the
rural cottager, instead of the aristocrat, who emblematized Englishness. He

endorsed the radical campaign for parliamentary reform and its deep critique of the political system. Yet, unlike most radicals, he based it not on abstract, universalist theory but on national belonging and local attachment. As James Grande suggested, he could be understood as a "Burkean radical," an apparent oxymoron that highlights his idiosyncratic ideological integration.[19]

Cobbett's attack on the financial system was blunt and direct. It was part of his nostalgic perception of English society before it was taken over by industrialists, financiers, and corrupt politicians. Yet most accounts of Cobbett overlooked a key component of his antifinancial ideology: his passionate condemnation of the Jews. At the same time, scholars of Jewish history, who were certainly aware of Cobbett's Judeophobia, dismissed him as an eccentric critic and did not pay adequate attention to his opinions, their contexts, and their resonance.

Jews loom as bêtes noires in Cobbett's writing. They epitomize in his mind the converged evils of both the modern system of finance and the corrupt political system.[20] This notion developed in his writing only gradually. Cobbett became immersed in the critique against finance in 1803, but at the time he made only a few anti-Jewish references that associated them with the defects of the financial system. His first major reference to the Jews was in the *Political Register* of June 1805, following the report of the inquiry commission appointed to investigate an alleged misappropriation of public funds by the navy.[21] For critics such as Cobbett, this was an exemplary case, demonstrating the damage wrought by a funding system reliant on perpetually extended debts:

> With the Jews, the money dealers, that vile race of men, who,
> to save what *they* call *public credit*, but which, in fact, is neither
> more nor less than a system by which they live at their ease upon
> the labour of the poor and upon the estates of the nobility, the
> gentry, and the clergy; with this race of men, amongst whom but
> too many of the [English] merchants may be included, any act, no
> matter how grossly illegal, how flagrantly corrupt, will be excused,
> and even applauded, if it be committed under the pretext of pre-
> serving *public credit*, in comparison with which the honour of their
> wives and daughters is something too trifling to mention.[22]

Despite vaguely touching on the timely issue of public credit, the passage seems highly generic, employing familiar anti-Jewish images but not perti-nent to a concrete relation of the Jews and English society. The Jews loom as a collective whose attachment with money-dealing and parasitic social conduct transcends history. Ahistorical as they are, they become a mere image that could encompass Christians as well ("many of the merchants"), a depiction of the Jews that is very similar to some writers of the late sixteenth- and early seventeenth centuries (see the Introduction and Chapter 2). Cobbett's last phrase is also telling in integrating gender and sexuality with the financial conduct of the Jews—a trend that has been increasing since the middle of the eighteenth century.

Cobbett resumed that criticism more than a year later, in an aggressive article published in September 1806 in the *Political Register* under the pen-name Ethnicus. Titled "Jewish Predominance," the piece entwined for the first time the economic nature of the Jews with the question of civil and parliamentary reform, a theme that would resonate in his consecutive works. As a historical rule, Cobbett argues, the treatment of the Jews by the regime "has always been milder, in proportion to the commercial advancement of the states in which they lived. How sadly forlorn were they, for example, in the pasturing countries of Assyria and Babylon! How different there the state of the homeless exile, hanging up his harp in despair on the willows, from that of our modern broker."[23]

The extreme level of commercialism attained by the British state and society implied a new and distinct civil approach to the Jews. Cobbett attacked both aspects. Rather than referring to the Jews as generic signifiers of economic depravity, as he had in the 1805 reference, he now addressed concrete conditions and questions. What made him address the Jewish civil status in England two and a half decades before this question became a parliamentary debate was probably his attentiveness to the Jewish emancipation in France, especially the encounter between Napoleon and the Sanhedrin in 1806–1807. "Jewish Predominance" was preceded by two other related articles in August and September 1806. Napoleon confronted the Sanhedrin with the Jews' practice of usury and their unproductive employment, and his concerns proved, Cobbett argued, the impossibility of turning Jews into productive citizens, contrary to initial revolutionary aspirations. Napoleon's engagement with the Jews proved that they were "not of a temper to submit to agriculture or mechanical trades; and let Bonaparte do what he can, he never shall make them regular artizans, any more than Pharaoh could make them brick makers." The civil approach to the Jews in France was contrasted to that in England: "Bonaparte must needs inquire *why they do not work* and conform to the institutions of his other subjects; whilst, in our commercial state, if they are *wealthy*, no other question is asked." This stark difference, Cobbett argued, evolved from the difference in the level of commercialism in each society.[24]

For Cobbett, the futile attempt by the French to turn the Jews into productive citizens testified to their governmental health, in contrast to England, where the financial power of the Jews was uncontested. The British government was trapped in the Jewish-commercial catch it had been developing for more than a century, making itself powerless against the interests of finance and speculation. He concluded: "Tremble ye statesmen, to touch this hallowed confederation? . . . The hair of a Jew's beard must not be singed, lest our gold become paper, our paper assignats; lest our stocks vanish into air and loans become impossible."[25] Cobbett did not relate directly to the question of Jewish emancipation, but through the French comparison it was fixed in the background. His key for civil inclusion was not confessional—he later endorsed the emancipation of Catholics—but rather the genuine sharing of the national interest. Jews had to remain excluded from citizenship not because of their religion but because their economic nature prevented them from taking part in it.

While the backdrop of Cobbett's anti-Jewish critique was Napoleon's approach to emancipation, it was triggered by a local event in England that symbolized in his mind the English approach to the question. On August 22, 1806, Abraham Goldsmid held a grand feast in his new country mansion, where he entertained prominent members of high society including the Prince of Wales and the Lord Chancellor.[26] Abraham and his brother Benjamin were the most prominent Jewish financiers at the time. Abraham was also dominant in the social reform scheme led by Joshua van Oven, discussed in the previous chapter. Associated with William Pitt, they contracted loans to the government for the wars against France and thereby gained a controlling influence in the financial market. The brothers' social practices—their philanthropy, the design of their country estates, and their hospitality—were calculated to build up their credit in both the social and financial senses.[27]

Goldsmid's move to his mansion in Morden was a conspicuous step intended to pave his way into English high society. For Cobbett, his impersonating a landed gentleman was the essence of social degradation, illustrating how the manipulators of the public credit system not only undermined the social fabric and ethics of the country but took over landed property. The danger of Jewish takeover of the English country, practically and

Figure 10. Medley
and Ridler,
*Portrait of Abraham
Goldsmid* (1810).

Courtesy of the Jewish
Theological Seminary
Library, New York.

symbolically, became an obsession. In a long diary passage from November 2, 1821, on his way through the park of Lord Carnarvon, Cobbett remarked that he "could not help calculating how long it might be before some Jew would begin to fix his eye upon Highclere [Castle], and talk of putting out the present owner."[28] In a letter to the Chancellor of the Exchequer published three years later in his *Weekly Register*, he elaborated further on that point, remarking that in one country, which contains about two hundred considerable mansions, only forty-four of the current owners belong to the families that held them thirty years ago. In four cases, the original owners are currently the tenants of "the Jews and Jobbers": "The victims of your System have been driven from their mansions they know not how; and they have seen horrible Jews walk in and take possession, they know not why. . . . A violent revolution leaves hope of change; but this Jewish revolution takes the property quietly away, according to due course of law, and leaves to the loser nothing but eyes to cry with, and hands wherewith to hang himself or cut his throat."[29] The Jewish danger to English society therefore has two

Painted by S. Drummond ARA   Engraved by T. Blood.
LONDON, Published by James Asperne N° 32, Cornhill 1st April 1815.

(Mr. Joshua Van Oven)

הרופא כ"ה יהושע וואן אובן יהייהו השם
לעדתו יקר תפארה .
לאהביו עדיה ועטרה .

Figure 11. Thomas Blood (after a painting by S. Drummond), *Portrait of Joshua van Oven* (1815). The Hebrew epigraph reads: "The surgeon, the right honorable Joshua van Oven, may God enliven him / To his community an honor and glory / to his loved ones ornament and crown."

Courtesy of the Jewish Theological Seminary Library, New York.

dimensions. It reorganizes society according to the benefits and features of the monied interest, but it also penetrates to the landed country life and undermines it by a piecemeal takeover.

"Jewish Predominance" targeted the Goldsmids as a metonym for systemic financial corruption. However, reviewing the *Political Register* of the preceding years demonstrates that this was a new approach. A year earlier, in 1805, Cobbett related to the Goldsmids in an indistinctive, practical tone—as agents of the system but not as a particular target.[30] Notably, the influence of the Goldsmids in the financial market was considerable already in 1805, and nothing changed it dramatically before Cobbett published the 1806 article. Apparently, his approach shifted from a vague and generic anti-Jewish disposition to an orchestrated attack on the Jews and the financial system.

What caused this change? I suggest it was triggered by the combination of two processes that occurred in 1805–1806 and affected Cobbett. The first was the deliberations on the Jews' status in France which, as mentioned earlier, attracted considerable attention in England. The *Monthly Repository*, among others, regularly reported on these events, and a year later the *Transactions of the Parisian Sanhedrim* [sic] was published in English, with other publications following.[31] The second was the development of Cobbett's distinct version of rural ideology in these very years, as mentioned earlier. In the summer of 1805, he moved to a country mansion in the village of Botley, near Southampton. He conspicuously immersed himself in rural life and took part in country meetings, which he endeavored to turn into a new platform for political activism.[32] Against this backdrop, I suggest, the housewarming of Abraham Goldsmid's mansion several months after Cobbett's move to the country triggered the shift in his attitude toward Jews. His rural radicalism became inherently combined with anti-Jewish ideology.

Conveniently for Cobbett, Goldsmid lost a fortune in one of his loan contracts to the government in 1810, and eventually committed suicide. Together with the eminent Baring banking firm, Goldsmid contracted an enormous loan of £12 million. A market slump followed by recession, and then the death of Francis Baring, drove Goldsmid into a deep depression, and he shot himself in his house in Morden on September 28. Goldsmid's death captured the headlines, and it caused a market crash and much public agitation. Cobbett exploited this and published a letter a few days after his death, later printed in *Paper against Gold*, on the absurdities and contradictions of the financial system. These were epitomized by what he described as the essence of Jewishness—inherent, constant, and irrational pursuit of financial gain, incompatible with the basic human desires of life, both private and national.

The incident is worthy of public attention, Cobbett suggests in the letter, because it offers "a more striking and satisfactory illustration, than any other that can be imagined, of the *loan making transactions.*" How can the death of one individual cause such a crisis? If the national credit and private investments depend so much on the fate of individuals and can be so easily manipulated, then the whole thing is nothing more than a gamble. What conceals this truth is the delusion that financiers like Goldsmid are deemed as "pillars" of the nation—a designation commonly used in the press after his death. This misleads the public to believe that Goldsmid's life and death are matters of national consequence, even more—according to some newspapers—than declarations of war and peace. This deception overshadows the real foundation of the nation, namely its traditional institutes and its industrious people, all of whom "become nothing, at the mention of the names of a couple of dealers in funds and paper-money!"[33]

One can see that Cobbett stopped employing Jewish adjectives and epithets merely as a readymade traditional form of othering and denunciation; for him, Jewishness became an integral feature of the modern financial condition. First, it demonstrates the breakdown of social relations and of the traditional responsibility of the higher class for the low. He reminds the readers of Goldsmid's feast, where "as much was consumed in an evening as would have maintained the whole village of Morden for a year." The much-publicized philanthropy of magnates such as Goldsmid does not evolve from a sense of charity or responsibility but rather is a calculated attempt to minimize public resentment of their immense profits, which are made at the cost of the destruction of the social order. Second, Jewishness emblematizes the modern fetish for money: Under the guise of Goldsmid's outward liberality and philanthropy, he is "a money-loving, a money-amassing Jew, and nothing more." His suicide proves this essential point, for it appears "that the thought of such a loss was more than his mind could bear; which latter is by no means wonderful, seeing that his soul was set upon gain; that all his views and notions of happiness centred in wealth. The lover, whose passion is too strong for his reason, destroys himself, because the object of that passion is dearer to him than life. Goldsmidt [sic] destroys himself, because wealth is dearer to him than life."[34] For Goldsmid, money has become disconnected from the concrete world. Moreover, in contrast to traditional money of precious metal, it is but a vacuous paper representation of abstract value.

The antidote to the paper-money fetish is living off the land. Cobbett denounces the English who invest their money in the funds instead of in land.[35] As for Jews, Cobbett does not even raise the possibility of having them work the land, as their character is fixed as an antonym to vital country life. While in the 1800s there were still no public voices calling for Jewish emancipation, Cobbett's engagement with Jewish emancipation in France and with the English financial system prefigures the discussion. His premise is decisive: Jews could never be emancipated because their economic nature contradicts the very idea. Foreshadowing Karl Marx's infamous notion, Cobbett rejects the option of emancipation *of* the Jews and views the desired reform as an emancipation *from* the Jews.

* * *

In 1809, at the apex of Cobbett's campaign against paper money and the system of public credit, an anonymous pamphlet was published in London: *An Essay on the Commercial Habits of the Jews.* Like Cobbett's writings, the tract reacts against the supposedly favorable inclination toward the Jews in England. It criticizes the Jews' influence on public finance and takes it as a basis for a discussion of their emancipation. Again, the economic nature of the Jews looms large: The pamphlet's fundamental notion is that, unlike other peoples, Jews are distinct in their fixed "primordial principles," a uniformity of character that reflects directly on economic life.[36] On this basis, the writer develops a fourfold analysis, which is then applied to the possibility of Jewish emancipation: The Jews are essentially (1) disposed to pecuniary gain; (2) devoid of moral restraints; (3) alien to the societies where they live and are driven by foreign interests; (4) inclined to monopolize.

While "normal" society is characterized by the varied dispositions of fathers and sons, which prevent the concentration of power in the same place for a long time, Jews are all "actuated by the same principle—the love, the sordid pleasure, of *amassing*"; they have "witnessed all the shades which diversify the manners of men, in different periods of society, from the extreme of barbarism to the present state of refinement, without having themselves been at all affected by the change." This enduring disposition means that the Jew is not checked by the moral restraints common to the rest of society, always retaining "the strongest vestiges of his original abasement, in his occasional and almost spontaneous depredations upon the property of his neighbours . . . as if governed by the instinct of inferior animals." This nonhuman imagery is constitutive and repetitive: The Jews are compared to "monsters of the deep," foreign weeds, insects, contagion, and their development is described as a "disgusting scene."[37]

Alien to morality, the Jews are depicted as essentially foreign, with no view of the common good. Jews have never evinced "a desire of co-operating with the natives of the countries, in which they were received." Instead, they have been particularly injurious to the national interest.[38] The devastating potential of these inclinations is manifested in the modern system of public finance, which allows ministers who pursue their private interests rather than the national interest to call on the support of creditors against the national welfare. Resonating some of the anti-Jewish arguments of 1753, the writer calls for exclusive reliance on English creditors; yet instead of that, he laments, "the Jews have been allowed to engross the largest proportion in most of the operations of this modern system of funding."[39]

This incompatibility of interests illuminates in turn the Jewish inclination to monopolize commerce. The historical concentration of Jews in towns has enabled them to erect monopolies against local traders, constraining the "free spirit of liberal enterprize, which is the genuine characteristic of commerce." Since the latter part of the eighteenth century, the problem has become all the more prevalent because of the Jewish monopolization of the new credit market, facilitated by the carelessness of British governments and their "ill-defined conceptions of the national interests." Consequently, the funds and national loans contribute "not so much to the welfare of the public, as to the interested speculations of alien adventurers."[40]

These interlocked characteristics, which resemble some of the accusations made by Cobbett, also reveal the difference between the two regarding political economy. The pamphlet does not condemn the Jews as the epitome of a corrupt system, but rather as its abusers. The Jews corrupt a system whose default is its proneness to manipulations against the true national interest, but which could otherwise prove productive. The system, then, need not be abolished but rather confined to national investors and administered with prudence.

In the second part of the pamphlet, the analysis of the Jews' economic character becomes the hinge of a discussion regarding their emancipation. Like Cobbett, the writer seems to have taken his cue from the developments in France, suggesting that Jewish emancipation in Britain is "not very distant." Jews will never become productive citizens, but the damage of their emancipation transcends the realm of production: It will debase the very foundations of English society by allowing the Jews to infuse their "peculiar system of monopoly" into both the landed and the trading sectors. Resonating Cobbett's attack on Goldsmid's fête, the writer warns against a Jewish takeover of country land that will undermine the "constitutional government of the country."[41]

Emancipation will also debase the English polity because the Jews do not cherish civil liberties and will never struggle to maintain them against despotic governments. On the contrary, "they will promote the encroachments of arbitrary power as the best groundwork whereon to erect the bulwark of their own mercenary interests." Similar to William Prynne's critique against read-mission, the author points to a convergence of interests of despotic rulers and Jews against the nation. Finally, as the Jews have no other outlook on society than a commercial one, they will take the precious civil rights "only as the objects of merchandise . . . they would produce in the market." Should the Jews be emancipated, the author concludes, their money fetish will corrupt not only the economic realm but also the very idea of citizenship.[42]

The author justifies the civil exclusion of Jews not by a restrictive ideology of political rights but by their alleged distinct socioeconomic features. Accordingly, other religious minorities, such as Catholics and Dissenters, do have an ethical claim for emancipation. This combination of inclusive liberalism toward non-Anglican Christians and the exclusion of Jews is shared with Cobbett. However, the writer of the *Essay* takes another step and contrasts the Jews' civil status with that of colonized people in the empire. The modern colonial condition, he argues, is another manifestation of the monopolizing spirit, which conjoins the accumulation of material power with enslavement, by the combined oppression of the sword and trade. Instead of spreading civilization and freedom, modern empires—Britain included—promote "the calamities and slavery of half the globe" by waging wars over the monopolization of sea and land.[43]

This corruptive force operates also domestically, making its way "into almost all the relations of private life." The monopolizing spirit denudes commerce of its morality. Commerce, argues the writer, has become an arena strictly divided into two fixed classes—the capitalists and their workers—where the "gradations from servitude to independence" have been destroyed: "An insuperable barrier is now placed between the fortunes of the trading capitalist and his dependents: An impenetrable line has disunited their interests; and they have become distinct classes of men. Merit has been stripped of her pretensions; and money alone can purchase a property in the common benefits of nature." The profits of the capitalist are "the spoils of violence, not the rewards of industry," and "will never be respected with the same religious reverence" as those achieved by honorable exertion.[44]

What role do Jews play in these global processes? The author admits that monopolistic pursuits are not confined to Jews. However, for Jews it is their exclusive activity. English society and polity are in a perilous historical moment, where the empowerment of the Jews, the expansion of monopolistic powers, and a frail financial system that can be easily manipulated against the public interest all intersect.

Beyond their different takes on the financial system, the writer of the *Essay* and Cobbett both introduced a new and powerful notion into the integrated discourse regarding the civil status of the Jews and finance: the idea that Jewish preoccupation with finance is inherent and hereditary. These were new weapons in the anti-Jewish arsenal, which did not have precedents in eighteenth-century discourse, not even in the hostile environment of the 1753 controversy. They signaled an evolving modern, racist attitude toward the Jews. Implied in this criticism were two essential premises. If the economic nature of the Jews was inherently fixed, then the question of Jewish civil integration was not a historical one. This claim countered the basic assumption of advocates of Jewish integration that the Jews' debased social condition evolved from prohibitive historical circumstances. Moreover, if the Jews' debasement was beyond history, it was also beyond conversion. Conversion had been a central argument of many of the advocates of Jewish rights since the seventeenth century, and it became again an instrumental notion in the early nineteenth century. Indeed, the first petition to the Parliament in favor of Jewish emancipation was made by members of the conversionist *Philo-Judaean Society* in 1827, and the central promoters of emancipation in the 1830s were evangelists. Plausibly then, Cobbett and the writer of the *Essay* implicitly engaged in their writing also with the dominant conversionist discourse that simmered from the 1790s, in which the questions of Jewish political rights and the millennium were tightly integrated.[45]

The anti-Jewish critique put forth by Cobbett and in the *Essay* is of historical importance because it aptly prefigures the leftist critique of the second half of the century, on which I touch in the Epilogue. Notwithstanding its future resonance and the assumed broad readership of the pieces—Cobbett being the most popular publicist of the time—the immediate impact of their ideas seems to have been low. Despite his vast readership, Cobbett's notions about the Jews, as Endelman indicated, remained idiosyncratic. In the following section, I will look into the economic arguments in favor of and against Jewish emancipation in the early debates in Parliament over the Jewish Emancipation Bill in the early 1830s. As we shall see, while Cobbett himself participated in some of them (he became an MP in 1832), the essential link he advocated between Jews and the corruption of finance did not gain momentum in the opposition discourse. The Jews' economic character and its relations with the development of modern finance—issues fundamental to the discussions of their relation with English society and polity during the long eighteenth century—ceased to be common preoccupations.

From the Public Sphere to Parliament

It took a relatively long time for the public discussion of Jewish emancipation to reach Parliament. The initiative materialized only in the early 1830s, as part of a series of reforms that expanded the scope of the political nation. In 1828 the Test and Corporation Acts were repealed, revoking the requirement that government officials take communion in the Church of England; in 1829 the Catholic Emancipation Act was passed, permitting Catholics to sit in Parliament; and in 1832 the Representation of the People Act (or Great Reform Act) introduced drastic reforms in the electoral system. Jews remained barred from taking civil offices due to the phrase "upon the true faith of a Christian" that remained in the new form of the oath, and the campaign for their emancipation began in 1830. The amended law did not pass for another twenty-eight years.[46]

In February 1830 several petitions in favor of Jewish emancipation were read in the House of Commons, and on April 5, the bill was introduced. Eventually, it fell in the second reading in the Commons, on May 17. In 1833, with the reformed Parliament, the bill was reintroduced and passed the three readings in the Commons, but fell in the House of Lords. It passed again in the Commons in 1834, 1836, 1841, 1848, 1849, 1851, 1853, 1856, and 1857, but was repeatedly defeated in the Lords.[47]

In the debates on the first two bills, before approval in the Commons, several representatives attempted to bring in some of the arguments and images from the 1800s. MP Sir Robert Inglis, a devoted evangelist passionately committed to the church order, said in the first reading of the 1830 bill that the interests of the Jews were hostile to the English interest, as seen in their alleged financial support of Napoleon. He warned that Jewish emancipation would commercialize franchise, as their capital would allow them to obtain seats—"for it was out of the question to suppose that they would ever obtain the unbought suffrages of the people." Resonating this warning, MP Charles Harrison-Batley warned that, should the Jews be permitted to sit in Parliament, they would "soon obtain as much influence there as they had already-possessed over the 3-per-cent consols."[48] Richard Grosvenor (Lord Belgrave), who was affiliated with the Whigs and supported the previous emancipation reforms, pushed these notions further in the second reading (May 17), rhetorically asking whether the Jew was to be considered an Englishman because he "negociated a loan upon the Stock Exchange for the benefit of this country, or that country, or any other country, provided it only squared with his own interest? Or was there the slightest reason for presuming that in his speculations he would give any decided preference to the interests of England?"[49]

His answer was that Jewishness and Englishness were essentially contradictory. Tory MP Henry Vane (Lord Darlington) related to a warning he had received that voting against emancipation would undermine future Jewish investment in the public funds. He replied that the Jews would be ready to lend money to the state just as before, for it was not for the sake of the country that they lent but for their own personal interests. He quoted Antonio's reply to Shylock: "If thou wilt lend this money, lend it not as to thy friends. . . . But lend it rather to thine enemy; Who, if he break, thou may'st with better face Exact the penalty." Darlington's allusion to *The Merchant of Venice* echoed another such use, in Thomas McLean's satirical magazine *The Looking Glass*, which featured a caricature of a Jew with a Shylockean appearance entering the House of Commons in the middle of MP Thomas Babington Macaulay's energetic speech in favor of Jewish emancipation. The Jew remarked, "It's liberty of Conscience my peoples vants—that's all," but from his pocket dangled a financial bill.[50]

Note that while opponents accused the Jews of abusing the system of public credit for their own interest, they did not attack the system itself. Cobbett's critical campaign against the funding system did not have much resonance in the parliamentary discourse. Apparently, in the eyes of their detractors, the Jews no longer represented a corruptive system that had to be abolished or at least limited, as argued during the eighteenth century, but instead represented a distinct case of corruption that needed to be addressed.

Apparently, the economic-oriented anti-Jewish rhetoric did not gain momentum among the opponents, and overall, economic anti-Jewish sentiments were negligible in the parliamentary opposition to emancipation. Advocates of the Jewish cause did not ascribe much weight to the economic anti-Jewish allegations. In 1833 MP Macaulay, the renowned Whig historian, referred in the second reading to Cobbett's casting of the Jews as a "money-getting race . . . averse to all honourable pursuits, and fit for nothing but those of usury," idols for which they "sacrificed all patriotic feelings and all social affections." This was an allegation, he said, that even the opponents "had too much knowledge and taste to bring," and he did not find it requiring a serious response.[51] Indeed, most opponents argued that there was no unique degradation of Jewish morality but that the problem with emancipation lay purely in religious difference. As future prime minister Sir Robert Peel—who opposed the bill and eventually supported it in 1845—said in his speech in 1830, "There is nothing in the conduct of the Jews themselves which ought to create the slightest prejudice against them." The problem was that, unlike Nonconformists and Roman Catholics, they "reject Christianity altogether"; hence if the bill were to pass it would follow "that every form of oath which requires a profession of the Christian faith must be abandoned."[52]

The same rhetorical line dominated the opposition to the bill in the House of Lords on August 1, 1833, where it fell 104 to 54 after having passed the Commons. The Duke of Gloucester thought the bill was outrageous but admitted that it was alarming only from a religious point of view, while "in a temporal point of view it was not of much consequence." Archbishop of Canterbury William Howley acknowledged that the Jews' "precepts of their morality were founded on the laws of the Prophets, and drawn from the Fountain of Holiness." The problem with emancipation lay not in the morality of the Jews, nor in their economy, but in its contradiction to the definition of England as a Christian polity and the fact that, unlike other religions, Judaism included "a positive contradiction of Christianity."[53]

There was one exception to that general trend of the opposition to Jewish emancipation, however. In the debates in 1848 and 1849, bishop of Oxford Samuel Wilberforce, the most vehement of all opponents in the House of Lords, denounced the Jews as "immersed in the pursuit of gain," resonating some of the economic anti-Jewish arguments from the early century.[54] Presumably, the trigger for Wilberforce's condemnation was the election of Lionel de Rothschild as a member of Parliament in 1847. It is telling, however, that despite Wilberforce's public influence, his line was not adopted by others.

Perhaps most indicative of the decline of the force of the economic charges is the fact that Cobbett himself hardly promoted them on the parliamentary floor. His last attempt to restore this criticism was a sermon published in his *Weekly Political Register* on March 9, 1833, titled "Good Friday, or the Murder of Jesus Christ by the Jews," later published as an independent pamphlet.[55] Cobbett endeavored to reintroduce economy to the discourse through the door of religion. The Jews opposed Jesus on the essence of his teaching to abstain from oppression of the weak. They wanted to execute him not because of his claim to be a king or a prophet but for overturning the tables of the moneychangers. Cobbett described the ancient Jews' passion "for accumulating money" as having "come down, unimpaired, to their descendants." This had a direct bearing on emancipation, for "what can be more pernicious than to give countenance and encouragement to a race, whose god is *gain* . . . who never labour in making, or causing to come, any thing useful to man," a propensity that seems to be "inborn with them." For Cobbett, this inherent feature of the Jews is consequential not only regarding their civil status but also the English nation itself, as without them, "it would have been impossible to carry on fiscal oppressions to the extent that we have beheld."[56]

Apparently, neither this nor Cobbett's previous anti-Jewish tracts had much influence. The linkage between the perils of finance and the Jews, which became enhanced during the eighteenth century, was no longer applicable. Instead, the debate revolved around the place of Christianity in the English constitution and the nature of political power and rights. David Feldman aptly demonstrated how the question of Jewish emancipation, which was not consequential in itself, came to stand for much larger issues in the context of the political conflicts of the mid-nineteenth century, caught in the crossfire between two camps that fiercely debated the very notion of the nation. This meant that the core of the debate was not Jewishness but rather Englishness and that the financial system was no longer part of the conflicts pertaining to this concern.[57]

* * *

The low resonance of Cobbett's anti-Jewish notions, I suggest, was part of broad public inattention to Jewish finance in this period, attested to by the low level of animosity toward the Rothschilds compared to their eighteenth-century predecessors, as well as to themselves later in the nineteenth century. In 1798 twenty-one-year-old Nathan Mayer Rothschild, the third son of the dynasty's founder, Mayer Amschel, settled in Manchester, to open a branch of the family business. His initial undertaking was textile trade, but after several years he moved to London, where he increasingly dealt with financial instruments and soon made a great profit. Toward the end of the Napoleonic Wars, he began dealing in bullion, making large contracts with the government, which proved highly profitable. By the 1820s he had made a fortune.[58] Despite becoming a well-known figure, he did not attract anti-Jewish criticism of the sort raised against Samson Gideon (see chapters 5 and 7). Public denunciation of the Rothschilds gained momentum only in the 1840s, and more so on the Continent than in England.[59] This is not to say that there were no attacks against them in England before that time, but that these came mainly from their competitors and lacked broad public resonance until the last third of the century.[60] Whereas Nathan's son, Lionel de Rothschild, was the face of the later campaign for emancipation, anti-Jewish economic arguments were ephemeral in the opposition.[61] As discussed in the Epilogue, the later criticism against the Rothschilds was of a radically new form. Perhaps another indication of the decrease in the public resonance of economic anti-Jewish notions was the transformation of Shylock's figure in the first third of the century from Charles Macklin's malevolent character to Edmund Kean's sympathetic one. Thus, over the first decades of the century, Shylock stopped signifying Jewish avarice.[62]

The difference between the place of finance in the emancipation debate and its place in the 1753 controversy is conspicuous. Why did the association of Jews with finance and its destructive sociopolitical effects lose force in the rhetoric of the opposition to Jewish emancipation? The crucial factor that changed was the general attitude of English society to the financial market. The bitter, expansive public critique of the national debt and the financial market waned after the first third of the century, which saw the transformation of political economy into a universal, abstract science. At stake were not national-historical specifics but rather an abstract notion of society, as an aggregation of profit-seeking universal individuals. David Ricardo's 1817 *On the Principles of Political Economy and Taxation* epitomized this change.[63]

As sociologist Alex Preda showed, the growing professionalization of finance did not exclude the public from the financial market but rather enabled growing public involvement in it. The depoliticization and "naturalization" of finance neutralized much of the moral import that had stigmatized it. After the first third of the century, public participation in the market grew significantly and steadily, in a process that was aptly termed "the domestication of speculation."[64] According to a contemporary estimation, by the middle of the century there were 268,191 individual stockholders in England.[65] In the course of the century, in the words of George Robb, "middle[-] and upper-class England truly had become a nation of shareholders."[66]

The consequences of these shifts transcended the socioeconomic realm. Literary scholars have argued for inherent relations between it and changing forms of literary representations. Mary Poovey demonstrated how paper credit was consistently naturalized during the first half of the century, directly related to new conceptions of literary value. As literary fiction became valuable and cherished, contemporaries became comfortable with the idea of paper money—the economic counterpart of fiction. Likewise, Patrick Brantlinger demonstrated the gradual endorsement of the national debt and the various financial instruments associated with it in parallel with the rise of literary

realism. The problem of debt and credit, he claimed, changed from a public
to an individual concern. The literary movement coincided with growing confidence in public finance and growing economic stability from the 1830s to the
mid-1870s, a period of prosperous capitalist accumulation.[67]

In the same way, I suggest, the changing nature of economic discourse
affected the conception of the Jews and their relation with the English polity.
In an environment that endorsed a financial market hinging on the national
debt, vehement anti-Jewish, anti-finance allegations such as Cobbett's did not
resonate much. One can sense the change by comparing the cultural role of
the notion of Jewishness in Thomas Mortimer's popular guide to the stock
exchange, published in 1761 (see Chapter 7), and a parallel guide published
anonymously in 1816 under the title *The Art of Stock-Jobbing Explained*, where
Jews played a marginal role.[68] Like the Jews-usury compound, which lost its
force in the second half of the seventeenth century after the practice of lending on interest was naturalized, as shown in Part I, the association of Jews
with the harms of the new system of finance was not effective for opponents
to Jewish emancipation when this system finally became broadly accepted.

Epilogue

This book argued that ideas about Jews and Judaism were an effective channel through which early modern English people made sense of their fast-evolving and financializing economy. As social, political, and economic conditions shifted during the long eighteenth century, so did the concerns they generated and the public attitudes to them. Yet while all these constantly changed, one trend persisted: the tendency to address economic concerns through the Jews. Although people thought differently about the Jews' relation to the economy and invoked divergent imageries thereof, they continually employed the Jew in their engagement with the financial world.

This brings us to the notion of the economic exceptionalism of the Jews—the idea that Jews are somehow endowed with unique economic genius that "normal" people lack.[1] As demonstrated by the endeavors of Joshua van Oven at the turn of the nineteenth century (see Chapter 8), the vast majority of the Jews in England actually lived in extreme poverty and lacked any occupational advantage or exceptional financial talent.[2] If we play a mind game and imagine an alternative history in which Jews arrived in England 150 years after their actual time of arrival, England's economic history would not have been substantially different. The impact of Jews on the overall development of the English economy would have been negligible. Nevertheless, as depicted in the earlier chapters, many social critics of the time did attribute economic savviness to Jews as such, particularly in the area of speculative finance. Thus, whereas in England of the long eighteenth century, Jewish economic performance was not exceptional, it was widely perceived to be so. What sense should we make of that?

A simple answer could be that Jews attracted such attention and were conceived as exceptional because they were situated in key economic positions on which public concerns revolved. However, as demonstrated in the previous chapters, there was only a partial correspondence between the concrete economic history of the Jews and stereotypes about them. At the height of the campaign against usury in the latter part of the sixteenth century, for instance, the image of the Jew was extensively used, yet there were no Jews in England (at least not legally). In contrast, when the English Rothschild branch gained unprecedented power in the 1820s, anti-Jewish economic stereotypes were in significant decline. This is not to say that the level of imagery was completely unfounded in reality, but rather that it depended on a distinct set of factors, pertaining to the specific context. Reality could be a trigger for an image that would quickly become independent from it and gain autonomous life. (Samson Gideon in the middle of the eighteenth century is an example of a figure who unleashed a powerful image with a life of its own.)

Instead, I suggest that what lent power to the enduring pattern of thinking about economy through the Jews was the communicative dimension of economy. The Financial Revolution depended on, and in turn incited, a revolution in communication.[3] To participate in the thriving securities market, people needed access to a credible flow of financial and political information. The development of new financial instruments, accordingly, was tightly connected with the development of a public sphere with effective means of communication, such as pamphlets and newspapers. Another crucial development of social media were the coffeehouses, which had consequential influence on the progress of the Financial Revolution. In the long eighteenth century, coffeehouses served as information hubs. From the middle of the seventeenth century, they proliferated quickly; by the end of the century, there were more than two thousand coffeehouses in and around London alone. No wonder, then, that up to the latter part of the eighteenth century, they served de facto as the London stock exchange. Coffeehouses were also sites where *dis*information was spread on a grand scale by people with financial interests, through both rumors and print.[4]

Jews were closely associated with this new economy of information. It was believed that the first coffeehouse in England was opened by a Jew in Oxford, in 1650.[5] Tory satirist Ned Ward wrote in 1714 about the "English Jews," who were pleased with "Coffee, Tea, and Whiggish News." Ward might have referred here not to real Jews but rather to the English whom he designated as such, but this proves the association of Jews with the coffeehouse culture all the more.[6] In particular, Jews were associated with the manipulation and monopoly of information, by which they gained control over the market. As the eighteenth-century historian of commerce Adam Anderson put it, they maintained "a regular Correspondence with those of their own Nation throughout all the World; whereby they are said to gain great and early Intelligence in their commercial Interests, so as to be too often an Over-match for others." The Jews, wrote the *Morning Post* offhandedly, "generally have the first intelligence."[7] Control of information meant control of the market. Many writers believed, moreover, that the Jews were financial schemers, who could "without the least embarrassment run through all the mazes of this labyrinth, yet will puzzle the steps of others who imagined themselves guided by an equally unerring clue of thread."[8]

At the same time the Jews were seen as a force that could promote integration. As Joseph Addison famously put it in the *Spectator* in 1712, "They are, indeed, so disseminated through all the trading Parts of the World, that they are become the Instruments by which the most distant Nations converse with one another, and by which Mankind are knit together in a general Correspondence."[9] Addison's analysis was itself contradictory. Ironically, while Jews facilitated the integration of humanity into one system, they were excluded from it. Their self-isolating customs "shut them out from all Table Conversation, and the most agreeable Intercourses of Life." In Richard Braverman's words, the Jews provided the lingua franca for civil society, but they themselves failed to master it.[10] Indeed, as famously quipped by Addison, "They are like the Pegs and Nails in a great Building, which, though they are but little valued in themselves, are absolutely necessary to keep the whole Frame together."[11] The Jews facilitate the unification of humanity, but, like the nails in a great building, are not conceived to be part of it. For Addison, the civilizing force of commerce not only promoted polite society but, consequently, expedited the spread of the true Gospel. Commerce, civility, and redemption are all entwined here: The Jews are the activators of this historical process by means of their integrative commerce; they are excluded from its benefits due to their self-isolation; and again, like pegs and nails that are blind to the meaning of their surroundings, they spread the Gospel by their universal presence, which exhibits and proves the Christian truth.

I wish to elucidate the linkage contemporaries perceived among economy, communication, and redemption by detouring through scriptural discourse once again, this time focusing on another episode—the cleansing of the temple by Jesus. According to the Synoptic Gospels, Jesus entered Jerusalem several days before the Crucifixion and purged the temple from the thriving commercial activities that were taking place there—moneychanging and trade in animals for sacrifice.[12] The episode was traditionally conceived as a campaign against commercialism and became emblematic of the Christian attitude to commerce. Indeed, biblical commentators emphasized the corruption that prevailed in the temple. To take but one example, the mid-seventeenth-century puritan John Trapp explained that the "covetous priests" would receive animals for sacrifice and then resell them. Contemporizing the criticism, he stated that "Christ is every day casting out of his Church all these money merchants, these sacrilegious simonists, both ministers and others, that make sale of holy things."[13]

Yet from the second half of the seventeenth century, many English commentators discarded the interpretation of the commercial vice in favor of a different understanding of the scriptural passage. They described the market as required to ensure the operation of the temple and saw the problem not in the commercial practices themselves but rather in their location. As articulated by the early eighteenth-century commentator Matthew Henry, "Lawful things, ill timed and ill placed, may become sinful things." Merchandise, he added, "is a good thing in the exchange, but not in the temple," for it made "the business of religion subservient to a secular interest."[14] Moreover, they emphasized that the commercial activity took place specifically in the Gentiles' Court, where the Jews themselves did not worship and thought they could put it to profane use. In Henry Hammond's words, Jesus rebuked them because it was "a house of prayer to the Gentiles, and therefore had a promise of Gods peculiar presence there."[15] This interpretation was increasingly adopted by English commentators, epitomizing what Anthony Waterman described as a favorable eighteenth-century English theological approach to market economy and an attempt to harmonize it with Christianity.[16]

Remarkably, English writers used the scene of Jesus and the money-changers as a reference point also in discussions of contemporary economic issues—specifically, on bills of exchange. Bills of exchange had been the backbone of commodity exchange and financial speculation alike since medieval times. They enabled their users to transfer funds to distant locations where they could be redeemed in local currency, and thus could be seen as instruments of economic networking and monetary translation. Over time they came to be used also for speculative purposes. Lacking any intrinsic value, not being secured by sovereign authorities, and vulnerable to deceptive practices by savvy manipulators, while at the same time facilitating a thriving network of global commerce, they came to symbolize both the advantageous and the destructive potential of abstract financial instruments.

As demonstrated by Francesca Trivellato, from the middle of the seventeenth century, European economic writers were preoccupied with the history and meaning of bills of exchange. One central means for that was a pseudohistorical legend that attributed the invention of bills of exchange to Jews who were persecuted and fled France during the Middle Ages. According to her, the legend was formulated by the French economic writer Étienne Cleirac, and subsequently spread by Jacques Savary (their bestselling works respectively published in 1647 and 1675). Through them, it was transmitted to dozens of works in most European languages, striking root well into the twentieth century. Trivellato illustrated how the legend allowed contemporaries to channel resentments over the financial system and distinguish—representationally—between "the promise and peril of credit," as her book is titled.[17]

While indeed many English writers employed the legend of the medieval Jewish invention of bills of exchange, there was also an English tendency to relate the discussion of this instrument (though not necessarily its invention) to the Second Temple.[18] My contention here is that the engagement with the biblical reading of the exchange in the temple intervened in the discourse about bills of exchange, and about the concerns over the financialization of the economy and society in general. Charles Molloy, the popular economic writer in the late seventeenth century, included a passage on the exchange carried out in the temple in his bestselling reader on commercial law, with which he opened the chapter on bills of exchange. This formula was adopted by many successive economic writers.[19] Malachy Postlethwayt, a prolific writer who translated from French the economic dictionary published by Savary's two sons, removed from the section on bills of exchange the legend of its Jewish medieval invention and in its stead incorporated the passage about the exchange in the temple.[20] The association of bills of exchange with the temple was articulated also by religious writers. Henry Hammond referred to the episode and explained that the tables that Jesus turned were of those who dealt for profit "in returning moneys, or in bills of exchange . . . that sort of men who (as Merchants among us) return money for others to some other place . . . giving then so much money here, for so much more in another place; where the thing that is paid for, is not so much the use of the money, as the conveying it from one place to another, or the saving others that trouble of conveyance."[21]

What is the meaning of the odd association between the history of modern credit and the practices in the temple? I want to return here from our scriptural detour to the communicative dimension of the economy in early modern discourse. The Jews of antiquity, according to the writers who promoted this association, had a twofold role: economic and spiritual. Materially, they advanced economic integration through exchange, as Jews and Gentiles from all over the ecumenical world gathered at the temple and necessarily brought with them different coinage and goods that they had to exchange.[22] Spiritually, the Jews had the responsibility of spreading the monotheistic word to disparate communities (again, including Gentiles). These two networks, the material and the spiritual, overlapped and converged at the temple. Applying the verse "for mine house shall be called an house of prayer for all people" (Isaiah 56:7, KJV), Jesus rebukes the Jews for letting the inferior material network override the temple's superior spiritual network. As the Jews neglected their communicative-spiritual role in favor of their communicative-material role—thereby failing to understand the meaning of the temple—they were eventually replaced: Their law was replaced by the Christian Gospel; their temple by Jesus; and themselves by *Verus Israel*. Thus, a new model of human integration was established.

What happened to the Jews' role of economic networking after the destruction of the temple? Some writers, such as Molloy, claimed that the Jews, after their exile, mainly developed manipulative financial practices, undermining social integration. In a sidenote to the discussion about bills of exchange, he added that the Jews introduced into England the practice of "dry exchange"—a financial manipulation that was meant to bypass the ban on usury.[23] In contrast, others proposed a pro-Jewish take, in the spirit of Montesquieu, who described the invention of bills of exchange by persecuted medieval Jews as a bypass of the rulers' arbitrary power.[24] While Montesquieu focused on the political aspect, some of his English adapters had a different interest in mind. Here is an indicative passage, taken from Scottish legal writer Stewart Kyd: "[The invention of bills of exchange] was reserved for an oppressed people, considered as the outcasts of mankind, in an unenlightened age, urged by the necessity of their situation, to introduce into Europe at least, if not to give birth to a method, by which the merchants, of religions the most remote from each other, could convey the means of procuring the values of their commodities, without the inconvenience of transporting gold or silver."[25]

In this version, what made the invention possible was the Jews' ostracism, which they had to overcome. It was no accident that the most excluded people in society invented an instrument that promoted networking on a far-reaching scale. At the center here was the invention's power to bridge and integrate people not only geographically remote but also culturally isolated. The excommunicated medieval Jews who introduced bills of exchange thus complemented the progressive process that the Jews of antiquity promoted—the material unification of humanity. I found this idea most aptly articulated in the words of John Francis, in his 1847 *History of the Bank of England*: "Their genius produced the wonderful invention of Bills of Exchange; an object, like the art of printing, become too familiar to be admired; the miracle has ceased, and its utility only remains; yet both are sources of civilization, and connect together as in one commonwealth, the whole universe."[26]

The legendary stories about the invention and development of bills of exchange elucidate the inherent conflict in the perceived link between Jews and economy: the tension between Jewish exclusionism and universalism. One can read this tension in the shifting interpretations of the moneychangers scene as well as in the contradictory descriptions of the role of medieval Jews in the development of bills of exchange. At the backdrop of these representations lies the fundamental Christian notion of supersession: Jews and their particular law have been replaced by the universal Christian spirit, under which the world is to be united. Yet the processes of economic modernization in early modern Europe, which had a marked globalizing effect, potentially confounded this model, for it introduced an alternative account of universal integration. As illustrated earlier in this Epilogue, such integration was conceived not as purely material but as communicative as well. In this account, the Jews become a central integrative force.

I want to return now to the point that opened this book. Early modern English people were increasingly concerned that their economic life was becoming impersonal and mediated. The modernization of the economy entailed its abstraction, which involved a fundamental sense of alienation. Since ancient times, Jews epitomized the stranger in Christian society, and this was also the case in England of the long eighteenth century. This takes us back to the conundrum of Jewish exceptionalism. Jews were seen as having exceptional financial skills, which were associated with their strangeness. While their economic exceptionalism was more imagined than real, it was deeply entrenched in early modern thought. And as such, it had real historical impact.

Such thought patterns, David Nirenberg demonstrates, were not unique to early modernity nor to England—they were (and are) deeply embedded in Western tradition. To some extent, they are trans-historical, enduring from late antiquity to our own days. The historian thus straddles both the endurance of the thought pattern and its concrete, contextual, shifting manifestations. While both are imperative for making sense of history, every explanation gravitates us toward one of the poles, that of continuity or that of change. In Nirenberg's words, one's choice of analytical focus "depends on whether you think the greater danger lies in inventing continuities or in forgetting them."[27]

A fitting illustration can be seen in the figure of Shylock, some of whose history was presented in this book, and which opened the Introduction. The figure had its roots in medieval anti-Jewish traditions and conveyed a harsh message in Shakespeare's society, which grappled with a new commercialized setting at the turn of the sixteenth century. Shylock was muted in the seventeenth century, reappeared as a comic villain at the beginning of the eighteenth, turned into a grave, cruel character in the middle of the century, and finally became a tragic figure who demonstrated the oppression of the Jews in the early nineteenth century. Through the rise of modern antisemitism in Europe from the late nineteenth century, the character became an archetype of Jewish evil and danger, taking another complex turn after the Holocaust. To point to two recent adaptations out of many, the character was featured in a 2020 Bollywood movie called *Shylock* and in a 2023 theater production it was reworked as a woman Shylock—a Jewish widow refugee from pogrom-invested Russia in 1930s London. Shylock's figure thus epitomizes the enduring potency of the trend of engaging society and economy through the Jew as well as its continual shifts. Accordingly, it raises the dilemma of whether each manifestation should be interpreted as a separate case within a concrete context, or as partaking in a long tradition.

This analytical tension affects how we deal with the history of antisemitism. Are different anti-Jewish manifestations better understood as symptoms of a coherent phenomenon or as independent occurrences? This links back to the pressing terminological dilemma presented in the Introduction regarding the analytical usefulness of the term *antisemitism*, whose advocates tend to see continuities where its opponents see changes. Each choice comes with a price; the question remains, what is the more reasonable price in every case?

In this interplay between continuity and change, the current book leans toward the explanatory importance of changes. If the pattern of thought of Jewish exceptionalism is a trans-historical given in the history of Western civilization—the baseline, if you will—then the primary task in understanding how people thought about Jews and what sense it made in their lives lies in deciphering those changes. While dislike of Jews or even Judeophobia was the norm in premodern England, I demonstrated in this book that it did not entail automatic exclusion, but rather varied ideas meeting different purposes. Accordingly, my focus was on the shifting of the meanings attached to the concept of "the Jew" in making sense of economic life. The discussion in Chapter 1 demonstrates this dynamic well: For various contextual reasons, some of which were coincidental, opponents of Jewish readmission in the 1650s discarded the prevailing anti-Jewish accusation of usury, whereas the advocates of readmission maintained it. As shown in this book, context and contingency played significant roles in the development of the uses of the Jew in European discourse, rather than an entrenched continuity of images and ideas. Yet on the other hand, without attention to the enduring patterns of thought, one may miss the significance of the specific changes. One may also miss the significance of indifference in certain contexts, which can only be gauged in relation to longue-durée conceptions. Accordingly, the changes should be evaluated against the general lines of continuity.

It is not only to changes in details that we need to direct our attention, but also to the fundamental ideas we tend to naturalize. Such is the very basic association of Jews and materiality, situated at the center of our discussion. From the dawn of Christianity, Jews and Judaism were equated with materiality. Israel of the Flesh was contrasted with the True Israel and true law of the spirit. This profound distinction was seen as reflected not only in the Jews' religious life but also in their avaricious economic behavior. However, the historical process of financialization and the rise of capitalism undermined this conventional perception of the Jew. As Peter Stallybrass brightly demonstrates along Marx's line of thought, capitalism is an antimaterial ideology: Its principle is the turning of material things into commodities, namely into items whose value does not lie in their objectiveness but is bound with their exchange. Capitalism's essence is the surpassing of materiality.[28] It is this momentum of capitalism that encapsulated the modern sense of estrangement—with which this book opened—permeating English society in the long eighteenth century. In this setting, Jews were conceived not as materialistic but as a force of abstraction—as epitomized most harshly in Marx's *On the Jewish Question*.[29] For good or bad, the *spirit* was returned to them, and the *flesh* taken away. For some, this could mean a fulfillment of the Christian drive for universal spirituality; for others, an inverted reality.

Notes

INTRODUCTION

1. For an overview, see Bruce G. Carruthers, "The Sociology of Money and Credit," in *The Handbook of Economic Sociology*, 2nd ed., ed. Neil J. Smelser and Richard Swedberg (Princeton, NJ: Princeton University Press, 2005), 355–78; Stephen Gudeman, *The Anthropology of Economy: Community, Market, and Culture* (Oxford: Blackwell, 2001).

2. Niklas Luhmann, *Trust and Power: Two Works by Niklas Luhmann* (Chichester: Wiley, 1979), 39–60; Anthony Giddens, *The Consequences of Modernity* (Stanford, CA: Stanford University Press, 1990), 80; for a brief discussion, see Carl Wennerlind, *Casualties of Credit: The English Financial Revolution, 1620–1720* (Cambridge, MA: Harvard University Press, 2011), 95.

3. Shylock's legal obsession is taken ad absurdum in his refusal to supply a doctor to prevent Antonio from bleeding to death: "Is it so nominated in the bond?" he asks Portia. When she replies that it should be an act of charity, he refuses—"I cannot find it. 'Tis not in the bond." William Shakespeare, *The Merchant of Venice*, act 4, scene 1.

4. *The Merchant*, act 4, scene 1.

5. *The Merchant*, act 4, scene 1.

6. For exemplary works that emphasize similar points, see David Nirenberg, *Anti-Judaism: The Western Tradition* (New York: W. W. Norton, 2013), chap. 8; Samuel Ajzenstat, "The Ubiquity of Contract in *The Merchant of Venice*," *Philosophy and Literature* 21, no. 2 (1997): 262–78.

7. Keith Wrightson, *Earthly Necessities: Economic Lives in Early Modern Britain, 1470–1750* (New Haven, CT: Yale University Press, 2002).

8. See, for instance, Wennerlind, *Casualties of Credit*; Bruce G. Carruthers, *City of Capital: Politics and Markets in the English Financial Revolution* (Princeton, NJ: Princeton University Press, 1999); Stuart Banner, *Anglo-American Securities Regulation: Cultural and Political Roots, 1690–1860* (New York: Cambridge University Press, 2002); Catherine Ingrassia, *Authorship, Commerce, and Gender in Early Eighteenth-Century England: A Culture of Paper Credit* (Cambridge: Cambridge University Press, 1998).

9. For a classic account of this intellectual movement, see Stephen G. Burnett, *Christian Hebraism in the Reformation Era (1500–1660): Authors, Books, and the Transmission of Jewish Learning* (Leiden: Brill, 2012); and Frank Edward Manuel, *The Broken Staff: Judaism Through Christian Eyes* (Cambridge, MA: Harvard University Press, 1992).

10. Achsah Guibbory, *Christian Identity, Jews, and Israel in Seventeenth-Century England* (Oxford: Oxford University Press, 2010); Andrew Crome, "English National Identity and the Readmission of the Jews, 1650–1656," *Journal of Ecclesiastical History* 66, no. 2 (2015): 280–301;

Eliane Glaser, *Judaism Without Jews: Philosemitism and Christian Polemic in Early Modern England* (Basingstoke: Palgrave Macmillan, 2007); David S. Katz, *Philo-Semitism and the Readmission of the Jews to England, 1603–1655* (Oxford: Clarendon Press, 1982); David B. Ruderman, *Connecting the Covenants: Judaism and the Search for Christian Identity in Eighteenth-Century England* (Philadelphia: University of Pennsylvania Press, 2007).

11. Naomi Tadmor, *The Social Universe of the English Bible: Scripture, Society, and Culture in Early Modern England* (Cambridge: Cambridge University Press, 2010); Christopher Hill, *The English Bible and the Seventeenth-Century Revolution* (London: Allen Lane, 1993); David Daniell, *The Bible in English: Its History and Influence* (New Haven, CT: Yale University Press, 2003).

12. David Hawkes, *The Culture of Usury in Renaissance England* (New York: Palgrave Macmillan, 2010).

13. Francesca Trivellato, *The Familiarity of Strangers: The Sephardic Diaspora, Livorno, and Cross-Cultural Trade in the Early Modern Period* (New Haven, CT: Yale University Press, 2009).

14. James Vernon, *Distant Strangers: How Britain Became Modern* (Berkeley: University of California Press, 2014).

15. Joshua Trachtenberg, *The Devil and the Jews: The Medieval Conception of the Jew and Its Relation to Modern Antisemitism* (Philadelphia: Jewish Publication Society of America, 1983), 188–95; Anthony Julius, *Trials of the Diaspora: A History of Anti-Semitism in England* (Oxford: Oxford University Press, 2010); Jerry Z. Muller, *Capitalism and the Jews* (Princeton, NJ: Princeton University Press, 2010), chap. 1; Derek Penslar, *Shylock's Children: Economics and Jewish Identity in Modern Europe* (Berkeley: University of California Press, 2001), 13–23.

16. On the association between Jews and usury in early modern England prior to the resettlement of Jews, see Eric Kerridge, *Usury, Interest, and the Reformation* (Aldershot: Ashgate, 2002), 21 and his references there; Hawkes, *The Culture of Usury in Renaissance England*, 67–71.

17. William Harrison, *The Description of England: The Classic Contemporary Account of Tudor Social Life* (Washington, DC: Folger Shakespeare Library, 1994 [1587]), 202–3. See also Raphael Holinshed, *The First and Second Volumes of Chronicles [. . .] to the Yeare 1586* (London, 1587), 189.

18. Thomas Wilson, *A Discourse upon Usury [. . .] with an Historical Introduction by R. H. Tawney* (London: G. Bell & Sons, 1925 [1572]), 283.

19. David Nirenberg, *Anti-Judaism*, chap. 8, and especially pp. 274–76.

20. For more precise figures and calculated demographic increase rates, see Keith Wrightson, *Earthly Necessities*, 120–28; E. A. Wrigley and Roger Schofield, *The Population History of England 1541–1871: A Reconstruction* (Cambridge: Cambridge University Press, 1989), 183, 528. On the economic impact of the demographic shifts, see ibid., 159–81; Craig Muldrew, *The Economy of Obligation: The Culture of Credit and Social Relations in Early Modern England* (Basingstoke: Macmillan, 1998), 15–59.

21. Wrightson, *Earthly Necessities*, 116–18, 128–31; Henry Phelps Brown and Sheila V. Hopkins, "Seven Centuries of the Prices of Consumables, Compared with Builders' Wage-Rates," *Economica* 23, no. 92 (1956): 296–314.

22. Muldrew, *The Economy of Obligation*, 15, 24–35, 99–103; Eric Kerridge, *Trade and Banking in Early Modern England* (Manchester: Manchester University Press, 1988), 92–97.

23. Muldrew, *The Economy of Obligation*, chaps. 4–7; Margaret R. Hunt, *The Middling Sort: Commerce, Gender, and the Family in England, 1680–1780* (Berkeley: University of

California Press, 1996), chap. 1; John Brewer, *The Sinews of Power: War, Money and the English State, 1688–1783* (Cambridge, MA: Harvard University Press, 1988), 186–88.

24. Muldrew, *The Economy of Obligation*, 96, 108.

25. Kerridge, *Trade and Banking in Early Modern England*, chap. 2; Muldrew, *The Economy of Obligation*, 103–19.

26. 3 Henry VII, c. 6 (1487), "An Acte Agaynst Usury and Unlawfull Bargaynes"; Norman L. Jones, *God and the Moneylenders: Usury and the Law in Early Modern England* (New York: Blackwell, 1989), 11–14, 24–29.

27. Kerridge, *Trade and Banking in Early Modern England*, 36–39; Wrightson, *Earthly Necessities*, 205–9. The interest cap was removed by the Usury Laws Repeal Act of 1854.

28. This is a central flaw of Benjamin Nelson's *The Idea of Usury*, which emphasized the economic-progressive aspects of Calvin's thought and deduced from them an actual historical change of attitude of both policymakers and the public; see Benjamin Nelson, *The Idea of Usury: From Tribal Brotherhood to Universal Otherhood* (Chicago: University of Chicago Press, 1969).

29. Jones, *God and the Moneylenders*, chap. 3, where he surveys typical credit relations and dynamics of the late sixteenth century; Joan Thirsk, *Economic Policy and Projects: The Development of a Consumer Society in Early Modern England* (Oxford: Clarendon Press, 1978).

30. In Jones's words: "Clearly by the early seventeenth century many thinkers no longer agreed with the traditional prohibition against usury: the reason for rejecting them was a new understanding of man's relationship with God" (163), and "The sufficient cause for the acceptance of lending at interest as a proper way to make money must lie in the moral theology that was the product of solifidian theology and Puritan demands for freedom of the conscience" (174). See esp. 153, 157, 163–66, 173–74.

31. Kerridge, *Usury, Interest, and the Reformation*; Johann Sommerville, "Sir Robert Filmer, Usury, and the Ideology of Order," in *Money and Political Economy in the Enlightenment*, ed. Daniel Carey (Oxford: Voltaire Foundation, 2014), 45–49.

32. Jones, *God and the Moneylenders*, 12–14.

33. Sommerville, "Sir Robert Filmer, Usury, and the Ideology of Order," 49–50.

34. James Steuart, *An Inquiry into the Principles of Political Oeconomy* (London, 1765), 595.

35. By the late seventeenth century, Jewish shareholding of the total sum of Bank of England stocks was only 0.016 percent. See J. A. Giuseppi, "Sephardi Jews and the Early Years of the Bank of England," *Transactions (Jewish Historical Society of England)* 19 (1955): 53–63; Peter G. M. Dickson, *The Financial Revolution in England: A Study in Development of Public Credit, 1688–1756* (New York: St. Martin's Press, 1967), 253–64.

36. Maxine Berg and Elizabeth Eger, eds., *Luxury in the Eighteenth Century: Debates, Desires and Delectable Goods* (New York: Palgrave Macmillan, 2003), introduction.

37. For a compelling discussion on the roles of luxury, material culture, and sociability in the eighteenth century and the relations among them, as well as on the debate over them, see Maxine Berg, *Luxury and Pleasure in Eighteenth-Century Britain* (Oxford University Press, 2007), 1–45; Berg and Eger, *Luxury in the Eighteenth Century*, chap. 1.

38. Derek Penslar, *Shylock's Children: Economics and Jewish Identity in Modern Europe* (Berkeley: University of California Press, 2001); Cornelia Aust, *The Jewish Economic Elite: Making Modern Europe* (Bloomington: Indiana University Press, 2018); Rebecca Kobrin and Adam Teller, eds., *Purchasing Power: The Economics of Modern Jewish History* (Philadelphia: University of Pennsylvania Press, 2015).

39. Jonathan Karp, *The Politics of Jewish Commerce: Economic Thought and Emancipation in Europe, 1638–1848* (Cambridge: Cambridge University Press, 2008); Francesca Trivellato, *The*

Promise and Peril of Credit: What a Forgotten Legend About Jews and Finance Tells Us About the Making of European Commercial Society (Princeton: Princeton University Press, 2019).

40. See the valuable discussion in Mark Knights, *Representation and Misrepresentation in Later Stuart Britain* (New York: Oxford University Press, 2005), 45–46.

41. For a review of the field, see Sina Rauschenbach and Jonathan Schorsch, "Postcolonial Approaches to the Early Modern Sephardic Atlantic," in *The Sephardic Atlantic: Colonial Histories and Postcolonial Perspectives*, ed. Sina Rauschenbach and Jonathan Schorsch (Cham: Springer, 2018), 1–20. The main contribution remains Jonathan Schorsch's *Jews and Blacks in the Early Modern World* (Cambridge: Cambridge University Press, 2004), esp. chaps. 2, 8–9. See also Stanley Mirvis, *The Jews of Eighteenth-Century Jamaica: A Testamentary History of a Diaspora in Transition* (New Haven, CT: Yale University Press, 2020); Aviva Ben-Ur, *Jewish Autonomy in a Slave Society: Suriname in the Atlantic World, 1651–1825* (Philadelphia: University of Pennsylvania Press, 2020).

42. Historian David Katz offers a programmatic articulation of such an approach; see David S. Katz, *The Jews in the History of England, 1485–1850* (Oxford: Clarendon Press, 1994), preface.

43. For illuminative discussions on the debate, see the introductions to the special issues of *American Historical Review* and *Zion*: Jonathan Judaken, "Introduction," *American Historical Review* 123, no. 4 (2018): 1122–38; Scott Ury and Guy Miron, "Antisemitism: On the Dialectical Relationship Between a Historical Concept and Contemporary Debates," *Zion* 85, no. 1–4 (2020): 7–30. Yehuda Bauer, "Problems of Contemporary Antisemitism," in *Varieties of Antisemitism: History, Ideology, Discourse*, ed. Murray Baumgarten, Peter Kenez, and Bruce Thompson (Newark: University of Delaware Press, 2009), 315.

44. Anthony Julius, *Trials of the Diaspora: A History of Anti-Semitism in England* (Oxford: Oxford University Press, 2010); Frank Felsenstein, *Anti-Semitic Stereotypes: A Paradigm of Otherness in English Popular Culture, 1660–1830* (Baltimore, MD: Johns Hopkins University Press, 1999).

45. Hannah Arendt, *The Origins of Totalitarianism* (New York: Harcourt Brace & Co., 1973), chap. 3.

46. Zygmunt Bauman, "Allosemitism: Premodern, Modern, Postmodern," in *Modernity, Culture and "the Jew,"* ed. Bryan Cheyette and Laura Marcus (Stanford, CA: Stanford University Press, 1998), 143–56.

47. Jonathan Karp and Adam Sutcliffe, "A Brief History of Philosemitism," in *Philosemitism in History*, ed. Jonathan Karp and Adam Sutcliffe (New York: Cambridge University Press, 2011), 2, 5–6.

48. Wennerlind, *Casualties of Credit*. Wennerlind follows the footsteps of Henry Roseveare, who also promoted a broader perspective of the change, stretching its beginning to the Restoration; see Henry Roseveare, *The Financial Revolution, 1660–1760* (London: Longman, 1991).

49. Patrick K. O'Brien and Nuno Palma, "Danger to the Old Lady of Threadneedle Street? The Bank Restriction Act and the Regime Shift to Paper Money, 1797–1821," *European Review of Economic History* 24, no. 2 (2020): 390–426. The 1797 Bank Restriction Act, which was in force until 1821, removed the requirement of the Bank of England to convert banknotes into gold on demand.

50. For a useful historiographic survey of economic Jewish history since the nineteenth century, see Kobrin and Teller, eds., *Purchasing Power*, introduction.

CHAPTER I

1. The most conclusive piece on the subject is still Katz, *Philo-Semitism and the Readmission of the Jews to England, 1603–1655.* For a recent accessible, broad account, see Steven M. Nadler, *Menasseh Ben Israel: Rabbi of Amsterdam* (New Haven, CT: Yale University Press, 2018).

2. The first proposal for Jewish readmission was suggested in 1607, from mercantilist motivation. See Edgar R. Samuel, "'Sir Thomas Shirley's Project for Jewes'—the Earliest Known Proposal for the Resettlement," *Transactions & Miscellanies* (Jewish Historical Society of England) 24 (1970): 195–97. For the broad resonance of the issue in contemporary press, see Lukas Erne, *Shakespeare and the Book Trade* (Cambridge: Cambridge University Press, 2013), 130–34.

3. Glaser, *Judaism Without Jews.*

4. Katz, *Philo-Semitism and the Readmission of the Jews to England,* 53, 63–71, 87–88; Guibbory, *Christian Identity, Jews, and Israel in Seventeenth-Century England,* chap. 7; Crome, "English National Identity and the Readmission of the Jews, 1650–1656."

5. James Shapiro, *Shakespeare and the Jews* (New York: Columbia University Press, 1996); Crome, "English National Identity and the Readmission of the Jews, 1650–1656"; Guibbory, *Christian Identity, Jews, and Israel in Seventeenth-Century England.*

6. Glaser, *Judaism Without Jews,* chap. 5; Jonathan A. Bush, "You're Gonna Miss Me When I'm Gone: Early Modern Common Law Discourse and the Case of the Jews," *Wisconsin Law Review* (1993): 1225–85.

7. Henry Jessey, *A Narrative of the Late Proceeds at White-Hall Concerning the Jews* (London, 1656); [Nathaniel Crouch], "The Proceedings of the Jews in England in the Year 1655," in *Two Journeys to Jerusalem* [. . .] (London, 1704), 167–73.

8. Katz, *Philo-Semitism and the Readmission of the Jews to England,* 7, 212; Don Patinkin, "Mercantilism and the Readmission of the Jews to England," *Jewish Social Studies* 8, no. 3 (1946): 161–78. Edgar Samuel's argument that the readmission attempt derived from Cromwell's mercantilist policy is an exception. Samuel points to an overlap of mercantile interest in Jews (by the Atlantic traders, versus the London traders whose interest lay with the Continent) and advocacy of readmission, which often also overlapped with Puritan tendencies. His argument is based on personal affiliations and not on textual evidence, hence even though it sheds important light on some of the players' motives, it does not capture the public dimension of the polemic; see Edgar Samuel, "The Readmission of the Jews to England in 1656, in the Context of English Economic Policy," *Jewish Historical Studies* 31 (1988): 153–69.

9. Benjamin Braude, "Les Contes Persans de Menasseh ben Israel: Polémique, Apologétique et Dissimulation à Amsterdam Au XVIIe Siècle," *Annales. Histoire, Sciences Sociales* 49, no. 5 (1994): 1107–38. The text was translated by Moses Wall and published in English in 1650, 1651, and 1652. On Menasseh ben Israel's translation strategies more broadly, see Sina Rauschenbach, "Christian Readings of Menasseh ben Israel: Translation and Retranslation in the Early Modern World," in *The Jew as Legitimation: Jewish-Gentile Relations Beyond Antisemitism and Philosemitism,* ed. David J. Wertheim (Cham: Springer, 2017), 63–81.

10. Menasseh ben Israel, *The Humble Addresses* (London, 1655), 1–2. For Menasseh ben Israel's mercantile argument, see Patinkin, "Mercantilism and the Readmission of the Jews to England," 164–65; Karp, *The Politics of Jewish Commerce,* 34–36.

11. Menasseh ben Israel, *The Humble Addresses,* 20–21.

12. Calendar of the Close Rolls Preserved in the Public Record Office, vol. 3, 1288–1296, 1904, 109.

13. For some examples of Tudor and Stuart historiography on the matter, see Benjamin Dew, "Jewish Exclusions: Eighteenth-Century Historians and the Expulsion of England's Jews," *Intellectual History Archive* 6 (2018): 1–10, esp. pp. 2–5. See also Gerard Malynes, *Lex Mercatoria* (London, 1622), 331; John Selden, *An Historical and Political Discourse of the Laws & Government of England*, ed. Nathaniel Bacon (London, 1682), 170–71.

14. Edward Coke, *Institutes of the Laws of England*, part 2 (London, 1642), 507. Coke gave a similar historical account in his discussion of the legal history of usury and explained the Jews' banishment as a consequence of the pious *Statutum de Judaismo*, which remedied their transgression against the English people and constitution. See Coke, *Institutes*, part 3, 1644, 151–52. This adds to Barbara Malament's argument that Coke had no so-called capitalist impetus but rather a conservative drive, contrary to what has been commonly suggested; Barbara Malament, "The 'Economic Liberalism' of Sir Edward Coke," *Yale Law Journal* 76, no. 7 (1967): 1321–58.

15. Coke's Judeophobia was apparent beyond the issue of usury—for instance, he objected to admitting Jews as witnesses. Contemporaries noted this feature; see, for example, Francis Plowden, *A Treatise upon the Law of Usury and Annuities* (London, 1797), 99.

16. Coke, *Institutes*, part 2, 1642, 507.

17. Coke, *Institutes*, part 3, 1644, 152. The 1545 Act Against Usury licensed loans of all sorts with a maximum interest rate of 10 percent. The statute was revoked in 1552 and revived by Elizabeth's parliament in the Act against Usury of 1571.

18. [Crouch], "Proceedings," 171–72.

19. Thomas Barlow, *Cases of Conscience* (London, 1692), 9. The pamphlet was written during the polemic but was published only in 1692. See Mordecai L. Wilensky, "Thomas Barlow's and John Dury's Attitude Towards the Readmission of the Jews to England," *Jewish Quarterly Review* 50, no. 2 (1959): 167–75.

20. Barlow, *Cases of Conscience*, 72.

21. Churchman Thomas Fuller (1608–1661) is an example of an anti-Jewish and anti-usury writer who arrived at a partly favorable position on readmission by relying on Coke's historiography. See Francis Fullwood [Thomas Fuller], *The Church-History of Britain* (London, 1655), 85–88. On Fuller's support of the Jewish case, see Florence Sandler, "Thomas Fuller's 'Pisgah-Sight of Palestine' as a Comment on the Politics of Its Time," *Huntington Library Quarterly* 41, no. 4 (1978): 317–43. Similarly, the lawyer Charles Molloy (1640–1690), whose best-selling legal textbook *De Jure Maritimo* was profoundly informed by Coke's writings, hinged the expulsion on usury and consequently claimed that withdrawing from usury was sufficient for readmission. Charles Molloy, *De Jure Maritimo et Navali*, 3rd ed. (London, 1682), 397–410. David Hume's telling account of medieval Anglo-Jewish relations relied on Coke's narrative but twisted the significance of usury. Thus, medieval Jews were indeed immersed in financial dealing, as the paragon of rational economics during a backward era. David Hume, *History of England* (London, 1762), vol. 1, 332–34, 420–21; vol. 2, 56–58, 63–64.

22. Prynne's writing was of the largest scope and exhibited profound historical investigation. It was succeeded by a revised edition and a second part, published in 1656. One can see that defenders of the Jewish cause directed their replies mainly to him. See, for instance, D. L., *Israels Condition and Cause Pleaded* (London, 1656), esp. 91–92, 102–6. On its political impact, see Katz, *Philo-Semitism and the Readmission of the Jews to England*, 221. The treatise was widely referred to throughout the subsequent two hundred years, and Prynne was even considered by some as the founder of Anglo-Jewish historiography; see S. Levy, "Anglo-Jewish Historiography," *Transactions (Jewish Historical Society of England)* 6 (1908): 1–20.

23. William Prynne, *A Short Demurrer to the Jewes* (London, 1656), 6, 119.

24. Prynne, *Demurrer*, part 1, 54–58; for parallel arguments in the second part of the *Demurrer*, see 14, 78–79, 88, 134. For the broader context of the expulsion, and the place of usury allegations in it, see Robert C. Stacey, "Parliamentary Negotiations and the Expulsion of the Jews from England," *Thirteenth-Century England* 6 (1997): 77–101. Prynne's assertion that moneylending played a circumscribed role in medieval Anglo-Jewish life is compatible with up-to-date historical research on the subject. See Julie Mell, *The Myth of the Medieval Jewish Moneylender*, vols. 1 and 2 (New York: Palgrave Macmillan, 2017–2018).

25. See in the second edition of the *Demurrer*, part 1, 35–38, 49–65; and part 2, 58, 62–64, 66–69, 77–79, 110–11, 103 [123], 134–35. Note that the pages are misnumbered. See also William Prynne, *The First-[third] Tome of an Exact Chronological Vindication and Historical Demonstration* (London, 1665), 153. On Prynne's debate with Coke, see Avrom Saltman, *The Jewish Question in 1655: Studies in Prynne's Demurrer* (Ramat-Gan: Bar-Ilan University Press, 1995), 85–93. For a contemporary relation to the conflict between Coke and Prynne, see Tovey D'Blossiers, *Anglia Judaica* (Oxford, 1738), 204–6, 236–38.

26. Prynne, *Demurrer*, part 1, 50.

27. He supported this claim, in part, by the precedent of Edward I's actions in Gascony in 1287, from which he "banished their persons by an express Decree, not only for their Usury but chiefly for their Infidelity and Enmity to Christs Cross. Therefore he did the like in England." See Prynne, *Demurrer*, part 1, 54.

28. Prynne, *Demurrer*, part 1, 5–6, 43. See also Karp, *The Politics of Jewish Commerce*, 37–42; J. G. A. Pocock, *The Ancient Constitution and the Feudal Law: A Study of English Historical Thought in the Seventeenth Century*, 2nd ed. (Cambridge: Cambridge University Press, 1987), 155–62.

29. John Miller, "The Long-Term Consequences of the English Revolution: Economic and Social Development," in *The Oxford Handbook of the English Revolution*, ed. Michael J. Braddick (Oxford: Oxford University Press, 2015), 506–7; Michael J. Braddick, *The Nerves of State: Taxation and the Financing of the English State, 1558–1714* (Manchester: Manchester University Press, 1996), 39; Muldrew, *The Economy of Obligation*, 96, 108–15; Judith M. Spicksley, "Women, 'Usury' and Credit in Early Modern England: The Case of the Maiden Investor," *Gender & History* 27, no. 2 (2015): 263–92 (see especially figure 1).

30. Jones, *God and the Moneylenders*. By the second half of the seventeenth century, the usury polemic concentrated on the question of the level of interest rather than on the morality of the practice. See Wrightson, *Earthly Necessities*; Joyce O. Appleby, *Economic Thought and Ideology in Seventeenth-Century England* (Princeton, NJ: Princeton University Press, 1978), esp. 70–71.

31. Prynne, *Demurrer*, part 1, 59. For medieval accounts, see Robin R. Mundill, *England's Jewish Solution: Experiment and Expulsion, 1262–1290* (Cambridge: Cambridge University Press, 2002), chap. 8. For early modern accounts, see this chapter, n. 13.

32. See also Alexander Ross, *A View of the Jewish Religion* (London, 1656), introduction; and James Howell, *Londinopolis* (London, 1657), 121–22, two anti-Jewish works that omitted usury as a reason for the expulsion.

33. William Hughes, *Anglo-Judæus* (London, 1656).

34. Thomas Collier, *A Brief Ansvver* (London, 1656), 7–8. Contemporaries were aware of Prynne's significance in the public polemic; see D'Blossiers, *Anglia Judaica*, 277–78.

35. In contrast to Benjamin Nelson's contention that the issue of usury (the "Deuteronomical issue") was of exceptional importance in the polemic, see Nelson, *The Idea of Usury*, 98.

36. Prynne, *Demurrer*, part 1, 119–20.

37. Katz, *The Jews in the History of England*, 107–34.

38. Blair Worden, "James Harrington and the Commonwealth of Oceana, 1656," in *Republicanism, Liberty, and Commercial Society, 1649–1776*, ed. David Wootton (Stanford, CA: Stanford University Press, 1994), 87–88; Jonathan Scott, *Commonwealth Principles: Republican Writing of the English Revolution* (Cambridge: Cambridge University Press, 2004); J. G. A. Pocock, "Historical Introduction," in *The Political Works of James Harrington*, ed. J. G. A. Pocock (Cambridge: Cambridge University Press, 1977).

39. See Blair Worden and David Wootton, "Harrington's Oceana: Origins and Aftermath, 1651–1660," in *Republicanism, Liberty and Commercial Society, 1649–1776*, ed. David Wootton (Stanford, CA: Stanford University Press, 1994), 113–19. In the wake of the Cromwellian Act for the Settlement of Ireland of 1652, the notion of settling Ireland was a concrete idea, and Adam Sutcliffe demonstrates that Harrington's scheme was a criticism of Cromwellian policy regarding both the Jews and Ireland; see Adam Sutcliffe, "The Philosemitic Moment? Judaism and Republicanism in Seventeenth-Century European Thought," in *Philosemitism in History*, 81–83. For a general view on Harrington and the Anglo-Jewish question see Karp, *The Politics of Jewish Commerce*, 53–57.

40. Harrington, *The Political Works of James Harrington*, 159 and 295.

41. Harrington, *The Political Works of James Harrington*, 159. Menasseh ben Israel, *Humble Addresses*, 2.

42. Fania Oz-Salzberger, "The Jewish Roots of Western Freedom," *Azure* 13 (2002): 88–132; Sutcliffe, "The Philosemitic Moment?"

43. Sutcliffe, "The Philosemitic Moment?"

44. A brief mention can be found in C. B. Macpherson, "Harrington's "Opportunity State" *Past & Present* 17, no. 1 (1960): 45–70 (at 56). *The Prerogative of Popular Government* was written as a reply to the royalist criticism from Matthew Wren in his *Considerations upon Mr. Harrington's Commonwealth of Oceana* (London, 1657). For a general analysis of Wren's debate with Harrington, see Pocock, "Historical Introduction," 83–89.

45. Harrington, *The Political Works of James Harrington*, 320–21; Worden, "James Harrington and the Commonwealth of Oceana, 1656," 86–89.

46. Harrington, *The Political Works of James Harrington*, 406.

47. Harrington, *The Political Works of James Harrington*, 407.

48. Harrington, *The Political Works of James Harrington*, 407. This does not entail that usury should not be regulated. Harrington suggested a 4 percent interest as a yardstick, thus making sure that the borrower may gain more than the lender.

49. Jones, *God and the Moneylenders*, 19, 24, 32–33.

50. This lends support to the claim made by Steve Pincus, "Neither Machiavellian Moment nor Possessive Individualism: Commercial Society and the Defenders of the English Commonwealth," *American Historical Review* 103, no. 3 (1998): 705–36. See also Justin Champion, "'Mysterious Politicks': Land, Credit and Commonwealth Political Economy, 1656–1722," in *Money and Political Economy in the Enlightenment*, ed. Daniel Carey (Oxford: Voltaire Foundation, 2014) 117–62.

51. Guibbory, *Christian Identity, Jews, and Israel in Seventeenth-Century England*, 176–78.

52. Petrus Cunaeus, *Petrus Cunaeus of the Common-Wealth of the Hebrews. Translated by C.B.* (London, 1653), chap. 2. Sutcliffe, "The Philosemitic Moment?" 71–76. An English translation of Cunaeus's work was published in 1653. On the centrality of the work, see Richard Tuck, *Philosophy and Government, 1572–1651* (Cambridge: Cambridge University Press, 1993), 167–69; François Laplanche, "Christian Erudition in the Sixteenth and Seventeenth Centuries and the

Hebrew State," *Hebraic Political Studies* 3, no. 1 (2008): 5–18; Eric Nelson, *The Hebrew Republic* (Cambridge, MA: Harvard University Press, 2010), introduction; Manuel, *The Broken Staff: Judaism Through Christian Eyes*, 115–28. For a broader view on Dutch Hebraism, see Theodor Dunkelgrün, "'Neerlands Israel': Political Theology, Christian Hebraism, Biblical Antiquarianism, and Historical Myth," in *Myth in History, History in Myth*, ed. Laura Cruz and Willem Frijhoff (Leiden: Brill, 2009), 201–36.

53. Salmasius, *Dissertatio de Foenore Trapezitico* (Leiden, 1640), 370–71. His previous works on usury were *De Usuris Liber* (1638) and *De Modo Usurarum* (1639), also published in Leiden. For a summary of Salmasius's works, see John T. Noonan, *The Scholastic Analysis of Usury* (Cambridge, MA: Harvard University Press, 1957), 370–73.

54. Hugo Grotius, *The Rights of War and Peace*, vol. 2 (Indianapolis, IN: Liberty Fund, 2005 [1625]), book 2, chap. 12, section 20.

55. See Jean Barbeyrac's note 10 on Grotius, *The Rights of War and Peace, book 2*, chap. 12, section 20.

56. Hugo Grotius, *Annotationes in Novum Testamentum*, vol. 3, published in Paris and Amsterdam in installments in 1641, 1646, and 1650. On Grotius's hermeneutics of historical interpretation, see Dirk van Miert, *The Emancipation of Biblical Philology in the Dutch Republic, 1590–1670* (Oxford: Oxford University Press, 2018), chap. 5; Mark Somos, *Secularisation and the Leiden Circle* (Leiden: Brill, 2011), chap. 5, esp. 401–2.

57. Nelson, *The Hebrew Republic*, 78–86; Lea Campos Boralevi, "James Harrington's 'Machiavellian' Anti-Machiavellism," *History of European Ideas* 37, no. 2 (2011): 113–19.

58. Marco Barducci, "Harrington, Grotius, and the Commonwealth of the Jews, 1656–1660," in *European Contexts for English Republicanism*, ed. Gaby Mahlberg and Dirk Wiemann (London: Routledge, 2016), 77–94.

59. Salmasius, *Dissertatio de Foenore Trapezitico* (Leiden, 1640), 370.

60. John Selden, *Table-talk* (London, 1689), 146.

61. The same can be said regarding Dutch society, which became, from the late sixteenth century, highly commercialized. About half the population lived in towns, and almost its entirety was highly interconnected within a vast commercial grid. Dutch economy enjoyed considerable available capital, which was reinvested in the major trading joint-stock companies. Studies on Dutch commercialism are abundant. See, as an example, Maarten R. Prak, *The Dutch Republic in the Seventeenth Century: The Golden Age* (Cambridge: Cambridge University Press, 2005), 75–135.

62. Molloy, *De Jure Maritimo*, 397–410.

CHAPTER 2

1. Hill, *The English Bible and the Seventeenth-Century Revolution*, 4–44; Adam Fox, "Religion and Popular Literate Culture in England," *Archiv für Reformationsgeschichte* 95, no. 1 (2004): 266–82, esp. 272–73 and nn. 12–13. On the central place of Bible reading in early modern English culture, see Tadmor, *The Social Universe of the English Bible*; David Norton, *A History of the English Bible as Literature* (Cambridge: Cambridge University Press, 2000); David Daniell, *The Bible in English: Its History and Influence*, esp. chaps. 8 and 27; Thomas Preston, "Biblical Criticism, Literature, and the Eighteenth-Century Reader," in *Books and Their Readers in Eighteenth-century England*, ed. Isabel Rivers (Leicester: Leicester University Press, 1982), 97–126; Scott Mandelbrote, "The English Bible and Its Readers in the Eighteenth Century," in

Books and Their Readers in Eighteenth-Century England: New Essays, ed. Isabel Rivers (London: Leicester University Press, 2001), 35–78.

2. The Tyndale Bible, Coverdale Bible, Matthew Bible, Great Bible, Geneva Bible, Bishops' Bible, Douay-Rheims Bible, and King James Bible are all English achievements of the sixteenth century. See S. L. Greenslade, "English Versions of the Bible, 1525–1611," in *The Cambridge History of the Bible*, vol. 3, ed. S. L. Greenslade (Cambridge: Cambridge University Press, 1963), 141–74; Tadmor, *The Social Universe of the English Bible*, introduction; see also Henry Wansbrough, "History and Impact of English Bible Translations," in *Hebrew Bible/Old Testament: The History of Its Interpretation*, vol. 2, ed. Magne Sæbø (Göttingen: Vandenhoeck & Ruprecht, 2008), 536–52. For the development of English Bible commentaries, see Ian Green, *Print and Protestantism in Early Modern England* (Oxford: Oxford University Press, 2001), chap. 2, especially 113–29, where a general introduction on Bible commentaries and annotations in early modern England is given.

3. Such bibliographies were published in 1637 by John Verneuil, reprinted in 1642; and in 1663 by William Crowe (sometimes attributed to John Osborne), reprinted in 1668.

4. Preston, "Biblical Criticism, Literature, and the Eighteenth-Century Reader." See James Boswell, *Life of Johnson* (London: Oxford University Press, 1953 [1791]), 757. Remarkably, by the early nineteenth century this genre was losing its grip on the public interest and became the reading matter of specialists; see Preston, "Biblical Criticism, Literature, and the Eighteenth-Century Reader," 122, and his references there.

5. Ambrose of Milan, *S. Ambrosii De Tobia: a Commentary, with an Introduction and Translation*, trans. Lois Miles Zucker (Washington, D.C.: The Catholic University of America, 1933), xv, 51. For the prevalence of this interpretation in early modern England, see Kerridge, *Usury, Interest, and the Reformation*, 17; Hawkes, *The Culture of Usury in Renaissance England*, 62–63.

6. *The holie Bible faithfully translated into English, out of the authentical Latin. Diligently conferred with the Hebrew, Greeke, and other editions in diuers languages [. . .] By the English College of Doway* (Douai, 1609–1610).

7. Andrew Willet, *Hexapla in Exodum, that is, A sixfold commentary upon the second booke of Moses called Exodus [. . .]* (London, 1608); *Hexapla in Leviticum [. . .]* (London, 1631). On usury, see 425–30 in the 1633 edition of Exodus, and 624–34 in the 1731 edition of Leviticus. In spite of this negative view of Jewish usury, Willet was a crucial figure among early seventeenth-century promoters of Jewish readmission and toleration in England, which he saw as a means for advancing their conversion. His treatise *De Universali et Nouissima Judaeorum Vocatione* (Cambridge, 1590) was the first English text dedicated to the calling of the Jews; see Jeffrey S. Shoulson, *Milton and the Rabbis: Hebraism, Hellenism, and Christianity* (New York: Columbia University Press, 2001), 30.

8. Roger Fenton, *A Treatise of Vsurie* (London, 1611), 45–46; Gerard Malynes, *Consuetudo, Vel Lex Mercatoria* (London, 1622), 328; Edward Coke, *Institutes of the Laws of England*, part 3 (London, 1644), 150. For more instances of the use of this explanation of the biblical permission to take usury of the stranger, see, for instance, Gabriel Powel, *Theologicall and Scholasticall Positions Concerning Vsurie Set Forth by Definitions* (Oxford, 1602), 21; Richard Capel, *Tentations Their Nature, Danger, Cure [. . .] To Which Is Added a Briefe Dispute, as Touching Restitution in the Case of Usury* (London 1633, 441 (a treatise that went through six editions in 25 years); Robert Bolton, *A Short and Priuate Discourse Betweene Mr. Bolton and One M.S. Concerning Vsury* (London 1637), 8, 21–22; Nathanael Homes, *Usury Is Injury* (London, 1640), 40–41; Christopher Jelinger, *Usury Stated Overthrown* (London, 1679), 177–78; John Weemes, *An Exposition*

of the Morall Lavv, or Ten Commandements of Almightie God Set Dovvne by Vvay of Exercitations (London, 1632), 205–6.

9. Hawkes, *The Culture of Usury in Renaissance England*, 71–79, and see his references there. Ainsworth first published his commentaries between 1617 and 1619 in Amsterdam, where he settled after being apprehended for his separatist opinions. The full *Annotations* were published in London in 1627. Arthur Jackson, *A help for the understanding of the Holy Scripture* (Cambridge, 1643) (see Leviticus 25:36 and Deuteronomy 21:20); Joseph Hall, *A plaine and familiar explication* (London, 1633) (see Deuteronomy 21:20); [John Downham, ed.], *Annotations upon all the books of the Old and New Testament* [. . .], vol. 1 (London, 1645) (see Deuteronomy 23:20). On the *Assembly's Annotations*, see Dean George Lampros, "A New Set of Spectacles: The Assembly's Annotations, 1645–1657," *Renaissance and Reformation* 31, no. 4 (2009): 33–46.

10. John Trapp, *A Clavis to the Bible. Or A new Comment upon the Pentateuch* (London, 1649–1650), 425–26. He adds that this is "their chief trade, and this is yielded by some as a reason why the Jews do so stink . . .because most of them are Usurers, lead sedentary lives, and use no bodily exercise." His *Annotations on the Old and New Testaments* was integrated and published in five volumes in London between 1654 and 1662. It gained great popularity and was still republished up to the mid-nineteenth century.

11. On Willet's idea of usury, see also Jones, *God and the Moneylenders*, 152–53; Sommerville, "Sir Robert Filmer, Usury, and the Ideology of Order," 43.

12. Gervase Babington [Miles Smith and T. C, eds.], *The workes of the Right Reuerend Father in God Gervase Babington* [. . .] (London, 1615), especially his notes on Exodus 22:25.

13. The quote is taken from John Mayer, "To the reader," in his *A Commentarie upon the Foure Evangelists and the Acts of the Apostles* (London, 1631).

14. John Mayer, *A Commentary upon the whole Old Testament* (London, 1653), 567 and 846.

15. Poole reached Isaiah 58 by his death, and the work was completed by his colleagues. For the attribution of each of the rest of the commentaries, see William Orme, *Bibliotheca Biblica* (London, 1824), 360. For the commentary's enormous success see Green, *Print and Protestantism in Early Modern England*, 121–22.

16. Matthew Poole, *Annotations upon the Holy Bible*, vol. 1 (London, 1683), 469–70. And he continues: "And though the word *brother* is oft times used in a general sense for *every man*, yet I think I may affirm that wheresoever the words *brother* and *stranger* are opposed in the Jewish law, the brother signifies the Israelite only, and the stranger signifies any person from what nation or religion soever, whether proselyted to the Jewish religion or not, and so it seems to be meant here" (italics in original).

17. Matthew Poole, *Annotations upon the Holy Bible*, vol. 1 (London, 1683), 469–70.

18. James Hodges, *Essays on several subjects* (London, 1710), 35–37. Hodges was concerned with Scotland's economic underdevelopment, and his conception of usury was plausibly part of that; see Colin Kidd, "North Britishness and the Nature of Eighteenth-Century British Patriotisms," *Historical Journal* 39, no. 2 (1996): 367–68.

19. T. P., *Usury Stated Being a Reply to Mr. Jelinger's Usurer Cast* (London, 1679), 86; *The Case of Usury Further Debated, in a Letter to the Author of Usury Stated* (London, 1684), 4–5.

20. Renée Jeffery, *Hugo Grotius in International Thought* (New York: Palgrave Macmillan, 2006), 52; on Grotius's influence on Harrington, see Barducci, "Harrington, Grotius, and the Commonwealth of the Jews, 1656–1660," 70–76.

21. Curiously enough, it was not in use in the *Annotations* on Luke's passage, yet this was already not the work of Poole himself.

22. See Simon Patrick, Robert Jameson, and William Dodd on Deuteronomy 23, and the Methodist Thomas Coke (1747–1814) in *A Commentary on the Old and New Testaments*, vol. 1 (London, 1801) (on Deuteronomy 23:19–20).

23. Richard Kidder, *A Commentary on the five books of Moses* (London, 1694); Simon Patrick, *A Commentary upon the fifth Book of Moses* (London, 1700). Patrick's commentary was highly popular and went through four editions in forty years. It was also published as part of *A Critical Commentary and Paraphrase of the Old and New Testaments, along with Commentaries of Lowth, Whitby and Arnald* (1727–1760), an edition that gained great influence. Patrick's was recommended by Dr. Johnson to Boswell as the best Bible commentary. See Green, *Print and Protestantism in Early Modern England*, 118. Patrick's commentary on Deuteronomy 23 was adopted by Samuel Humphreys (1697–1737) in his compilation of Bible commentary: *The Sacred Books of the Old and New Testament*, vol. 1 (London, 1735).

24. Matthew Henry, *An exposition of the five books of Moses* [. . .] (London, 1707). See this explicit argument also in his commentary on Nehemiah 5. By the turn of the century, ten editions of his commentary had been published, and by the mid-nineteenth-century, fifteen more. See Ian Green, *Print and Protestantism in Early Modern England*, 118–19. Along with Matthew Poole and Simon Patrick's commentaries, his was one of the most widely read and esteemed in the eighteenth century; see Preston, "Biblical Criticism, Literature, and the Eighteenth-Century Reader."

25. [Robert Jameson], *A critical and practical exposition of the Pentateuch, with notes, theological, moral, philosophical, critical, and historical* [. . .] (London, 1748).

26. John Gill, *An Exposition of the Old Testament*, vols. 1 and 2 (London, 1765). In his commentary on Deuteronomy 23 he writes: "As the Jews were chiefly employed in husbandry, and not merchandise, they had but little occasion to borrow, and when they did could not afford to pay interest, as persons concerned in merchandise, whose gains are great, are able to do; and it is but reasonable that such persons should; but that the Israelites, when poor and in distress, might not be bowed down under their burdens, this law is made for their relief." See also his commentary on Leviticus 25:37, where he conjugates the saying that "if persons borrow money to gain by it, to carry on a greater trade, or to make purchase with it, it is but reasonable that the lender should have a share of profit arising from thence."

27. Thomas Pyle, *A paraphrase with short and useful notes on the books of the Old Testament, part I* [. . .] *for the use of families* [. . .], vol. 1 (Exodus) and vol. 2 (Deuteronomy), (London, 1717). While I suggest that the main channel of transmission of the new interpretive outlook was Grotius's NT commentary, it is telling that some of the later English commentators attributed it to other sources. In his interpretation on Deuteronomy 23, William Dodd referred to Harrington and concluded from his thesis that usury is forbidden only when "it might come to overthrow the balance or foundation of the government." See William Dodd, *A commentary on the books of the Old and New Testament* [...], vol. 1 (London, 1770). Robert Jameson on Deuteronomy 23 went so far as to attribute this explanation to Josephus, despite the fact that the latter did not refer to the issue at all.

28. Matthew Henry's commentary on Deuteronomy 23:19–20, in his *An Exposition of the five books of Moses* [. . .] (London, 1707).

29. John Trapp, *A commentary or exposition upon the books of Ezra, Nehemiah, Esther, Job and Psalms* (London, 1657), 63–65.

30. "Our Saviour doth no more patronize usury here than he doth injustice, Luke 16:1; theft, 1 Thessalonians 5:2; dancing, Matthew 11:17; Olympic games, 1 Corinthians 9:24." John

Trapp, *A commentary or exposition upon all the books of the New Testament* [...] (London, 1656), see his commentary on Matthew 25:27.

31. In a similar vein, see also John Lightfoot, *The works of the reverend and learned John Lightfoot* [. . .] (London, 1684), *Hebrew and Talmudic Exercitations*, vol. 2, 247.

32. Poole's commentary on Ezekiel was edited by Henry Hurst. For other contrasting comparisons, see Proverbs 28:8; Isaiah 58:6; Micah 3:2; Nahum 3:16; Ecclesiastes 5:10.

33. See the commentaries of Matthew Poole (edited by Henry Hurst after Poole's death), Simon Patrick, and Matthew Henry.

34. Matthew Poole, *Annotations upon the Holy Bible*, vol. 2 (London, 1685).

35. Richard Baxter, *A paraphrase on the New Testament with notes* (London, 1685); Matthew Henry, *An exposition of all the books of the Old and New Testament* [...] 3rd ed. vol. 5 (London, 1725), 184–85.

36. Richard Baxter, *A Christian Directory* (London, 1673), 126; Edward Stillingfleet, *A letter to a Deist* (London, 1677), 119–22.

37. Steven Pincus, *1688: The First Modern Revolution* (New Haven, CT: Yale University Press, 2014), chap. 13; N. H. Keeble, *Calendar of the Correspondence of Richard Baxter* (Oxford: Clarendon Press, 1991). Richard Baxter, *Reliquiae Baxterianae* (London, 1696). Baxter related to both Stillingfleet and Poole, together with Simon Patrick and others, as "the best and ablest of the Conformists." Baxter, *Reliquiae Baxterianae* § 40.

38. For the shift toward commercialism that English divines underwent in the second half of the seventeenth century, in contrast to previous decades, see Charles A. Knight, "The *Spectator's* Moral Economy," *Modern Philology* 91, no. 2 (1993): 161–79 (164); Charles H. George and Katherine George, *The Protestant Mind of the English Reformation, 1570–1640* (Princeton, NJ: Princeton University Press, 1961), 166–73; Richard B. Schlatter, *The Social Ideas of Religious Leaders 1660–1688* (London: Oxford University Press, 1940), 158–86; Anthony Waterman, *Political Economy and Christian Theology Since the Enlightenment: Essays in Intellectual History* (London: Palgrave Macmillan, 2004), chap. 7.

39. Pincus, *1688*, chap. 12.

40. Justifications were made already in medieval times. For a brief account of medieval caveats on lending with interest, see Joseph Shatzmiller, *Shylock Reconsidered: Jews, Moneylending, and Medieval Society* (Berkeley: University of California Press, 1990), 45. For later engagements with the practical problem of moneylending, see this volume, introduction, n. 25, and also Sir Robert Filmer, *A discourse whether it may be lawful to take use for money* (London, 1678 [1652; written originally in 1630]).

41. The distinction was rooted in the Bible and was developed by the early church (*Verus Israel* vs. the Jews). For this and other examples, see "Israelite, n. and adj.," OED Online, December 2022 (Oxford University Press), https://www.oed.com/view/Entry/100204?redirectedFrom =israelite& (accessed March 01, 2023). On the Continent, this separation was much stronger than in England, where the two terms were used more fluidly. On the continental distinction, see Yaacov Deutsch, *Judaism in Christian Eyes: Ethnographic Descriptions of Jews and Judaism in Early Modern Europe* (Oxford: Oxford University Press, 2012), 40–41; on the English ambiguity, see James Shapiro, *Shakespeare and the Jews*, 174, and note 33 there; Achsah Guibbory, "England, Israel, and the Jews in Milton's Prose, 1649–1660," in *Milton and the Jews*, ed. Douglas A. Brooks (New York: Cambridge University Press, 2008), 24–34; Shoulson, *Milton and the Rabbis*, chap. 1.

42. Fleury, *A Short History of the Israelites* (London, 1756), part 2, 52–56. The work was published with the approbation of the bishop of Meaux, Jacques-Bénigne Bossuet. In 1683 it

was translated into English (translator unknown) under the title *The Manners of the Israelites*. It was republished in English in 1756 (under the title *A Short History of the Israelites*) and in 1786 in Newcastle. Curiously, each of the English editions was translated anew. All references are made to the 1756 edition, from which the quotes are taken. It saw another nine reprints, based on the 1756 edition, by the middle of the nineteenth century. Remarkably, I did not note significant changes among the translations.

43. Fleury, *A Short History of the Israelites*, 1–4. On the utopian dimension of Fleury's text, see Adam Sutcliffe, *Judaism and Enlightenment* (New York: Cambridge University Press, 2005), 56–57.

44. Lionel Rothkrug, *Opposition to Louis XIV: The Political and Social Origins of French Enlightenment* (Princeton, NJ: Princeton University Press, 1965), chap. 5.

45. Henry C. Clark, *Compass of Society: Commerce and Absolutism in Old-Regime France* (Lanham, MD: Lexington Books, 2007), 54–58; Istvan Hont, "The Early Enlightenment Debate on Commerce and Luxury," in *The Cambridge History of Eighteenth-Century Political Thought*, ed. Mark Goldie and Robert Wokler (Cambridge: Cambridge University Press, 2006), 377–418; Rothkrug, *Opposition to Louis XIV*, 242–49. Fleury's other work central to this economic-political line was his *Pensées politiques*, presumably written between 1670 and 1675. See Rothkrug, *Opposition to Louis XIV*, 244, n. 13. Hont, "The Early Enlightenment Debate on Commerce and Luxury," 384–85.

46. Calmet's *Commentaire littéral sur tous les livres de l'Ancien et du Nouveau Testament* was first published in French between 1707 and 1716 and went through many editions as well as some translations. For Calmet's general exegetical attitude, see John W. Rogerson, "Early Old Testament Critics in the Roman Catholic Church—Focusing on the Pentateuch," in *Hebrew Bible/Old Testament: The History of Its Interpretation*, ed. Magne Sæbø, vol. 2 (Göttingen: Vandenhoeck & Ruprecht, 2008), 837–50. His works include many references to the works of Fleury.

47. See his commentary on Exodus in A. Augustin Calmet, *Commentaire littéral sur tous les livres de l'Ancien et du Nouveau Testament*, vol. 2 (Paris, 1717), 311–14. See also his commentary on Deuteronomy 23, Psalms 15, and the NT passages. The *Dictionnaire* was published in English in 1732, and then revised in 1795 (translated by Samuel D'Oyly and John Colson) as *An Historical, Critical, Geographical, Chronological, and Etymological Dictionary of the Holy Bible*. See vol. 3 (London, 1732), 140–41.

48. Trivellato, *The Promise and Peril of Credit*, chap. 6. Understanding the prohibition on usury along the traditional lines was a commonplace among later eighteenth-century French writers. Henri Grégoire, advocate of Jewish emancipation in revolutionary France, related to the problem of Jewish usury and blamed the Jews for having "extended the land of Canaan every where, in order that they might have a right to find Ammonites and Philistines throughout the whole earth." See Henri Grégoire, *Essai sur la régénération physique, morale et politique des Juifs* (Metz, 1789), 66.

49. Hont, "The Early Enlightenment Debate on Commerce and Luxury," 388–89.

50. Jonathan Sheehan, *The Enlightenment Bible: Translation, Scholarship, Culture* (Princeton: Princeton University Press, 2005), 182–216.

51. Richard J. Ross, "Distinguishing Eternal from Transient Law: Natural Law and the Judicial Laws of Moses," *Past & Present* 217, no. 1 (November 1, 2012): 79–115.

52. Tadmor, *The Social Universe of the English Bible*; see also Preston, "Biblical Criticism, Literature, and the Eighteenth-Century Reader."

53. See, for instance, the commentaries of Babington and Willet discussed earlier.

54. See Nelson, *The Idea of Usury*; Norman L. Jones, *God and the Moneylenders*.

55. One exception is Bishop Gervaise Babington, discussed earlier.

56. See Blair Worden, "The Question of Secularization," in *A Nation Transformed: England After the Restoration*, ed. Alan Houston and Steve Pincus (Cambridge: Cambridge University Press, 2001), 20–40; for a general consideration of the topic, see John C. Sommerville, *The Secularization of Early Modern England: From Religious Culture to Religious Faith* (New York: Oxford University Press, 1992), chap. 1, 13. Sheehan, *The Enlightenment Bible*, preface.

57. José Casanova, "Secularization," in *International Encyclopedia of the Social and Behavioral Sciences*, ed. N. J. Smelser and B. Baltes (St. Louis: Elsevier Science & Technology, 2001), 13786–91. For more on the process of secularization in tandem with religious thought and commitment, see William J. Bulman, *Anglican Enlightenment: Orientalism, Religion and Politics in England and Its Empire, 1648–1715* (Cambridge: Cambridge University Press, 2015); Mark Somos, *Secularisation and the Leiden Circle* (Leiden: Brill, 2011), introduction.

58. For a broader perspective on the Israelite–Jewish distinction, see this chapter, n. 40.

CHAPTER 3

1. Joan-Pau Rubiés, "Travel Writing as a Genre: Facts, Fictions and the Invention of a Scientific Discourse in Early Modern Europe," *Journeys* 1, no. 1 (July 1, 2000): 5–35; Anthony Pagden, *The Enlightenment: And Why It Still Matters* (Oxford: Oxford University Press, 2015), chap. 4.

2. For a general view of early modern ethnology and its concerns, see Guy G. Stroumsa, *A New Science: The Discovery of Religion in the Age of Reason* (Cambridge, MA: Harvard University Press, 2010), chap. 1.

3. The first edition, not extant, was published in 1558; ten subsequent editions were published in the following thirty years, and nine more in the second half of the seventeenth century. Lucien Wolf suggested that the great interest in the postbiblical history of the Jews should be understood against the backdrop of the spread of the English Bible at the time. On the translation and subsequent adaptations of Josippon, see Lucien Wolf, "'Josippon' in England," *Transactions (Jewish Historical Society of England)* 6 (1908): 277–88.

4. Eva J. Holmberg, *Jews in the Early Modern English Imagination: A Scattered Nation* (Farnham: Ashgate, 2012).

5. Joan Pau Rubiés and Jas Elsner, "Introduction," in *Voyages and Visions: Towards a Cultural History of Travel*, ed. Jás Elsner and Joan-Pau Rubiés (London: Reaktion, 1999), 1–56; Rubiés, "Travel Writing as a Genre."

6. David Armitage, "Purchas, Samuel (bap. 1577, d. 1626)," *Oxford Dictionary of National Biography* (Oxford: Oxford University Press, 2004). Expanded versions were published in 1614, 1617, and 1625, which relied in part on manuscripts borrowed from Richard Hakluyt, the great compiler of travel accounts preceding Purchas.

7. Samuel Purchas, *Purchas his pilgrimage* (London, 1613), 137.

8. "For in every citee the Iewes kepe open shops of vsurie, takyng gaiges [securities] of ordinarie for .xv. in the hundred by the yeere . . . by reason wherof the Iewes are out of measure wealthie in those parties." William Thomas, *The historye of Italye* (London, 1549), 76–77.

9. Moryson was born to a well-off family and renounced a profitable church position in favor of traveling. His first journey (1591–1595) took place in Europe, and the second (1595–1597) included the Ottoman Empire and the Holy Land. His account was published in Latin and then in English in 1617. He died before publishing his full account and left some chapters in

manuscript (written between 1617 and 1620) that included a synthetic account of the Jews. These were published by Charles Hughes in 1903; see Fynes Moryson and Charles Hughes, *Shakespeare's Europe: A Survey of the Condition of Europe at the End of the 16th Century*, 2nd ed. (New York: B. Blom, 1967), xl–xli. On the general dynamic of economic exploitation facilitated by the Jews, see 487. For his analysis of the matters in Italy and the German lands, see Fynes Moryson, *An itinerary vvritten by Fynes Moryson Gent.* (London, 1617), 173, 195, 211. See also Robert Fage, *A description of the whole world* (London, 1658), 24–25.

10. Samuel Clarke, *A geographicall description of all the countries in the known world* (London, 1657), 135. See also his offensive on the contemporary toleration of usury, *Medulla Theologiae* (London, 1659); G.H., *Memorabilia Mundi* (London, 1670), 148 (variously attributed to G. Hooker and G. Hussey); Peter Heylyn, *Mikrokosmos. A little description of the great world* (Oxford, 1625), 222 (this was an augmented version of his 1621 *Microcosmus*, but it is only here that he emphasized Jewish usury).

11. Peter Heylyn, *Cosmographie* (London, 1652), 106. This was an expanded edition of his work, where he reiterated much of his views, including his depiction of the Jews. It is plausible that the impetus for this elaboration was the intensifying discussion on the readmission of the Jews in England, as I describe in Chapter 1. On Heylyn's work, see Anthony Milton, *Laudian and Royalist Polemic in Seventeenth-Century England: The Career and Writings of Peter Heylyn* (Manchester: Manchester University Press, 2007), 152–58.

12. See, for example, Thomas Coryate, *Coryat's crudities; reprinted from the edition of 1611*, vol. 1 (London, 1776), 301.

13. George Sandys, *A relation of a journey began an: dom: 1610* (London, 1615), 146–48. See also Purchas, *Purchas his pilgrimage*, vol. 2 (London, 1625), 1306–7; William Biddulph, *The Travels of Certaine Englishmen* (London, 1609), 74. See Eva J. Holmberg, "Jews of All Trades: Jews and Their Professions in Early Modern English Travel Writing," *Journeys* 14, no. 2 (2013): 27–49.

14. Holmberg, "Jews of All Trades"; Nabil Matar, "Blount, Sir Henry (1602–1682)," *Oxford Dictionary of National Biography* (Oxford: Oxford University Press, 2004).

15. Henry Blount, *A voyage into the levant*, 4th ed. (London, 1650; first published in 1636), 207–9.

16. Blount, *A voyage into the levant*, 223–24. Blount's explanation of the Jewish condition was adopted, at times almost verbatim, in James Howell's *Familiar Letters*. Writing to Lord Clifford at Knasburgh, Howell depicted the Jewish condition along a similar narrative of degeneration, from a primitive simplicity into deceitful and self-enriching "Broakers and Lombardeers" as a result of the pressing necessities they endured. He repeated this narrative in his introduction to the *Warre of the Jews*, which he translated in 1652. James Howell, *Epistolae Ho-Elianae Familiar Letters* (London, 1650 [1645]), 198–200. See also his epistle to "Dr. B.," ibid., pp. 10–11.

17. The ambassador was Sir Henry Wotton. On the background of writing the treatise, see Mark R. Cohen, "Leone da Modena's Riti: A Seventeenth-Century Plea for Social Toleration of Jews," *Jewish Social Studies* 34, no. 4 (1972): 289–95; Deutsch, *Judaism in Christian Eyes*, 73–74; Katz, *Philo-Semitism and the Readmission of the Jews to England, 1603–1655*, 184, and his references in n. 78. The work gained its influence through its translation into French in 1674 (expanded edition in 1681) by the celebrated scholar Richard Simon. Curiously, it was retranslated into English from Simon's edition and republished in 1707 and 1711.

18. Leone Modena, *The history of the rites, customes, and manner of life, of the present Jews* (London, 1650), 83–85; see also Cohen, "Leone da Modena's Riti," 310–11. Both English and French translations of Modena seem to be decently loyal to the original in the sections

I examined. However, both seem to have taken a similar liberty in modifying the order of this sentence, thus augmenting the Jewish vice. While Modena apologized for contemporary Jewish usury on the grounds that they have no other means of living, unlike their brethren according to nature (the Gentiles), therefore they justify it as lawful ("ma perche non hanno in che intramettersi par vivere, come gl'altrri fratelli per natura, pretendono di poterlo far lecitamente"), English and French translations changed the order of the sentence: for they have "no other way of Livelihood left them, but onely this of Usury; they allege it to be Lawful for Them to do this, as well as for the rest of their Brethren by Nature" (1650 edition). Modena hints at the maltreatment of the Jews by the Christians, in spite of their being their brethren according to nature; Edmund Childmead and Simon, the translators, point to the maltreatment of the Christians by the Jews, in spite of their being their brethren according to nature.

19. Luzzatto's treatise apparently had great influence on Menasseh ben Israel, including his defense of Jewish usury, and later on other thinkers (also non-Jews), among them John Toland. An extensive discussion is offered by Karp, *The Politics of Jewish Commerce*, 21–27.

20. Benjamin Arbel, "Mediterranean Jewish Diasporas and the Bill of Exchange: Coping with a Foreign Financial Instrument (Fourteenth to Seventeenth Centuries)," in *Union in Separation*, ed. Georg Christ, Franz-Julius Morche, et al. (Rome: Viella, 2015), 539–40.

21. Cohen, "Leone da Modena's Riti," 293.

22. Stephen G. Burnett, *From Christian Hebraism to Jewish Studies: Johannes Buxtorf (1564–1629) and Hebrew Learning in the Seventeenth Century* (Leiden: Brill, 1996), chap. 3.

23. Buxtorf and Modena had significant influence in seventeenth-century England, and they came to represent competing attitudes toward the Jews. Numerous writers adapted Buxtorf's accounts, such as Samuel Purchas, Alexander Ross, William Prynne, and Lancelot Addison. An English translation of *The Jewish Synagogue* was published in 1657 under Buxtorf's name. During the readmission polemic, Jewish ethnographies were employed to highlight Jews' benevolence or depravity, and Modena's account was pitted against Buxtorf's. See, for instance, Joseph Copley, *The case of the Jews is altered* [. . .] *A vindication of the Jewes from the false imputations laid upon them* (London, 1656), 3–4. On the textual borrowing from Buxtorf by English writers, see Deutsch, *Judaism in Christian Eyes*, 41.

24. See Stroumsa, *A New Science*, 68–76; Jacqueline Hall, "'Ceremonies et Coutumes Qui s'Observent Aujourd'hui Parmi les Juiffs': An Important but Little-Known Work by Richard Simon," *Nottingham French Studies* 18, no. 2 (1979): 14–26.

25. Richard Simon, *Comparaison des cérémonies des Juifs et de la discipline de l'Eglise* [. . .] *pour servir de supplément au livre qui a pour titre, cérémonies et coutumes qui s'observent aujourd'hui parmi les Juifs* [. . .] (Paris, 1681), chap. 3. On Simon's translation of the sections on usury in comparison with the original, see this chapter, n. 18.

26. [Leone Modena and Richard Simon], *Cérémonies et coutumes qui s'observent aujourd'hui parmi les juifs* (Paris, 1674,) preface, section xxiv, unpaginated.

27. [Simon Ockley, translator and editor], *The history of the present Jews throughout the world* (London, 1707), 1711. Ockley was the vicar of Swavesey and an orientalist.

28. For an extensive study of Picart and Bernard's work, see Lynn Avery Hunt, Margaret C. Jacob, and W. W. Mijnhardt, *The Book That Changed Europe: Picart & Bernard's "Religious Ceremonies of the World"* (Cambridge, MA: Harvard University Press, 2010), esp. chap. 7, which deals with the treatment of Judaism. Both works were translated into English during the eighteenth century.

29. Jacques Basnage, *The history of the Jews from Jesus Christ to the present time* (London, 1708), 652. On the influence of Modena's *Rites* on Basnage, see Cohen, "Leone da Modena's

Riti," 317; Jonathan M. Elukin, "Jacques Basnage and the History of the Jews: Anti-Catholic Polemic and Historical Allegory in the Republic of Letters," *Journal of the History of Ideas* 53, no. 4 (1992): 603–30.

30. [Moses Marcus], *The Ceremonies of the Present Jews* (London, 1728), 22. On Marcus, see Ruderman, *Connecting the Covenants*. Isaac Abendana, *Discourses of the ecclesiastical and civil polity of the Jews* (London, 1706). For background on Abendana, see David S. Katz, "The Abendana Brothers and the Christian Hebraists of Seventeenth-Century England," *Journal of Ecclesiastical History* 40, no. 1 (1989): 45–50; Gamaliel ben Pedahzur [Abraham Mears], *The book of religion, ceremonies, and prayers of the Jews* (London, 1738); David Levi, *A succinct account of the rites and ceremonies of the Jews* (London, 1782).

31. Lancelot Addison, *West Barbary* (Oxford, 1671), 178; Lancelot Addison, *The Present State of the Jews* (London, 1675), 9–10. A new edition was published a year later, in which the title lost its geographical focus and related generally to the present state of the Jews, which was a catchier title and plausibly appealed to a wider audience interested in Jewish ethnography in the wake of the readmission polemic. For a broader look at Addison, in his full intellectual, religious, and political contexts, see William J. Bulman, *Anglican Enlightenment: Orientalism, Religion and Politics in England and Its Empire, 1648–1715* (Cambridge: Cambridge University Press, 2015).

32. John Ogilby, *Africa* (London, 1670), 150.

33. Aaron Hill, *A full and just account of the present state of the Ottoman empire in all its branches* (London, 1709), 79, 257; *The letters of Lady Wortley Montagu*, vol. 2 (London, 1763), 96–97; Thomas Nugent, *Travels Through Germany*, vol. 1 (London, 1768), 45.

34. Richard Chandler, *Travels in Asia Minor* (Oxford, 1775); See also, for instance, *Frederick Calvert Baron Baltimore, A tour to the east, in the years 1763, and 1764* (London, 1767); Elizabeth Berkeley Craven, *A journey through the Crimea to Constantinople* (London, 1789); Thomas Martyn, *A tour through Italy* (London, 1791).

35. Samuel Sharp, *Letters from Italy, describing the customs and manners of that country* (London, 1767), 262–63 (letter 49, Bologna, May 9, 1766).

36. For some representative works, see Kim I. Parker, *The Biblical Politics of John Locke* (Waterloo, ON: Wilfrid Laurier University Press, 2004); Fania Oz-Salzberger, "John Locke and Political Hebraism," in *Political Hebraism: Judaic Sources in Early Modern Political Thought*, ed. Gordon Schochet, Fania Oz-Salzberger, and Meirav Jones (Jerusalem: Shalem Press, 2008), 231–56; Jason Rosenblatt, *Renaissance England's Chief Rabbi* (Oxford: Oxford University Press, 2006); Gary Remer, "After Machiavelli and Hobbes: James Harrington's Commonwealth of Israel," in *Political Hebraism: Judaic Sources in Early Modern Political Thought*, ed. Gordon Schochet, Fania Oz-Salzberger, and Meirav Jones (Jerusalem: Shalem Press, 2008), 207–30.

37. Thomas Seccombe [revised by Stephen J. Barnett], "Lewis, Thomas (b. 1689, d. in or after 1737)," *Oxford Dictionary of National Biography* (Oxford: Oxford University Press, 2004). Thomas Lewis, *Origines Hebrææ: The Antiquities of the Hebrew Republick* [. . .], vol. 1 (London, 1725), chap. 12, 183–85.

38. William Whiston, *The horeb covenant reviv'd* (London, 1730), 64–65.

39. Moses Lowman, *A dissertation on the civil government of the Hebrews* (London, 1745), 190, 236–39.

40. *An universal history, from the earliest account of time to the present*, vol. 2 (Dublin, 1745), 367–68, in the explanatory notes, and 402–18. On the history and the context of the publication, see Guido Abbattista, "The Business of Paternoster Row: Towards a Publishing History of the 'Universal History' (1736–65)," *Publishing History* 17 (1985): 5–59.

41. James Home, *The scripture history of the Jews and their Republick*, vol. 1 (London, 1737), 393–94.

42. Edward Ryan, *The history of the effects of religion on mankind* (London, 1788), 97. A similar portrayal of Israelite society can be found in the work of the Scottish minister Duncan Shaw (1727–1794), *The history and philosophy of Judaism* (Edinburgh, 1787), esp. 135–36.

43. See Stroumsa, *A New Science*, 58; Deutsch, *Judaism in Christian Eyes*, 39–40; Sutcliffe, *Judaism and Enlightenment*, 56–57.

44. Fleury, *A short history of the Israelites* (London, 1756), part 2, chap. 5, 52–56, and chap. 4, 49–51.

45. William Hurd, *New universal history of the religious rites, ceremonies, and customs of the whole world* (London, 1780 [reprinted in 1799 and 1814]). Each section received a similar scope of text, around ten pages. To the history of the modern Jews were added six large prints.

46. Hurd, *New universal history of the religious rites, ceremonies, and customs of the whole world*, 22–23.

47. Hurd, *New universal history of the religious rites, ceremonies, and customs of the whole world*, 23. Mistakenly it was printed Edward III.

48. Hurd, *New universal history of the religious rites, ceremonies, and customs of the whole world*, 7–8, 11.

49. For the roots of such a stance, see Ross, "Distinguishing Eternal from Transient Law," 79–115.

50. Mark Somos, *Secularisation and the Leiden Circle*, introduction.

51. See, for instance, Sir Robert Filmer, *A discourse whether it may be lawful to take use for money* (London, 1678 [1652, written originally in 1630]).

52. Julian Hoppit, "Attitudes to Credit in Britain, 1680–1790," *Historical Journal* 33, no. 2 (1990): 305–22.

53. Ronald Schechter, *Obstinate Hebrews: Representations of Jews in France, 1715–1815* (Berkeley: University of California Press, 2003), 60, 90–91. See also the renowned treatise *Essai sur la régénération physique, morale et politique des juifs* by the Franco-Jewish emancipation advocate Henri Grégoire. On Fleury's influence on Grégoire, see Rita Hermon-Belot, "The Abbe Gregoire's Program for the Jews: Social Reform and Spiritual Project," in *The Abbé Grégoire and His World*, ed. Jeremy D. Popkin and Richard H. Popkin (Dordrecht: Springer, 2000), 13–26; Francesca Trivellato, "Between Usury and the 'Spirit of Commerce': Images of Jews and Credit from Montesquieu to the Debate on Emancipation in Eighteenth-Century France," *French Historical Studies* 39, no. 4 (2016): 645–83.

54. This fluidity is apparent in the equally pejorative use of the terms *Israelites* or *Hebrews* during the 1753 Jew Bill polemic, to be discussed in Chapter 5. On the continental distinction between Hebrews and Jews, see Chapter 2, n. 53.

55. Marcel Gauchet, *The Disenchantment of the World: A Political History of Religion* (Princeton, NJ: Princeton University Press, 1997); Keith M. Baker, "Enlightenment and the Institution of Society: Notes for a Conceptual History," in *Main Trends in Cultural History: Ten Essays*, ed. Willem Melching and Wyger Velema (Amsterdam: Rodopi, 1994), 95–120; David A. Bell, *The Cult of the Nation in France: Inventing Nationalism, 1680–1800* (Cambridge, MA: Harvard Univeristy Press, 2001), 24–40; Dror Wahrman, *The Making of the Modern Self: Identity and Culture in Eighteenth-Century England* (New Haven, CT: Yale University Press, 2007), 198–202. See also Jonathan Sheehan and Dror Wahrman, *Invisible Hands: Self-Organization and the Eighteenth Century* (Chicago: University of Chicago Press, 2015), preface.

56. Han F. Vermeulen, *Before Boas: The Genesis of Ethnography and Ethnology in the German Enlightenment* (Lincoln: University of Nebraska Press, 2015), conclusion, and esp. 452–53. The effectiveness of ethnological thought in the reading of the Bible is especially revealing and supports Richard Popkin's argument that Bible criticism was a major influence on the development of the Science of Man. See Richard Popkin, "Bible Criticism and Social Science," in *Methodological and Historical Essays in the Natural and Social Sciences*, ed. Robert S. Cohen and Marx W. Wartofsky (Dordrecht: Springer, 1974), 339–60.

57. Thomas Mun, *A discourse of trade* (London, 1621); Mun, *England's treasure by forraign trade* (London, 1664[written in 1623]). Edward Misselden, *Free trade, or, the means to make trade flourish* (London, 1622); Misselden, *The circle of commerce* (London, 1623). For a general overview and analysis of their significance, see Appleby, *Economic Thought and Ideology in Seventeenth-Century England*, 37–51. For the significance of this intellectual basis for the subsequent Financial Revolution, see Wennerlind, *Casualties of Credit*.

58. Appleby, *Economic Thought and Ideology in Seventeenth-Century England*, 63–70, 87–97; William Letwin, *The Origins of Scientific Economics* (Abingdon: Routledge, 2013), chap. 3, and esp. 81–82.

59. Wrightson, *Earthly Necessities*, 229–48. By 1700 most of the labor force in England was not occupied in agriculture; see C. G. A. Clay, *Economic Expansion and Social Change: England, 1500–1700*, vol. 2 (Cambridge: Cambridge University Press, 1984), 98–102; Pincus, *1688*, 52–59.

60. Appleby, *Economic Thought and Ideology in Seventeenth-Century England*, 63–70, 87–93.

61. Pasi Ihalainen, *Protestant Nations Redefined: Changing Perceptions of National Identity in the Rhetoric of the English, Dutch, and Swedish Public Churches, 1685–1772* (Leiden: Brill, 2005), 109. On the gradual detachment of Milton from Israel as an image for England, see Achsah Guibbory, "England, Israel, and the Jews in Milton's Prose, 1649–1660," 24–34; Fania Oz-Salzberger also argues for such a dismissal of the biblical model, but relates it to the intellectuals of the Scottish Enlightenment: Fania Oz-Salzberger, "The Jewish Roots of Western Freedom."

62. Linda Colley, *Britons: Forging the Nation* (New Haven, CT: Yale University Press, 1992), 30–34.

CHAPTER 4

Note to epigraph: James Steuart, *An inquiry into the principles of political oeconomy* (London, 1765), 595.

1. Dickson, *The Financial Revolution in England*; Wennerlind, *Casualties of Credit*; Carruthers, *City of Capital*; Ingrassia, *Authorship, Commerce, and Gender in Early Eighteenth-Century England*.

2. Luhmann, *Trust*, 39–60; Giddens, *The Consequences of Modernity*, 80; for a brief discussion see Wennerlind, *Casualties of Credit*, 95.

3. Dickson, *The Financial Revolution in England*; Dwyryd W. Jones, *War and Economy in the Age of William III and Marlborough* (Oxford: B. Blackwell, 1988); Brewer, *The Sinews of Power*; Larry Neal, "How It All Began: The Monetary and Financial Architecture of Europe During the First Global Capital Markets, 1648–1815," *Financial History Review* 7, no. 2 (2000): 117–40; Anne L. Murphy, *The Origins of English Financial Markets: Investment and Speculation Before the South Sea Bubble* (Cambridge: Cambridge University Press, 2009).

4. Douglass C. North and Barry R. Weingast, "Constitutions and Commitment: The Evolution of Institutions Governing Public Choice in Seventeenth-Century England," *Journal of Economic History* 49, no. 4 (1989): 803–32; David Stasavage, *Public Debt and the Birth of the Democratic State: France and Great Britain, 1688–1789* (Cambridge: Cambridge University Press, 2008).

5. Wennerlind, *Casualties of Credit.*

6. Wennerlind, *Casualties of Credit,* 8 and his references there.

7. Patrick K. O' Brien and Philip A. Hunt, "The Rise of a Fiscal State in England, 1485–1815," *Historical Research* 66, no. 160 (1993): 134.

8. Stasavage, *Public Debt and the Birth of the Democratic State,* 77.

9. For the gripping social concerns in the early eighteenth century regarding the new culture of credit, see, among many works, Wahrman, *The Making of the Modern Self,* 207–10; Patrick Brantlinger, *Fictions of State: Culture and Credit in Britain, 1694–1994* (Ithaca, NY: Cornell University Press, 1996), chap. 2; John G. A. Pocock, *Virtue, Commerce, and History: Essays on Political Thought and History, Chiefly in the Eighteenth Century* (Cambridge: Cambridge University Press, 1985), 110–12; John G. A. Pocock, *The Machiavellian Moment* (Princeton, NJ: Princeton University Press, 2009), chap. 13.

10. Justin Champion, "'Mysterious Politicks': Land, Credit and Commonwealth Political Economy," 135–42; Colin Nicholson, *Writing and the Rise of Finance: Capital Satires of the Early Eighteenth Century* (Cambridge: Cambridge University Press, 1994), 63–71.

11. Dickson, *The Financial Revolution in England,* chap. 20; Carruthers, *City of Capital,* 13. While the number of shareholders of the Royal African Company in 1671, for instance, was 200 (holding a capital of £0.1 million), the number of Bank of England shareholders in 1694 was 1,509 (holding a capital of £1.2 million); see Ranald C. Michie, *The London Stock Exchange: A History* (Oxford: Oxford University Press, 2001), 15–16.

12. Sandra Sherman, *Finance and Fictionality in the Early Eighteenth Century: Accounting for Defoe* (New York: Cambridge University Press, 2005), 18; Dickson, *The Financial Revolution in England,* appendix D. During 1720, the number climbed to 6,846, with an average book value per transaction of £871.30. By 1739 there were about 15,000 transactions per year, and at the end of the War of Jenkins' Ear in 1748 there were 35,000. See Dickson, *The Financial Revolution in England,* 511.

13. Banner, *Anglo-American Securities Regulation,* 94; Dickson, *The Financial Revolution in England,* 285–86.

14. Peter Earle, *The Making of the English Middle Class: Business, Society, and Family Life in London, 1660–1730* (Berkeley: University of California Press, 1989), 146–51; Jerry White, *A Great and Monstrous Thing: London in the Eighteenth Century* (Cambridge, MA: Harvard University Press, 2013), 307–13; Edward V. Morgan, *The Stock Exchange: Its History and Functions,* 2nd ed. (London: Elek Books, 1969), 3; Jones, *War and Economy in the Age of William III and Marlborough,* 286.

15. Banner, *Anglo-American Securities Regulation,* chap. 1; Hoppit, "Attitudes to Credit in Britain, 1680–1790"; H. V. Bowen, "'The Pests of Human Society': Stockbrokers, Jobbers and Speculators in Mid-Eighteenth-Century Britain," *History* 78, no. 252 (1993): 38–53. All were aptly articulated by Daniel Defoe, *The villainy of stock-jobbers detected* (London, 1701). On gambling, see, for instance, George Gordon, *The history of our national debts and taxes, from the year MDCLXXXVIII, to the present year MDCCLII,* part 3 (London, [1752]), 36. Sheehan and Wahrman, *Invisible Hands,* chap. 3.

16. Daniel Defoe, *An essay upon projects* (London, 1697), introduction; B.E., *A new dictionary of the terms ancient and modern of the canting crew* (London, 1699).

17. *Mirth and wisdom in a miscellany of different characters* (London, 1703), 30, 56. On the figure of the stockjobber, see Bowen, "'The Pests of Human Society.'"

18. Defoe, *An essay upon projects*, 29–30.

19. Wennerlind, *Casualties of Credit*, 109–10; Natasha Glaisyer, *The Culture of Commerce in England, 1660–1720* (Woodbridge: Boydell Press, 2006), 31–32.

20. *Mirth and wisdom in a miscellany of different characters* (London, 1703), 55–56.

21. For a more detailed map, see "A New & Correct Plan of all The Houses destroyed and damaged by the FIRE which began in Exchange-Alley, Cornhill, On Friday, March 25th, 1748," published in *London Magazine, or, Gentleman's Monthly Intelligencer*, 1748 (publisher R. Baldwin). The map is available at: https://mapco.net/cornhill/fire.htm, Mapco—Map and Plan Collection Online [accessed February 28, 2023]. Jonathan's Coffee House is located in the western part of the map, and Garraway's is a little southeast of it.

22. [Daniel Defoe], *The anatomy of Exchange-Alley: or, a system of stock-jobbing* (London, 1719), 35.

23. John Perceval (Lord Egmont), *An essay on the means of discharging the public debt* (London, 1763), introduction.

24. Bowen, "'The Pests of Human Society.'" It was reckoned in 1776 that three-sevenths of the debt was owned by the Dutch. Paul Langford, *A Polite and Commercial People: England 1727–1783* (New York: Oxford University Press, 1994), 642.

25. Dudley Abrahams, "Jew Brokers of the City of London," *Miscellanies (Jewish Historical Society of England)* 3 (1937): 80–94; Dickson, *The Financial Revolution in England*, 493–95, 516–17. Several historians note that the number of 12 was not included in the 100 limit but on top of it, but this seems inadequate with the phrasing of the act. See "William III, 1696–7: An Act to restraine the Number and ill Practice of Brokers and Stock-Jobbers. Chapter XXXII. Rot. Parl. 8 & 9 Gul. III. p.11.nu.1.," in *Statutes of the Realm*, vol. 7 (1695–1701), ed. John Raithby (s.l, 1820), 285–87.

26. Harold Pollins, *Economic History of the Jews in England* (Rutherford, NJ: Fairleigh Dickinson University Press, 1982), 53–57. For contemporary conceptions, see, for instance, John Mottley, *A survey of the cities of London and Westminster*, vol. 2 (London, 1733–1735), 408–9; Tovey D'Blossiers, *Anglia Judaica* (Oxford, 1738), 297–98.

27. By the late seventeenth century, Jewish shareholding of the total sum of Bank of England stocks was only 0.016 percent. See Giuseppi, "Sephardi Jews and the Early Years of the Bank of England"; Dickson, *The Financial Revolution in England*, 253–64.

28. Ann M. Carlos, Karen Maguire, and Larry Neal, "'A Knavish People . . . ': London Jewry and the Stock Market During the South Sea Bubble," *Business History* 50, no. 6 (2008): 728–48.

29. Lucy S. Sutherland, "Samson Gideon: Eighteenth Century Jewish Financier," *Transactions (Jewish Historical Society of England)*, 17 (1951): 79–90; Dickson, *The Financial Revolution in England*, 222–28, 230–36.

30. Jean-Christophe Agnew, *Worlds Apart: The Market and the Theater in Anglo-American Thought, 1550–1750* (Cambridge: Cambridge University Press, 1988), preface.

31. Gillian Russell, "Theatrical Culture," in *The Cambridge Companion to English Literature, 1740–1830*, ed. Thomas Keymer and Jon Mee (Cambridge: Cambridge University Press, 2004), 100–118.

32. Agnew, *Worlds Apart: The Market and the Theater in Anglo-American Thought*, preface.

1. Pocock, *Virtue, Commerce, and History*, 48–49, 66–67, 107–110.

2. Kathleen Wilson, *The Sense of the People: Politics, Culture, and Imperialism in England, 1715–1785* (Cambridge: Cambridge University Press, 1995), 185–205.

3. For the fullest treatment of the subject, see the classical study by Thomas W. Perry, *Public Opinion, Propaganda, and Politics in Eighteenth-Century England: A Study of the Jew Bill of 1753* (Cambridge, MA: Harvard University Press, 1962); also Katz, *The Jews in the History of England, 1485–1850*; and Todd M. Endelman, *The Jews of Britain: 1656 to 2000* (Berkeley: University of California Press, 2002), whose accounts are based on Perry's.

4. Robert Liberles, "The Jews and Their Bill: Jewish Motivations in the Controversy of 1753," *Jewish History* 2, no. 2 (Fall 1987): 29–36.

5. For the course of the parliamentary events, see Perry, *Public Opinion*, 46–54. For a general survey on the opposition material, see ibid., 89–95, 100–11, 117–21; Israel Solomons, "Satirical and Political Prints on the Jews' Naturalisation Bill, 1753," *Transactions (Jewish Historical Society of England)* 6 (1908): 205–33.

6. Felsenstein, *Anti-Semitic Stereotypes*, chap. 8; Bernard Glassman, *Protean Prejudice: Anti-Semitism in England's Age of Reason* (Atlanta: Scholars Press, 1998), chap. 8.

7. Perry, *Public Opinion*; Katz, *Jews in the History of England*.

8. The response was severe, compared, for instance, to the response to the 1708 Act for Naturalising Foreign Protestants, which was also unpopular and was repealed three years after being enacted. See Daniel Statt, *Foreigners and Englishmen: The Controversy over Immigration and Population, 1660–1760* (Newark: University of Delaware Press, 1995), chap. 8.

9. Perry, *Public Opinion*, 178.

10. Todd Endelman, *The Jews of Georgian England, 1714–1830: Tradition and Change in a Liberal Society* (Ann Arbor: University of Michigan Press, 1999 [1979]), 89–90. See more generally 59–64 and 88–91.

11. Shapiro, *Shakespeare and the Jews*, chap. 7; Dana Y. Rabin, *Britain and Its Internal Others, 1750–1800: Under Rule of Law* (Manchester: Manchester University Press 2017), chap. 1; Dana Rabin, "The Jew Bill of 1753: Masculinity, Virility, and the Nation," *Eighteenth-Century Studies* 39, no. 2 (2006): 157–71; Dana Rabin, "Seeing Jews and Gypsies in 1753," *Cultural and Social History* 7, no. 1 (2010): 35–58; Michael Ragussis, *Theatrical Nation: Jews and Other Outlandish Englishmen in Georgian Britain* (Philadelphia: University of Pennsylvania Press, 2012); Andrew Crome, "The 1753 'Jew Bill' Controversy: Jewish Restoration to Palestine, Biblical Prophecy, and English National Identity," *English Historical Review* 130, no. 547 (2015): 1449–78.

12. This was the second petition out of four (two in favor and two against the bill) presented to the House of Commons on May 21–22. See Perry, *Public Opinion*, 54–62. An important exception to the focus on religious rhetoric is Jonathan Karp's contribution in *The Politics of Jewish Commerce*, chap. 3, which focuses on the conceptual uses of the Jews by political economist Josiah Tucker during and following the polemic. This chapter seeks instead to illuminate wide-ranging socioeconomic concerns and their projection on the public agitation over the bill.

13. See the discussion in the Commons on the repeal of the bill on November 27, in William Cobbett, *The Parliamentary History of England*, vol. 15 (London, 1813), 144–45. See also Horace Walpole's reflections, ibid., 152.

14. This is not to say that religious themes and arguments were totally absent in parliamentary discussions, but these were raised mainly pertaining to the capability of the establishment to contain religious differences.

15. For a general analysis, see Perry, *Public Opinion*, 78–89. On colonial commerce in the parliamentary debate on the Jew Bill, see Sheldon J. Godfrey and Judith C. Godfrey, *Search Out the Land: The Jews and the Growth of Equality in British Colonial America, 1740–1867* (Montreal: McGill-Queen's University Press, 1995), 52–54.

16. Cobbett, *Parliamentary History*, vol. 14 (London, 1813), 1376.

17. Cobbett, *Parliamentary History*, vol. 14, 1378, 1386–87, 1402.

18. Cobbett, *Parliamentary History*, vol. 14, 1393; see also MP Nicholas Fazakerley's similar concerns, ibid., 1409.

19. Cobbett, *Parliamentary History*, vol. 14, 1390–92. Barnard proposes that Jews might prove beneficial in countries that had already set their trade but still lacked either capital or commercial connections. On this point, see Karp, *The Politics of Jewish Commerce*, 85.

20. This is because, by being globally dispersed, they have a detailed knowledge of changing supplies and demands. See Cobbett, *Parliamentary History*, vol. 14, 1397.

21. For earlier versions of the Whig-Tory debate on the open/closed nature of the economic system, see Steven Pincus, "The State and Civil Society in Early Modern England: Capitalism, Causation and Habermas's Bourgeois Public Sphere," in *The Politics of the Public Sphere in Early Modern England*, ed. Peter Lake and Steve Pincus (Manchester: Manchester University Press, 2007), 213–31.

22. Pocock, *Virtue, Commerce, and History*, 110–12.

23. Cobbett, *Parliamentary History*, vol. 14, 1405.

24. Cobbett, *Parliamentary History*, vol. 14, 1405.

25. Cobbett, *Parliamentary History*, vol. 14, 1411–12. The threats posed by the new economic-political system and the centrality of Jews in it were recurrent themes in the press and pamphleteering in the subsequent months.

26. Cobbett, *Parliamentary History*, vol. 14, 1394, 1366.

27. Cobbett, *Parliamentary History*, vol. 14, 1424.

28. Cobbett, *Parliamentary History*, vol. 14, 1424. On other aspects of his speech, see Perry, *Public Opinion*, 65–67.

29. Cobbett, *Parliamentary History*, vol. 14, 1386–87.

30. Apparently, he does not mean only Jews. Cobbett, *Parliamentary History*, vol. 14, 1413, and also Lord Dupplin's speech (ibid., 1376, 1378).

31. Cobbett, *Parliamentary History*, vol. 14, 1402.

32. Cobbett, *Parliamentary History*, vol. 14, 1402. See also the discussion in Chapter 4.

33. Wilson, *The Sense of the People*, 185–205; Bob Harris, "The London Evening Post and Mid-Eighteenth-Century British Politics," *English Historical Review* 110, no. 439 (November 1995): 1132–56 (1144).

34. *London Evening Post* (hereafter *LEP*), May 22–24, 1753.

35. *LEP*, July 28–31, 1753.

36. *LEP*, June 28–30, 1753.

37. *LEP*, September 13–15, 1753.

38 *LEP*, October 30–November 1, 1753. On the eighteenth-century concerns about luxury and its social impact, see Maxine Berg, *Luxury and Pleasure in Eighteenth-Century Britain* (Oxford: Oxford University Press, 2007), 1–45.

39. *LEP*, October 25–27, 1753. See also the letter of "John Christian" in *LEP*, August 28–30, 1753, arguing that it was "for want of a due Regard to Religion and to a Depravation of Manners that such an Act could have ever been thought upon"; and *A collection of the best pieces in prose and verse against the naturalization of the Jews* (London, 1753), 43–44.

40. See *LEP*, June 19–21, 1753. Also *LEP*, May 22–24, 1753; *LEP*, July 26–28, 1753.

41. *LEP*, October 25–27, 1753.

42. Felsenstein, *Anti-Semitic Stereotypes*, 207–10; Dana Y. Rabin, "The Jew Bill of 1753: Masculinity, Virility, and the Nation," *Eighteenth-Century Studies* 39, no. 2 (2006): 157–71. See my discussion in Chapter 7 on Figure 2, and n. 41 there.

43. William Romaine, *An answer to a pamphlet, entitled, Considerations on the bill to permit persons professing the Jewish religion to be naturalized* (London, 1753), 5. Romaine's account of Jewish history relies on William Prynne, *Short Demurrer*, part 1, on which I elaborated in Chapter 1. See also *An appeal to the throne against the naturalization of the Jewish nation* (London, 1753), 5–6.

44. Romaine, *Answer to a pamphlet*, 39–40. It is likely that Romaine also contributed letters to *LEP* focusing on the religious aspects of the polemic; see Harris, "The London Evening Post," 1136–38.

45. *Read's Weekly Journal*, July 28, 1753. For another example, see *LEP*, July 24–26, 1753.

46. *LEP*, May 24–26, 1753; *LEP*, July 26–28, 1753; *LEP*, August 14–16, 1753.

47. *LEP*, October 18–20, 1753.

48. Other pictures purchased included *Peter Denying His Master* and *Judas Betraying Him for Thirty Pieces of Silver*, designed as presents to bill-supporting bishops. See *Connoisseur* 1, no. 2 (February 1754): 9–11. The association of English people with Judas, favoring base money over their religion, was commonly used in the polemic.

49. *Public Advertiser*, November 26, 1753. Examples of this motif are abundant, some of which can be found in the references in the following n. 49.

50. See, for example, Roy S. Wolper, "Circumcision as Polemic in the Jew Bill of 1753: The Cutter Cut," *Eighteenth-Century Life* 7, no. 3 (May 1982): 28–36; Felsenstein, *Anti-Semitic Stereotypes*, 137–47; Shapiro, *Shakespeare and the Jews*, chap. 4, 111.

51. Wolper, "Circumcision as Polemic"; Rabin, *Britain and Its Internal Others*, chap. 1; Rabin, "The Jew Bill of 1753"; Madge Dresser, "Minority Rites: The Strange History of Circumcision in English Thought," *Jewish Culture and History* 1, no. 1 (August 1998): 72–87; Caroline Gonda, "Queer Doings in Oxford: The Christian's New Warning Piece (1753)," in *Queer People: Negotiations and Expressions of Homosexuality, 1700–1800*, ed. Chris Mounsey and Caroline Gonda (Lewisburg, PA: Bucknell University Press, 2007), 261–73.

52. Literature on the motif of gender in the discourse on commercialism is vast. See, for example, Pocock, *Virtue, Commerce, and History*, 114; Catherine Ingrassia, "The Pleasure of Business and the Business of Pleasure: Gender, Credit, and the South Sea Bubble," *Studies in Eighteenth-Century Culture* 24 (1995): 191–210; Natasha Glaisyer, "'A Due Circulation in the Veins of the Publick': Imagining Credit in Late Seventeenth- and Early Eighteenth-Century England," *Eighteenth Century* 46, no. 3 (Fall 2005): 277–97; Kimberly S. Latta, "The Mistress of the Marriage Market: Gender and Economic Ideology in Defoe's 'Review,'" *English Literary History* 69, no. 2 (Summer 2002): 359–83; E. J. Clery, *The Feminization Debate in Eighteenth-Century Britain: Literature, Commerce and Luxury* (Houndmills: Palgrave Macmillan, 2004).

53. Clery, *The Feminization Debate*; Wilson, *The Sense of the People*, 185–205.

54. *LEP*, July 28–31, 1753.

55. See, for example, *The Christian's New Warning Piece* (London, 1753); *LEP*, August 4–7, 1753; Wolper, "Circumcision as Polemic."

56. For other examples of this trope in visual material, see Wolper, "Circumcision as Polemic."

57. The image refers to the book of Esther, and on the top of the broadside one reads the verse, "And in every Province, and in every City . . . the fear of the Jews fell upon them" (Esther

8:17). One cannot ignore the implicit allusion to the story of Jesus entering Jerusalem on a donkey, fulfilling Zechariah's prophecy (Matthew 21:1–9; Luke 19:28–39; Mark 11:1–11). The image on the left features Jews hailing their entrance to London as a promised land designated "New Jerusalem." Attached to the image is the text of "The Prophesies of Shylock."

58. "The Grand Conference or the Jew Predominant" (1753), Catalogue of Political and Personal Satires in the Department of Prints and Drawings in the British Museum (3203). The print is available on the British Museum's internet site at: https://www.britishmuseum.org /collection/object/P_1868-0808-3936.

59. *LEP*, July 26–28, 1753. For a survey of accusations of Jews coin clipping in the Middle Ages, see Joe G. Hillaby and Caroline Hillaby, *The Palgrave Dictionary of Medieval Anglo-Jewish History* (Houndmills: Palgrave Macmillan, 2013), 103–9. Most notable was the coin-clipping crisis in 1278. King Edward I ordered the arrest of hundreds of Jews suspected of coin clipping, of whom more than three hundred were executed.

60. *LEP*, October 18–20, 1753. The theme is frequent in many of the sources. A telling instance is found in the anonymous *The Christian's New Warning Piece*, where the rabbi preaches on the story of Dinah before circumcising E. T. Bart (based on the Whig candidate for Oxfordshire, Sir Edward Turner). For a broader view of the uses of the story in eighteenth-century English social discourse, see Rabin, *Britain and Its Internal Others*, chap. 1

61. *LEP*, May 26–29, 1753. Harris, "London Evening Post," 1145–47.

62. *Read's Weekly Journal*, October 20, 1753; *Remarks on the Reverend Mr. Tucker's letter on naturalizations* (London, 1753), 26. The writer alludes to biblical phrases castigating Israel for its lack of social solidarity.

63. *LEP*, August 21–23, 1753.

64. See Chapter 3. For a straightforward articulation of this line, see Philo-Patriae, *Further considerations on the act to permit persons professing the Jewish religion, to be Naturalized by Parliament. In a Second Letter* (London, 1753), 6–7.

65. For the centrality of visual images in constructing Jewish racial difference during the polemic, see Isaiah Shachar, "The Emergence of the Modern Pictorial Stereotype of 'the Jews' in England," *Folklore Research Centre Studies, Jerusalem* 5 (1975), 331–64; Rabin, "Seeing Jews and Gypsies in 1753." For a broad view on the construction of differences in the eighteenth century, see, for example, Richard Popkin, "Medicine, Racism, Anti-Semitism: A Dimension of Enlightenment Culture," in *The Languages of Psyche: Mind and Body in Enlightenment Thought*, ed. G. S. Rousseau (Berkeley: University of California Press, 1990), 405–43.

66. *Read's Weekly Journal*, September 9, 1753; ibid., October 6, 1753. Moreover, it was argued, they would start competing with the English over employment.

67. *Read's Weekly Journal*, October 6, 1753.

68. *Public Advertiser*, November 19, 1753. The writer relates to Philo-Patriae's [Edmund Keene?] booklet, *Considerations on the bill to permit persons professing the Jewish religion to be naturalized by Parliament* (London, 1753), 36–37.

69. Jonas Hanway, *A review of the proposed naturalization of the Jews* (London, 1753), 73–74.

70. Hanway, *A review of the proposed naturalization of the Jews*, 75–76, 98.

71. Hanway, *A review of the proposed naturalization of the Jews*, chaps. 7, 10.

72. It is telling that to some degree the practicality of Hanway's view was not so far from the view of seventeenth-century Jewish apologists such as Luzzatto and Menasseh ben Israel, as presented in Karp, *The Politics of Jewish Commerce*, 21–37.

73. *LEP*, October 1–3, 1754.

74. Karp, *Politics of Jewish Commerce*, 72–93, where he elaborates on the part of Tucker in the polemic. See also W. George Shelton, *Dean Tucker and Eighteenth-Century Economic and Political Thought* (London: Palgrave Macmillan, 1981), 79–87. Tucker was an eminent political economic thinker and perhaps the nongovernmental figure most identified with the Jewish cause, dubbed by the *LEP* as "Josiah ben Tucker ben Judas Iscariot" and the "Jew Chaplain of B[risto]l."

75. For some background on these bills, all proposed by MP Robert Nugent, see Statt, *Foreigners and Englishmen*, 209–12.

76. An initial comparison is offered in Statt, *Foreigners and Englishmen*, chap. 8; see also Salim Rashid, "Josiah Tucker, Anglican Anti-Semitism, and the Jew Bill of 1753," *Historical Magazine of the Protestant Episcopal Church* 51, no. 2 (June 1982): 191–201. A thorough comparative examination has yet to be conducted.

77. Wilson, *The Sense of the People*, 185–205.

78. Quoted in Karp, *Politics of Jewish Commerce*, 89.

79. *LEP*, June 5–7, 1753; *LEP*, July 19–21, 1753; *LEP*, June 28–30, 1753.

80. *LEP*, July 19–21, 1753.

81. *LEP*, June 28–30, 1753. The essay relates to the pamphlet published anonymously by Philip Carteret Webb, *The bill, permitting the Jews to be naturalized by Parliament, having been misrepresented* (London, 1753).

82. For more pamphlets dealing with these themes, see Hanway, *A review of the proposed naturalization*, 70; *Some considerations on the naturalization of the Jews [. . .] by J. E. Gent.* (London, 1753), 9, 11, 68–74; George Coningesby, *The Jewish naturalization considered* (London, 1753), 5–6. For more occurrences of such discussions in the press, see also *LEP*, August 21–23, 1753; *Read's Weekly Journal*, October 20, 1753.

83. See, for instance, Philo-Patriae, *Further Considerations*, 36; *An earnest and serious address to the freeholders and electors of Great-Britain* (London, 1753), 29–30.

84. Statt, *Foreigners and Englishmen*, 218–19.

85. Philo-Patriae, *Further Considerations*, 6–7.

86. Justin Champion, "Toleration and Citizenship in Enlightenment England: John Toland and the Naturalization of the Jews, 1714–1753," in *Toleration in Enlightenment Europe*, ed. Ole Peter Grell and Roy Porter (Cambridge: Cambridge University Press, 2000), 133–56.

87. See, for example, Philo-Patriae, *Considerations on the Bill* and *Further Considerations*; Edward Weston, *Diaspora* (London, 1754); Josiah Tucker, *A second letter to a friend concerning naturalizations* (London, 1753); *Some thoughts on the reasonableness of a general naturalization: addressed to those of all denominations who act upon Whig-Principles* (London, 1753); T. F, "A Letter from a Clergyman in the Country, to His Friend in Town," in *The Other side of the question*, ed. Roger Flexman (London, 1753), 35–42.

88. Most significant was William Prynne, *Short Demurrer*.

89. The 1709 Protestant Naturalization Act was repealed in 1712 after intense public clamor, being then the longest-lived achievement of naturalization in Britain.

90. Rabin, *Britain and Its Internal Others*, chap. 1; G. Yogev, *Diamonds and Coral: Anglo-Dutch Jews and Eighteenth-Century Trade* (New York: Leicester University Press, 1978); Stephen A. Fortune, *Merchants and Jews: The Struggle for British West Indian Commerce, 1650–1750* (Gainesville: University Presses of Florida, 1984).

91. It is telling that the execution of the 1740 measure by local colonial administrations was far from compliant. Local English colonists, apparently, were much more concerned with questions of identity regarding their non-Anglican neighboring colonists than were parliamentarians

and the public as a whole in the metropole. For valuable discussions on the tension of imperial expansion and citizenship, see Kathleen Wilson, *The Island Race: Englishness, Empire and Gender in the Eighteenth Century* (London: Taylor & Francis, 2002), chap. 1; Jessica Roitman, "Creating Confusion in the Colonies: Jews, Citizenship, and the Dutch and British Atlantics," *Itinerario* 36, no. 2 (August 2012): 55–90. On the hardships of civil integration of Jews in the British colonies, see C. S. Monaco, "Port Jews or a People of the Diaspora? A Critique of the Port Jew Concept," *Jewish Social Studies* 15, no. 2 (Winter 2009): 137–66; Godfrey and Godfrey, *Search Out the Land*, chap. 3. For a different perspective on British imperialism and the Jews, see Eitan Bar-Yosef, "'Green and Pleasant Lands': England and the Holy Land in Plebeian Millenarian Culture, c. 1790–1820," in *A New Imperial History: Culture, Identity, and Modernity in Britain and the Empire, 1660–1840*, ed. Kathleen Wilson (Cambridge: Cambridge University Press, 2004), 155–75.

92. See, for example, Sheehan and Wahrman, *Invisible Hands*, chap. 3.

CHAPTER 6

Note to epigraph: Richard Cumberland, *The Note of Hand; or, Trip to Newmarket* (London, 1774), 8.

1. Muller, *Capitalism and the Jews*; Felsenstein, *Anti-Semitic Stereotypes*, 201.

2. Michael Ragussis, *Theatrical Nation: Jews and Other Outlandish Englishmen in Georgian Britain* (Philadelphia: University of Pennsylvania Press, 2012).

3. As referred to in Stephen Gosson, *The schoole of abuse* (London, 1579), 22.

4. *The Jew of Malta* was written around 1590 and first staged in 1592, becoming very successful. *The Merchant of Venice* was written between 1596 and 1598, first performed probably in 1605, and first published in 1623. See Darryll Grantley, *Historical Dictionary of British Theatre: Early Period* (Lanham, MD: Scarecrow Press, 2013), 221–222, 285–286.

5. Pejorative allusions to Jews continued. See Fernando Cioni, "Visualizing and Performing Jewishness: Jews and 'Shylocks' on Stage from the Restoration to Late Romanticism," in *Speaking Pictures: The Visual/Verbal Nexus of Dramatic Performance*, ed. Virginia M. Vaughan, Fernando Cioni, and Jacquelyn Bessel (Madison, NJ: Fairleigh Dickinson University Press, 2010), 141–43. Remarkably, at the same time that Jewish characters dwindled, there was growing interest in theatrical adaptations of the Jewish history of antiquity, for instance *The Jewes tragedy* (1662), *The destruction of Jerusalem by Titus Vespasian* (1677), *Herod and Mariamne* (1673), and *Caligula* (1698).

6. Frans de Bruyn, "Reference Guide to Shakespeare in the Eighteenth Century," in *Shakespeare in the Eighteenth Century*, ed. Fiona Ritchie and Peter Sabor (Cambridge: Cambridge University Press, 2012), 349. On the little that is known about productions of the *Merchant* before the eighteenth century, see Toby Lelyveld, *Shylock on the Stage* (London: Routledge, 2014), 9–11.

7. On Granville's production, see Lelyveld, *Shylock on the Stage*, 14–20; J. Harold Wilson, "Granville's Stock-Jobbing Jew," *Philological Quarterly* 13, no. 1 (1934): 1–15. On Dogget's performance of the part and the contemporary attitude to it, see Wilson, "Granville's Stock-Jobbing Jew," 12–15.

8. George Granville Lansdowne, *The Jew of Venice* (London, 1701), 12 and 20. The rubbing of ambiguities between good and evil into a polarized struggle was a prevalent trend in

Shakespeare's adaptations. See Jean I. Marsden, *The Re-Imagined Text: Shakespeare, Adaptation, & Eighteenth-Century Literary Theory* (Lexington: University Press of Kentucky, 1995), 13–29.

9. Granville, *The Jew of Venice*, prologue.

10. Eveline Cruickshanks, "Granville, George, Baron Lansdowne (1666–1735)," *Oxford Dictionary of National Biography* (Oxford: Oxford University Press, 2004).

11. Abba Rubin, *Images in Transition: The English Jew in English Literature, 1660–1830* (Westport, CT: Greenwood Press, 1984), 53.

12. Thomas Baker, *Hampstead Heath* (London, 1706), 54. The play was initially written as *An act at Oxford*, but was banned as it offended the university, and Baker revised it before it was performed in Drury Lane in 1705.

13. For exceptional instances of cursory references to Jews in relation to the stock market, see *The pretenders* (London, 1698), 46–47; *The Slip* (London, 1715), 17; *A bold stroke for a wife* (London, 1718), 63; *The fashionable lady* (London, 1730), 61, 83.

14. See, for instance, Thomas Shadwell, *The volunteers, or, The stock-jobbers* (London, 1693); Thomas D'Urfey, *The Richmond Heiress* (London, 1693); Peter Anthony Motteux, *Love's a jest* (London, 1696); Thomas Dilke, *The City Lady* (London, 1697); Thomas D'Urfey, *The bath, or, The Western Lass,* (London, 1701; Charles Johnson, *The wife's relief: or, The husband's cure* (London, 1712); William Taverner, *The female advocates: or, the Frantick Stock-Jobber* (London, 1713); Charles Molloy, *The coquet* (London, 1718).

15. *Exchange-Alley: or, the stock-jobber turn'd gentleman; with the humours of our modern projectors. A tragi-comical farce* (London, 1720), 26.

16. *South Sea; or the Biters Bit* (London, 1720), 16. See also *Money the mistress* (1726), by Thomas Southerne, which is set in a multinational context that exhibits the universality of economic corruption, and does not employ the Jews (who are present in the play) as a target for this criticism.

17. Thomas Gordon, *The creed of an independent Whig* (London, 1720), 22; Thomas Odell, *The Chimera* (London, 1721), 34.

18. Margaret Jacob, "Was the Eighteenth-Century Republican Essentially Anticapitalist?" *Republics of Letters: A Journal for the Study of Knowledge, Politics, and the Arts* 2, no. 1 (2010): 15–19; Trivellato, *The Promise and Peril of Credit*, chap. 7, n. 108; Frans de Bruyn, "Reading Het Groote Tafereel Der Dwaasheid: An Emblem Book of the Folly of Speculation in the Bubble Year 1720," *Eighteenth-Century Life* 24, no. 2 (2000): 1–42. In contrast to the prevalent Dutch anti-Jewish sentiment, English plays that attacked the mania of financial speculation ignored the Jews; see, for instance William Chetwood's *South Sea; or the Biters Bit* (London, 1720), and *The stock-jobbers: or, The humours of Exchange-Alley* (London, 1720).

19. B. B., *A historical and law treatise against the Jews and Judaism* (London, 1703), 17. It was printed in 1733 under the title *Britannia's fortune-teller*.

20. Rowe's critique is quoted in Brian Vickers, *William Shakespeare: The Critical Heritage—Volume 2, 1693–1733* (New York: Routledge, 2013), 96.

21. John Dryden, *Love triumphant* (London, 1694), 11. Thomas Baker, *Hampstead Heath* (London, 1706); the quotes are taken from 11, 33, 55.

22. Here, the Beau Jew is named Manasseh ben Israel. The money-gender relations between the aspiring Jew and the crafty girl is clearly expressed by her demand, "Give me the money," and his reply, "Give me a kiss den [then]"; *The jew decoy'd; or the progress of a harlot* (London, 1733), 18.

23. *The jew decoy'd; or the progress of a harlot*, 14, 32.

24. James Kirkman, *Memoirs of the life of Charles Macklin* (London, 1799), vol. 1, 259–64. See also William Cooke, *Memoirs of Charles Macklin*, 2nd ed. (London, 1806), 89–95, and William Worthen Appleton, *Charles Macklin: An Actor's Life* (Cambridge, MA: Harvard University Press, 1960), 46 and chap. 9. The *Merchant* was performed 316 times from 1741 to 1800, making it the ninth most popular Shakespearian play in the century. It opened the season in Drury Lane of 1742, 1746, and 1747, see Robert Shaughnessy, "Shakespeare and the London Stage," in *Shakespeare in the Eighteenth Century* (Cambridge: Cambridge University Press, 2012), 161–84.

25. See for instance Felsenstein, *Anti-Semitic Stereotypes*, 178–84.

26. I have consulted *Eighteenth Century Collections Online, Eighteenth Century Journals, British Periodicals, Seventeenth and Eighteenth Century Burney Collection Newspapers* and Google Books. The term was used a few times by Alexander Pope but never in relation to Jews; see *An Epistle to the Right Honourable Richard Earl of Burlington* (London, 1731), 6; *Of the Use of Riches* (London, 1733), 8; *Ethic Epistles, Satires, &c.* (London, 1735), 56. A similar instance, in which "bloody Shylock" is used to denote cruelty with no relation to Jews, is found in *Remarks on Some Passages in a Letter to the Clergy of the Church of England* [. . .] *By a Clergyman of the Church of England* (London, 1722), 13. In the *Original Weekly Journal* of May 14, 1720, a letter to the author is signed as Martha Shylock, yet it does not relate to economic vices or Jews whatsoever.

27 *Memoirs of the nobility, gentry, &c. of Thule: or, the Island of Love*, vol. 1 (London, 1742–1744), 60–61; *The Westminster Journal or New Weekly Miscellany*, July 2, 1743 (reprinted in the *London Magazine and Monthly Chronologer* [London, July 1744], 350–352); *Adventures Under-ground* (London, 1750), 15–20. On the earthquakes that shook London on February 8 and March 8, 1750, see George S. Rousseau, "The London Earthquakes of 1750," *Journal of World History* 11, no. 3 (1968): 436–51.

28. Michael Ragussis, *Theatrical Nation*, 113–16.

29. On the context of this development, see Michael Caines, *Shakespeare and the Eighteenth Century* (Oxford: Oxford University Press, 2013), 64–70; Marsden, *The Re-Imagined Text*, 75–77.

30. [Henry Fielding, plausibly with David Garrick], *Miss Lucy in town* (London, 1742). References were made to 15–16, 22, 32–33.

31. Ragussis, *Theatrical Nation*, 96–98.

32. *Miss Lucy in Town*, 17–18, 39.

33. Charles Macklin, *Love à la Mode* (London, 1793), 18. Beau Mordecai is constructed after the model of Fielding's Zorobabel (in *Miss Lucy in Town*, 1742) and William Hogarth's Mordecai (in the *Harlot's Progress*, 1732). The play was produced by Garrick as an afterpiece and gained great commercial success for Macklin after a series of failed projects.

34. Arthur Murphy, "The Temple of Laverna," *Gray's Inn Journal* (February 17, 1752): 150; reprinted in *The Craftsman*, June 16, 1753, and in *A Collection of the best pieces in prose and verse against the naturalization of the Jews* (London, 1753), 17–25.

35. Murphy, "The Temple of Laverna." The allusion of this figure of Caiphas to Samson Gideon was explicit for contemporaries. He is depicted as seeking to assimilate with the English, and some doubt his Jewishness. Also, he is asked why he does not offer himself as an MP, and answers that he is not interested in honor, but his son will be a noble (152). These fit contemporary public knowledge of the historical figure of Gideon.

36. Arthur Murphy, ed., *Gray's Inn Journal* 2 (London, 1756), no. 80 (April 27, 1754): 185–86. See also the use of the name "Abraham Shylock" as a witness in a satirical trial of a Jewish stockjobber: ibid., vol. 2, no. 65 (January 12, 1754): 80–81; and of "Rubens Shylock": ibid., vol. 2, no. 101 (September 21, 1754): 323.

37. Phanuel Bacon, *The taxes, A dramatick entertainment* (London, 1757). It was a typical piece by Bacon, whose dramatic works were mostly satirical and comical but also carried unambiguous moral messages, attempting to vitalize patriotic ideals of integrity and austerity. It is likely that the play was not intended to be performed.

38. See, for instance, Arthur Murphy's *The Citizen* (1761), William Kenrick's successful comic opera *The lady of the manor* (1778), Paul Jodrell's *A widow and no widow* (1779), and Thomas Holcroft's comedy *The road to ruin* (1792).

39. Richard Cumberland, *The fashionable lover* (London, 1772). The quote is taken from p. 42. Richard Cumberland, *The note of hand* (London, 1774), 8. As one of the characters in *The fashionable lover* attests, every failing gamester has his Jew, his "only doctor in a desperate case," who ushers him into the door of death. His interlocutor replies that the Jew is "more of the lawyer than the doctor," for "he makes you sign and seal as long as you have effects" (16).

40. Samuel Foote, *The Nabob* (London, 1778; first staged 1772), esp. 40–41; Eglantine Wallace, *The ton, or, follies of fashion* (London, 1788), esp. 89; Thomas Holcroft, *Duplicity* (London, 1781), esp. 28.

41. [Richard Brinsley Sheridan], *The School for Scandal* (London, 1781), act 3, scene 1. See also the reference to Shylock in act 2, scene 3. Ragussis, *Theatrical Nation*, 104–7.

42. See, for instance, *The profligates levee, or the Knight's interview with Israel the Jew & Tommy Bloodsucker* (1777), Catalogue of Political and Personal Satires, Department of Prints and Drawings, the British Museum (5423). The image is available on the British Museum's internet site at: https://www.britishmuseum.org/collection/object/P_1868-0808-4551. James Scawen, MP for Surrey, is faced by creditors: The two figures on the right (a man and woman) are Jews. Scawen was notorious for his gaming and had to sell large portions of his estates.

43. For a valuable study of John King, see Todd Endelman, "The Checkered Career of 'Jew' King: A Study in Anglo-Jewish Social History," *AJS Review* 7 (1982): 69–100. King was only a representative of what contemporaries saw as predominant Jewish involvement in personal moneylending to extravagant well-born Englishmen (see ibid., 74–76). Thomas Holcroft, who wrote the play *Duplicity* (1781) mentioned earlier, dined frequented at King's house, but probably only in the 1790s. On King's relations with literary talents, see Michael Scrivener, "The Philosopher and the Moneylender: The Relationship Between William Godwin and John King," in *Godwinian Moments*, ed. Robert M. Maniquis and Victoria Myers (Toronto: University of Toronto Press, 2015), 241–60.

44. Lewis O'Beirne, *The Generous Imposter* (London, 1781); Miles Peter Andrews, *Dissipation* (London, 1781). In the latter, Ephraim Labradore, the Jew, claims that there is no social or religious difference that "money bags could not rub out." When his daughter takes his possessions and runs away with a pretentious French noble, he cries at the discovery, echoing Shylock, "My papers! my bonds! my deeds!"; see 10–11, 77.

45. [A Lady], *The South Briton* (London, 1774). They reconcile and come to "detest national distinctions," being the "children of the same empire"; see 57, 72. Ragussis, *Theatrical Nation*, 52–53.

46. The quote is taken from *The South Briton*, 22. The Englishman presents him as a "little Israelite" with correspondents in all parts and admits that "all our remittances passed thro' his hands; he had a golden harvest, and like a true Hebrew reaped it clean" (*The South Briton*, 6).

47. *The South Briton*, 45.

48. John O'Keefe, *The Young Quaker* (Dublin, 1784). It was performed every year from 1783 to 1800, and well into the nineteenth century. O'Keeffe used again the figure of the Jewish

financial contriver in *The Little Hunch-Back* (1789). [Richard Brinsley Sheridan], *The duenna or Double elopement* (London, 1775). The play amassed 254 showings by the end of the century. Linda V. Troost, "The Characterizing Power of Song in Sheridan's *The Duenna*," *Eighteenth-Century Studies* 20, no. 2 (1986): 153–72. On the conflicting pro- and anti-Jewish trajectories in the production of *The Duenna* and its reception, see Uri Erman, "The Operatic Voice of Leoni the Jew: Between the Synagogue and the Theater in Late Georgian Britain," *Journal of British Studies* 56, no. 2 (2017): 301–7.

49. Endelman, "The Checkered Career of 'Jew' King," 69–100.

50. Margaret Holford, *Neither's the Man* (London, 1799), 10, 27, 72, and 14, respectively. Apparently, the play did not enjoy a great success.

51. Holford, *Neither's the Man*, 59–60. See also 26–27.

52. I Holford, *Neither's the Man*, 76.

53. Rudolph E. Raspe, preface to his translation of Gotthold Lessing's *Nathan the Wise* (London, 1781). The play was translated again into English by William Taylor in 1805.

54. Richard Cumberland, *The Observer*, no. 64 (London, 1785; see the 1786 compilation, vol. 3, 26–38). See Jean I. Marsden, "Richard Cumberland's *The Jew* and the Benevolence of the Audience: Performance and Religious Tolerance," *Eighteenth-Century Studies* 48, no. 4 (2015): 457–77. On the public literary debate, see Ragussis, *Theatrical Nation*, 112–17.

55. Richard Cumberland, *The Observer*, no. 113–18 (London, 1785; see the 1788 compilation, vol. 4, 176–233).

56. Ragussis, *Theatrical Nation*, 107–10, 112–17.

57. The central philo-Jewish literary works of the time were Edgeworth's *Harrington* (1817) and Scott's *Ivanhoe* (1819), which brought a profound change in the literary representations of Jews in England.

58. He explains that his benevolence derives from applying this motto to religious faith: "I always minds de main chance. The panker [banker], on whom I draw for payment, is Providence." After he is moved by Emily's gratitude, he quits the tender situation: "Well, well—I must mind ma pusiness—I must take care of de main chance." Thomas Dibdin, *The Jew and the Doctor* (London, 1800), esp. 8–11.

59. *The Critical Review, Or, Annals of Literature*, vol. 30 (London, 1800), 227–28.

60. Thomas Dibdin, *The School for Prejudices* (London, 1801), 82.

61. *Laugh when you can; or, the monstrous droll jester* [. . .] *To which is added, The benevolent Jew, as recited at the Royalty Theatre* (London [1795?]), 59–60, reprinted in Michael Scrivener, *Jewish Representation in British Literature 1780–1840: After Shylock* (New York: Palgrave Macmillan, 2016), 63–64.

62. Marsden, "Richard Cumberland's *The Jew* and the Benevolence of the Audience," 466.

63. It has been suggested that one of the impacts of the 1737 Licensing Act was an inclination to turn to indirect means for criticizing the authorities; see "Nationalism," in *The Encyclopedia of British Literature 1660–1789* (Hoboken, NJ: Wiley Blackwell, 2015), 829–38 (834–35). It is presumably another backdrop that explains why theatrical critique of the financial-political system through the figure of the Jew became an efficient method, as it could evade censorship. I thank Uri Erman for raising this point.

64. See, for instance, *LEP*, July 12–14, 1753; and Arthur Murphy, "The Temple of Laverna," *Gray's Inn Journal*, February 17, 1752 (reprinted in *The Craftsman*, June 16, 1753, and in *A Collection of the best pieces in prose and verse against the naturalization of the Jews* [London, 1753], 17–25); Arthur Murphy, ed., *The Gray's Inn Journal*, vol. 2(London, 1756), no. 80 (April

27, 1754): 185–86; *The grand question debated* [. . .] *whether it would be expedient to abolish the public debt* (London [1755?]).

CHAPTER 7

Note to epigraph: Thomas Erskine, *Reflections on gaming, annuities, and usurious contracts* (*London, 1776*), 17–18.

1. In the same treatise Erskine denotes a person who profits from jobbing in securities as "a Jew, or a nominal Christian"; see 36, 39.

2. *Essays, I. On the public debt. II. On paper-money, banking, &c. III. On frugality* [. . .] (London, 1755), 9–10. The treatise was variously attributed to Patrick Murray, fifth Lord Elibank, and Alexander Montgomerie, tenth Earl of Eglinton.

3. [Aristarchus], *The grand question debated: after the dialogistic manner of Lucian, whether it would be expedient to abolish the public debt* (London, [1755?]), 22, and other similar references *passim*. The figure of the Jew that the text features is named "Zorobabel Pickpocket." This is another example of the intertextuality of different contemporary genres, the writer borrowing Zorobabel the stockjobber from *Miss Lucy in Town* (1741).

4. *The Connoisseur*, no. 137, September 9, 1756 (3rd ed., vol. 4 [London, 1756]), 243.

5. This exclamation was unrelated to the actual parliamentary discussion in which it took place, which dealt with a crisis with Spain in the Falkland Islands. *The Parliamentary History of England,* vol. 16 (London, 1813), 1121 (House of Commons, Nov. 22,1770).

6. Pollins, *Economic History of the Jews in England,* 56–57. The petition is inserted in Tovey D'Blossiers, *Anglia Judaica* (Oxford, 1738), 297–98; John Mottley, *A survey of the cities of London and Westminster,* vol. 2 (London, 1733–1735), 408–9.

7. *The Art of Stock-jobbing: A poem, in Imitation of Horace's Art of Poetry. By a Gideonite* (London, 1746); *A winter evening's conversation in a club of Jews, Dutcmen [sic], French refugees, and English Stock-jobbers* [. . .] (London, 1748), 4.

8. Harold Levy, "'Emunat Omen' by Meyer Schomberg," *Transactions (Jewish Historical Society of England)* 20 (1959): 101–11, see sheets 5–8; for a general background on the treatise and the writer, see Edgar R. Samuel, "Dr. Meyer Schomberg's Attack on the Jews of London, 1746," *Transactions (Jewish Historical Society of England)* 20 (1959): 83–100.

9. See also in *A winter evening's conversation,* where Gideon makes sure the interests of the poor Jewish stockjobbers are not hurt by Barnard's measures for the 1748 subscription (esp. 12, 30); in *"The Temple of Laverna"* (*Gray's Inn Journal,* Feb. 17, 1752) and *Adventures under-ground* (London, 1750), where Gideon is conceived by his fellow Jews as the promoter of the Jews' salvation; and in the satirical print on the Jew Bill, *Vox Populi, Vox Dei, or, the Jew Act Repealed* (reprinted in Israel Solomons, "Satirical and Political Prints on the Jews' Naturalisation Bill, 1753," *Transactions (Jewish Historical Society of England)* 6 [1908]: 227–28).

10. *A winter evening's conversation,* 17.

11. Bowen, "'The Pests of Human Society,'" 38–39; Pollins, *Economic History of the Jews in England,* 57–58.

12. Michie, *The London Stock Exchange,* 31; Sydney R. Cope, "Stock-Brokers Find a Home: How Stock-Exchange Came to Be Established in Sweetings Alley in 1773," *Guildhall Studies in London History* 2, no. 4 (1977): 212–19; Edward Stringham, "The Emergence of the London Stock Exchange as a Self-Policing Club," *Journal of Private Enterprise* 17, no. 2 (Spring 2002): 1–19. The new institution charged a daily admission of six pence.

13. Banner, *Anglo-American Securities Regulation*, 94–95; Brewer, *The Sinews of Power*, 210; Earle, *The Making of the English Middle Class*, 146–51; Langford, *A Polite and Commercial People*, 642.

14. Harriet Guest, "'These Neuter Somethings': Gender Difference and Commercial Culture in Mid-Eighteenth-Century England," in *Refiguring Revolutions: Aesthetics and Politics from the English Revolution to the Romantic Revolution*, ed. Kevin Sharpe and Steven N. Zwicker (Berkeley: University of California Press, 1998), 173–94.

15. Endelman, *The Jews of Britain*, 104–5.

16. Cecil Roth in *A History of the Jews in England*, 3rd ed. (Oxford: Clarendon Press, 1964), 222–23, claimed that the event "left behind no rancour." See also Perry, *Public Opinion*, 76–77; Katz, *The Jews in the History of England*.

17. S. R. Cope, "The Stock Exchange Revisited: A New Look at the Market in Securities in London in the Eighteenth Century," *Economica* 45, no. 177 (February 1978): 4. According to Mortimer's account in the last edition, the previous publications amounted to 50,000 copies.

18. Thomas Mortimer, *Every man his own broker*, 2nd edition (London, 1761), 3–4 and 23–24.

19. Thus in the first edition, p. xviii. In the second edition it was altered to "the tribe of Gilead," with an additional footnote "apologizing" for the editorial mistake in the first edition (see p. xviii–xix).

20. Mortimer, *Every man his own broker* (London, 1761), preface.

21. On the uses of the feminine image of credit in the early eighteenth century, see Kimberly S. Latta, "The Mistress of the Marriage Market," 359–83; Catherine Ingrassia, "The Pleasure of Business and the Business of Pleasure: Gender, Credit, and the South Sea Bubble," *Studies in Eighteenth-Century Culture* 24, no. 1 (June 24, 2010): 191–210; Glaisyer, "'A Due Circulation in the Veins of the Publick,'" 277–97, f. 14.

22. Pocock, *The Machiavellian Moment*, 252–54; J. G. A. Pocock, *Virtue, Commerce, and History*, 99; Ingrassia, "The Pleasure of Business and the Business of Pleasure."

23. Latta, "The Mistress of the Marriage Market"; Sandra Sherman, "Lady Credit No Lady; or, The Case of Defoe's 'Coy Mistress,' Truly Stat'd," *Texas Studies in Literature and Language* 37, no. 2 (1995): 185–214.

24. Edward J. Hundert, *The Enlightenment's Fable: Bernard Mandeville and the Discovery of Society* (Cambridge: Cambridge University Press, 1994), 209.

25. Mortimer, *Every man his own broker* (London, 1761), xxi–xxiv.

26. Thomas Mortimer, *Every man his own broker*, 3rd edition (London, 1761), xvii.

27. Mortimer, *Every man his own broker*, xix and 70.

28. See, for instance, David Hawkes, *Shakespeare and Economic Theory* (London: Bloomsbury, 2015); Emma J. Clery, *The Feminization Debate*.

29. William Fordyce Mavor, *Youth's miscellany; or, a father's gift to his children* [. . .] *intended to promote a love of virtue and learning, to correct the judgment, to improve the taste, and to humanize the mind* (London, 1798), 17.

30. This appears in a manuscript of the play that exists in the archive of the Garrick Club, London, and dates to 1759 or 1760. Seemingly, it is the only manuscript of the play that survived, as no copy exists in the Larpent Plays. I thank the staff of the Garrick Club Library and Collections for their kind assistance.

31. [Robert Baddeley], *Moses and Shadrac; or a Specimen of Jewish Education*, John Larpent Plays 517 (unprinted). It was a one-act piece performed eight times as an interlude at Drury Lane in the 1780s. William van Lennep et al., *London Stage, 1660–1800* (Carbondale: Southern

Illinois University Press, 1968); [Robert Baddeley], *A specimen of Jewish Courtship*, John Larpent Plays 765 (unprinted), was performed in March 1787.

32. See *The Boarding School Miss*, presented in Richard Jodrell's *Select dramatic pieces* (London, 1787), where Shadrach is mentioned as a rich, detestable Jew; Isaac Jackman, *The man of parts, or, a trip to London* (Dublin, 1795), a farce where a Jew met on a London street is named Shadrach and is described as "thief of the world"; or Thomas Dibdin, *Jane of Pentonville; or the Jew in jeopardy* (1796), an intermezzo that featured Shadrach as a Jewish pawnbroker (the play was staged at Sadler's Wells, but we have no full text of it [see *Observer*, July 1, 1798]).

33. *The school of Roscius, or theatrical orator* (London, 1792), 65–68. The prologue was written and performed by the actor Henry Lee.

34. Joseph Moser, *The Adventures of Timothy Twig*, vol. 2 (London, 1794). For the print, see Jewish Theological Seminary of America Library and Frank Felsenstein, *The Jew as Other: A Century of English Caricature, 1730–1830: An Exhibition, April 6–July 31, 1995* (New York: Library of the Jewish Theological Seminary of America, 1995).

35. Richard Brinsley Peake, *The Bottle Imp* (London, 1828). The play was based on the tale "The Spirit in the Glass Bottle." James Cobb, *A House to be Sold* (London, 1802 [after *Maison a vendre*, a comedy by Alexandre Duval]). See also *Ninetta; or the Maid of Palaiseau*, first performed in February 1830 in Covent Garden, where a side character of a Jewish beggar is named Shadrach; (*The European Magazine, and London Review*, 50 [August 1806]: 177 ; the humorous song "Shadrach the Orangeman, or, the Biter Bit," in *Melodist, and Mirthful Olio; An Elegant Collection of the Most Popular Songs, Recitations, Glees, Duets* [. . .], vol. 3 (London, 1829), 370–71.

36. Thomas Dibdin, *The Jew and the Doctor* (London, 1800).

37. Thomas Mortimer, *Every man his own broker*, 2nd edition (London, 1761), iv.

38. The apocalyptic imagery of the book of Daniel loomed prominently among radical religious thinkers such as the Fifth Monarchists, other radicals of the mid-seventeenth century, and radicals of the later eighteenth century. On such contexts, see, for instance, Andrew Crome, *Christian Zionism and English National Identity, 1600–1850* (Cham: Springer, 2018); Christopher Rowland, "The Book of Daniel and the Radical Critique of Empire: An Essay in Apocalyptic Hermeneutics," in *The Book of Daniel: Composition and Reception*, vol. 2 (Leiden: Brill, 2001), 447–67. Jews in England were also contemplating on the book of Daniel to draw eschatological insights on similar historical contexts; see, for instance, Eliakim ben Abraham [Jacob Hart], *Aśarah ma'amarot* (London, 1795 [Hebrew]). Menasseh ben Israel himself was deeply informed by the book of Daniel, and dedicated a treatise to its interpretation; see Steven M. Nadler, *Menasseh Ben Israel: Rabbi of Amsterdam* (New Haven, CT: Yale University Press, 2018), 187–93.

39. See, for instance, the ending of Jonathan Swift's "The Run upon The Bankers" (1720), referred to in Colin Nicholson, *Writing and the Rise of Finance: Capital Satires of the Early Eighteenth Century* (Cambridge: Cambridge University Press, 1994), 75.

40. *Adventures under-ground* (London, 1750), 15–20.

41. *The Repository: for the Use of the Christian electors of Great Britain; in opposition to all Jews, Turks, and Infidels* (London, 1753), 33, cited in Shapiro, *Shakespeare and the Jews*, 218.

42. See also the discussion of the image in Chapter 5 as part of the discussion on the trope of circumcision, and in Chapter 5, n. 56. The image on the left features Jews hailing their entrance to London as a promised land designated "New Jerusalem." Attached to the image is the text of "The Prophesies of Shylock." See also the print "Vox Populi Vox Dei or the Jew Act Repealed," Catalogue of Political and Personal Satires, Department of Prints and Drawings,

British Museum (3202). The image is available on the British Museum's website at: https:// www.britishmuseum.org/collection/object/P_1868-0808-3933.

43. Thomas H. Luxon, "A Second Daniel: The Jew and the 'True Jew' in *The Merchant of Venice*," *Early Modern Literary Studies* 4, no. 3 (1999): 1–37.

44. Macklin Diary, f. 117, Folger Library. Quoted in William W. Appleton, *Charles Macklin; an Actor's Life* (Cambridge, MA: Harvard University Press, 1960), 46.

45. Robert Baddeley, *Moses and Shadrac; or, A Specimen of Jewish Education*, John Larpent Plays 517 (unprinted).

46. Crome, *Christian Zionism and English National Identity, 1600–1850*.

CHAPTER 8

1. For a brief description of the print see, M. Dorothy George, *Catalogue of Prints and Drawings in the British Museum: Division I—Political and Personal Satires*, vol. 5 (London: British Museum, 1935), 280.

2. Frank Felsenstein interprets the image as conveying "a sense of the fallen state of those who had once been God's chosen people." See Felsenstein, *Anti-Semitic Stereotypes*, 216. The bag of money and the coins are common attributes of the figure of Judas in Christian visual culture; see Richard Viladesau, "Judas Iscariot—Visual Arts," *Encyclopedia of the Bible and Its Reception*, vol. 14, ed. Hans-Josef Klauck (Berlin: de Gruyter, 2009), 951–53.

3. The estimation of Jewish demography is taken from Endelman, *The Jews of Georgian England*, 171–73; Vivian D. Lipman, "Sephardi and Other Jewish Immigrants in England in the Eighteenth Century," in *Migration and Settlement: Proceedings of the Anglo-American Jewish Historical Conference* [. . .] *July 1970* (London: Jewish Historical Society of England, 1971). The general estimation for London is taken from E. A. Wrigley, "A Simple Model of London's Importance in Changing English Society and Economy 1650–1750," *Past & Present*, no. 37 (1967): 44–70. It should be remarked that the presence of Jews differentiated according to the district. In the eastern parts of the City of London, Jews were highly present and visible, accounting for 10 percent of the population in certain areas. In the parish of Duke's Place, they comprised a third of the inhabitants. See Katz, *The Jews in the History of England*, 184–85.

4. Endelman, *The Jews of Britain*, 41–43; Pollins, *Economic History of the Jews in England*, 62.

5. Pollins, *Economic History of the Jews in England*, 62–65; Katz, *The Jews in the History of England*, 266–67.

6. Endelman, *The Jews of Georgian England*, 297–300. On crime in London in the eighteenth century, see Frank McLynn, *Crime and Punishment in Eighteenth-Century England* (London: Routledge, 1989), chap. 1.

7. The general data is taken from the digital database of the Old Bailey Proceedings Online, at https://www.oldbaileyonline.org/ It should be noted that the numbers for the 1770s are inaccurate because since the beginning of the American Revolution, transportation to the North American colonies stopped. It should also be stressed that these numbers relate to the trial verdicts, not to the actual punishment executed. Between 1780 and 1810, for instance, less than a third of the convicts sentenced to death were executed, and about 40 percent of the convicts sentenced to transportation were exiled. A useful resource for examining penal outcomes is the database *The Digital Panopticon: Tracing London Convicts in Britain and Australia, 1780–1925* (www.digitalpanopticon.org).

8. Patrick Colquhoun, *A treatise on the police of the metropolis*, 3rd ed. (London, 1796), vii.

9. Clive Emsley, *Crime and Society in England, 1750–1900*, 3rd ed. (Harlow: Longman, 2005), 56–63; Endelman, *The Jews of Georgian England*, 173–76, 192–94.

10. William Blackstone, *Commentaries on the laws of England*, 4th ed. (Oxford, 1770), book 4, ch. 10, section 9.

11. Endelman, *The Jews of Georgian England*, 194–96. James Stansbury, who was executed for robbery, mentioned before his death that many Jews receive stolen goods from burglars and that Samuel Levi was especially prominent among them. See *Penny London Post or The Morning Advertiser*, March 18–20, 1745.

12. Apparently, Chitty was never apprehended. Old Bailey Proceedings Online (www .oldbaileyonline.org, version 8.0, accessed November 3, 2021), Ordinary of Newgate's Account, October 1748 (OA17481028).

13. Endelman, *The Jews of Georgian England*, 196. See also the testimony of David Davis, who received information about a gang of six Jews who specialized in trading stolen goods and shipping them to Holland, in Old Bailey Proceedings Online (www.oldbaileyonline.org, version 8.0, accessed October 24, 2021), October 1757, trial of Abraham Bareive (t17571026–20).

14. Endelman, *The Jews of Georgian England*, 297–300.

15. Terachina was tried at least once and was acquitted. See *London Evening Post*, September 12–15, 1767; Old Bailey Proceedings Online (www.oldbaileyonline.org, version 8.0, accessed November 3, 2021), February 1769, trial of Abraham Terachina (t17690222–30). Cowen's name is found in the Justices' Working Documents from September 1765, in a list of defendants sent to correction. London Metropolitan Archives LL ref: LMSMPS505520073.

16. The information he gave under oath on June 1, 1767, where he implicates Israel Cowen and Lazarus Abraham as receivers of stolen goods, is available on the *London Lives* Database: Middlesex Sessions, Sessions Papers—Justices' Working Documents June 1767, *London Lives, 1690–1800* (www.londonlives.org, version 2.0, accessed November 16, 2022), London Metropolitan Archives LL ref: LMSMPS505720014.

17. For the proceedings of Cowen's trial, see Old Bailey Proceedings Online (www .oldbaileyonline.org, version 8.0, accessed October 24, 2021), June 1767, trial of Edward Williams, Thomas Peak, Israel Cowen (t17670603–43).

18. *Public Advertiser*, January 21, 1764.

19. *Public Advertiser*, January 21, 1764; *London Chronicle*, February 25–28, 1764. The details given in the *London Chronicle* do not appear in the Proceedings of the Old Bailey; see Old Bailey Proceedings Online (www.oldbaileyonline.org, version 8.0, accessed October 24, 2021), February 1764, trial of Isaac Usher Philip Abrahams, otherwise Scampy Richard Munday Joseph Taylor, otherwise Turner John Carpenter, otherwise Huckle (t17640222–49).

20. Henry Fielding, *An enquiry into the causes of the late increase of robbers*, 2nd ed. (London, 1751), 107.

21. Ned Ward's *The London-spy compleat*, 8th ed. (London, 1718 [first published in 1700]), which was concerned with London's low life and dedicated a substantial volume to crime, referred very pejoratively to Jews in many instances but never associated them with crime. Charles Hithin's *True discovery of the conduct of receivers and thief-takers* (London, 1718), which focused on the trade in stolen goods, never mentioned Jews. Likewise, Bernard Mandeville's *Enquiry into the causes of the frequent executions at Tyburn* (London, 1725), which highlighted the social system that facilitated the flourishing of robberies, never mentioned them. See also the anonymous *An Effectual scheme for the immediate preventing of street robberies* (London, 1731).

22. See *Public Advertiser*, July 21, 1766; Endelman, *The Jews of Georgian England*, 196–97, 201–2.

23. Cecil Roth, *Anglo-Jewish Letters (1158–1917)* (London: Soncino Press, 1938). *Lloyd's Evening Post*, May 30–June 2, 1766, issue 1388. See also Stephen Massil, "Naphtali Hart Myers (1711–1788): New Yorker and Londoner," *Jewish Historical Studies* 43 (2011): 97–124.

24. *London Chronicle*, April 11–13, 1765; also in the *Gazetteer and New Daily Advertiser*, April 12, and *London Evening Post*, April 11–13. Neither do such accusations appear in the information sworn against them, found in the Justices' Working Documents, London Metropolitan Archives LL ref: LMOBPS450090087. See the Old Bailey Proceedings Online (www .oldbaileyonline.org, version 8.0, accessed October 24, 2021), May 1765, trial of Rosa, wife of Jacob Samuel Abigal Samuel (t17650522–15).

25. *Morning Post*, December 6, 1775. Quoted in Endelman, *The Jews of Georgian England*, 202; *Public Advertiser*, November 12, 1777.

26. William Jackson, *New and complete Newgate calendar*, vol. 2 (London, 1795), 147.

27. William Blizard, *Desultory reflections on police* (London, 1785), 44 (my italics).

28. On the increasing eighteenth-century tendency to think in terms of "systems," see Jonathan Sheehan and Dror Wahrman, *Invisible Hands: Self-Organization and the Eighteenth Century* (Chicago: University of Chicago Press, 2015); Clifford Siskin, *System: The Shaping of Modern Knowledge* (Cambridge, MA: MIT Press, 2016).

29. Thomas Hobbes, *Leviathan* (London, 1651), part 2, chap. 22.

30. The book was first published in the 1770s, with new, shortened editions, until the beginning of the nineteenth century. Richard King, *The frauds of London detected* (London, n.d); sometimes under the title *The new cheats of London exposed*. The quote is taken from 104.

31. King, *The frauds of London detected*, 107.

32. For a general view on the work, see Leon Radzinowicz, *A History of English Criminal Law and Its Administration from 1750*, vol. 3 (London: Stevens and Sons, 1948), chap. 9, esp. 221–23.

33. Patrick Colquhoun, *A treatise on the police of the metropolis*, 1st ed. (London, 1796), 166–68, 187–88. For the value estimations of property loss, see the sixth edition (1800), 609–13. On top of these one should add theft and pilfering from quays, dockyards, ships, etc.—which presumably also involved Jewish receivers of the stolen goods. Colquhoun estimates these plunders amounted to £450 thousand annually. On the Jewish involvement in receiving and dispensing stolen goods, see Endelman, *The Jews of Georgian England*, 194–96, 206.

34. Colquhoun, *A treatise on the police of the metropolis*, 1st ed. (1796), 118–19. He remarks that the Jews concentrate on copper money and foreign coins; in the enlarged second edition (1796) he emphasized the Jewish role in the production and dissemination of foreign counterfeited money (130).

35. Colquhoun, *A treatise on the police of the metropolis*, 1st ed. (1796), 176.

36. Colquhoun, *A treatise on the police of the metropolis*, 1st ed. (1796), 168. Todd Endelman touches on this point, in Endelman, *The Jews of Georgian England*, 213–14.

37. Colquhoun, *A treatise on the police of the metropolis*, 2nd ed. (1796), 188 (and a less elaborate version in the first edition,184).

38. Colquhoun, *A treatise on the police of the metropolis*, 2nd ed. (1796), 43–44.

39. Colquhoun, *A treatise on the police of the metropolis*, 6th ed. (1800), 319–22.

40. Colquhoun, *A treatise on the police of the metropolis*, 6th ed. (1800), 319–22.

41. Patrick Colquhoun, *A Treatise on the Wealth, Power, and Resources of the British Empire* (London, 1814), 115–16.

42. Colquhoun, *A treatise on the police of the metropolis*, 6th ed. (1800), 37 and 637. The idea of harnessing the Jewish elite to the improvement of the poor appeared already in the first

edition of the book, but Colquhoun elaborated on it further, especially in the sixth edition (1800), calling for an educational and occupational scheme supported by a legislative intervention; see 319–22 and 637.

43. Christian Wilhelm von Dohm, *Ueber die bürgerliche Verbesserung der Juden* (Berlin, 1781–83); and Henri Grégoire, *Essai sur la régénération physique, morale et politique des Juifs* (Metz, 1788). On Dohm, see Jonathan Karp, *The Politics of Jewish Commerce: Economic Thought and Emancipation in Europe, 1638–1848* (Cambridge: Cambridge University Press, 2008), chap. 4; and Shmuel Feiner, *The Jewish Enlightenment* (Philadelphia: University of Pennsylvania Press, 2004), 119–27.On Grégoire, see Alyssa Goldstein Sepinwall, *The Abbé Grégoire and the French Revolution: The Making of Modern Universalism* (Berkeley: University of California Press, 2004), chap. 3; Rita Hermon-Belot, "The Abbé Grégoire's Program for the Jews: Social Reform and Spiritual Project," in *The Abbé Grégoire and His World*, ed. Jeremy D. Popkin and Richard H. Popkin (Dordrecht: Springer, 2000), 13–26; Ronald Schechter, *Obstinate Hebrews: Representations of Jews in France, 1715–1815* (Berkeley: University of California Press, 2003), 87–95.

44. According to Ursula Henriques, the utilitarian approach to the question of Jewish civil status in England, which characterized also Colquhoun, was inspired by Grégoire's treatise on the Jews (1789), which was translated into English in 1791. Ursula Henriques, *Religious Toleration in England, 1787–1833* (London: Routledge and Kegan Paul, 1961), chap. 6.

45. Dohm, *Concerning the Amelioration of the Civil Status of the Jews* (1781), English translation in Paul R. Mendes-Flohr and Jehuda Reinharz, eds., *The Jew in the Modern World: A Documentary History*, 2nd ed. (Oxford: Oxford University Press, 1995), 28–36; Henri Grégoire, *An essay on the [ph]ysical, moral, and political reformation of the Jews* [. . .] (London, 1791), chaps. 11–14, and esp. 88–92, 102, 105. It is telling that Grégoire based his scheme on Claude Fleury's influential work (already a century old), claiming that, because agriculture was a fundamental of Jewish historical constitution before their exile, it could—and should—be revived, for the benefit of all. See Grégoire, *Essay*, chap. 17.

46. See Schechter, *Obstinate Hebrews*, 119–26, 218–19; as scholars have shown, the concrete economic reality was different from its depiction. Alsacian Jews were a minority among creditors, despite the outrage against them. See Trivellato, *The Promise and Peril of Credit*, 145, and her reference there.

47. On Colquhoun's political-economic views, see Paul Tonks, "Leviathan's Defenders: Scottish Historical Discourse and the Political Economy of Progress," in *The Empire of Credit: The Financial Revolution in the British Atlantic World, 1688–1815*, ed. Christopher J. Finlay and Daniel Carey (Dublin: Irish Academic Press, 2011), 73–94. The quote is taken from Colquhoun, *A Treatise on the Wealth, Power and Resources of the British Empire in Every Quarter of the World* [. . .] (London, 1814), chap. 7, esp. pp. 276–91.

48. In 1802, van Oven published the correspondence with a preface under the title *Letters on the Present State of the Jewish Poor in the Metropolis, with Propositions for Ameliorating Their Condition by Improving the Morals of the Youth of Both Sexes, and Rendering Their Labour Useful and Productive in General* (London, 1802); see also Parliamentary Debates, House of Commons, February 25, 1802, 63–64. For more information on the scheme, see Endelman, *The Jews of Georgian England*, 231–36. For the substance of the petition to the Parliament, see Levi Alexander, *Answer to Mr. Joshua Van Oven's Letters on the Present State of the Jewish Poor in London* [. . .] (London, 1802).

49. Heather Shore, *London's Criminal Underworlds, c. 1720–c. 1930: A Social and Cultural History* (New York: Palgrave Macmillan, 2015), 13–14, and her references there. Three

sensational pamphlets on his life were published in 1829–1830, and he became, as one commentator in *Fraser's Magazine for Town and Country* lamented, "a hero of romance" (*Fraser's Magazine*, "Influence of Newspapers," 4:20 [1831]: 130).

CHAPTER 9

1. Endelman, *The Jews of Britain*, chap. 2.

2. See David Cesarani, "British Jews," in *The Emancipation of Catholics, Jews and Protestants: Minorities and the Nation State in Nineteenth-Century Europe*, ed. Rainer Liedtke and Stephan Wendehorst (New York: Manchester University Press, 1999), 33–55.

3. Michael C. N. Salbstein, *The Emancipation of the Jews in Britain: The Question of the Admission of the Jews to Parliament, 1828–1860* (Rutherford, NJ: Fairleigh Dickinson University Press, 1982), chap. 3.

4. In the first two decades of the eighteenth century, anti-Dissenting riots were frequent, and during the Jacobite uprising of the 1740s, the same was true against Catholics. The Gordon Riots of 1780, sparked by the Roman Catholic Relief Act of 1778, and attacks on Dissenters in the early 1790s, sparked by their support of the French Revolution, were notable incidents. See Jeremy Gregory, *The Routledge Companion to Britain in the Eighteenth Century, 1688–1820* (New York: Routledge, 2007); Colin Haydon, "Religious Minorities in England," in *A Companion to Eighteenth-Century Britain*, ed. H. T. Dickinson (Malden, MA: Blackwell, 2002), 241–51.

5. Rudolph E. Raspe, preface to his translation of Gotthold Lessing's *Nathan the wise* (London, 1781); William Taylor, preface to his translation of *Nathan the Wise* (London, 1805). Contemporary reviews, however, were not so enthusiastic about the piece. See, for instance: *La Belle Assemblée, Or Bell's Court and Fashionable Magazine*, vol. 1 (London, 1806), 15–16; *The Poetical Register, and Repository of Fugitive Poetry for 1805*, vol. 5 (London,1807), 501–2. See also Ragussis, *Theatrical Nation*, 113.

6. Ragussis, *Theatrical Nation*, 107–17, and epilogue.

7. *The Monthly Visitor, and Entertaining Pocket Companion*, vol. 1 (January, 1797), 49–55 (quoted in Ragussis, *Theatrical Nation*, 114).

8. Richard Hole, "An Apology for the Character and Conduct of Shylock," *Essays, by a society of gentlemen, at Exeter* (Exeter, 1796), 555–56. On Hole's essay, see the different interpretations of Michael Scrivener, *Jewish Representation in British Literature 1780–1840: After Shylock* (New York: Palgrave Macmillan, 2016), 91; and Judith Page, *Imperfect Sympathies: Jews and Judaism in British Romantic Literature and Culture* (New York: Palgrave Macmillan, 2004), 68–69.

9. *Monthly Magazine*, no. 1 (February 1796): iii. See David Chandler, "'A Sort of Bird's Eye View of the British Land of Letters': 'The Monthly Magazine' and Its Reviewers, 1796–1811," *Studies in Bibliography* 52 (1999): 169–79; the quote is taken from 169.

10. *Monthly Magazine*, no. 1 (February 1796): 12–15; *Monthly Magazine*, no. 2 (March 1796): 102.

11. Albert O. Hirschman, *The Passions and the Interests: Political Arguments for Capitalism Before Its Triumph* (Princeton, NJ: Princeton University Press, 2013 [1977]).

12. Charles de Secondat, Baron de Montesquieu, *Montesquieu: The Spirit of the Laws* (Cambridge: Cambridge University Press, 1989), book 21, chap. 20. On the uses of the account of the development and spread of bills of exchange in early modern and modern European thought, see Trivellato, *The Promise and Peril of Credit*. I will discuss this topic in the Epilogue.

13. Samuel Taylor Coleridge, *Essays on His Times in "The Morning Post" and "The Courier,"* ed. David V. Erdman, vol. 3 (London: Routledge & Kegan Paul; Princeton, NJ: Princeton University Press, 1978), 144–45. See the discussion in Felsenstein, *Anti-Semitic Stereotypes,* 220–21.

14. *Monthly Magazine,* no. 3 (April 1796): 200.

15. On Hazlitt's project and its tight relation with a new interpretation of the character of Shylock, see Page, *Imperfect Sympathies,* 46–73. William Hazlitt, "Emancipation of the Jews," *Tatler,* March 28, 1831.

16. On contemporary estimation of Cobbett's public influence, see William Hazlitt, "Character of Cobbett," in Hazzlitt, *Table Talk, Essays on Men and Manners,* 2nd ed. (London, 1822), 1:115–34; Leigh Hunt, *White Hat,* November 13, 1819, quoted in *The Opinions of William Cobbett,* ed. James Grande, John Stevenson, and Richard Thomas (Farnham: Ashgate, 2013), 3.

17. James Grande, *William Cobbett, the Press and Rural England: Radicalism and the Fourth Estate, 1792–1835* (Basingstoke: Palgrave Macmillan, 2014), chap. 2. When war resumed in 1803, Cobbett was commissioned by the government to write an address that would inspire the public with nationalistic martial spirit. The anonymous tract, "Important Considerations for the People of This Kingdom," was disseminated to every parish in England and Wales.

18. Quoted in Grande, *William Cobbett, the Press and Rural England,* 64.

19. Grande, *William Cobbett, the Press and Rural England,* chap. 3.

20. For a broad view on Cobbett's anti-Jewish sentiments, see John W. Osborne, "William Cobbett's Anti-Semitism," *Historian* 47, no. 1 (1984): 86–92.

21. Roger Morriss, *Naval Power and British Culture, 1760–1850: Public Trust and Government Ideology* (London: Routledge, 2004), 183–85; Gary D. Hutchison, "'The Manager in Distress': Reaction to the Impeachment of Henry Dundas, 1805–7," *Parliamentary History* 36, no. 2 (2017): 198–217.

22. *Cobbett's Weekly Political Register* 7, no. 23 (June 8, 1805): 891 (italics in original).

23. This refers to Abraham Goldsmid (see the discussion later in this chapter).

24. *Cobbett's Weekly Political Register* 10, no. 10 (September 6, 1806): 403–4 (italics in original).

25. *Cobbett's Weekly Political Register,* (September 6, 1806): 405.

26. For a description of the mansion and the event itself, taken from contemporary press, see Katie Fretwell, "The Fete of Abraham Goldsmid: A Regency Garden Tragedy," *London Gardener* 5 (1999).

27. For a detailed account of their business methods and impact, see S. R. Cope, "The Goldsmids and the Development of the London Money Market During the Napoleonic Wars," *Economica* 9, no. 34 (1942): 180–206. On the Goldsmids' social attempts and their self-construction as an integrated Anglo-Jewish elite, see Endelman, *The Jews of Georgian England,* 251–55; Mark L. Schoenfield, "Abraham Goldsmid: Money Magician in the Popular Press," in *British Romanticism and the Jews: History, Culture, Literature,* ed. Sheila A. Spector (New York: Palgrave Macmillan, 2008), 37–60.

28. Ironically, Almina Wombwell, presumably the illegitimate daughter of Alfred de Rothschild, married George Herbert, 5th Earl of Carnarvon, in 1895 and became the châtelaine of Highclere Castle.

29. *Cobbett's Weekly Political Register* 49, no. 10 (March 6, 1824 [London, 1835]). See also his letter "On the Remedy for the Evils that now afflict the Kingdom," *Weekly Political Register* 41, no. 2 (January 12, 1822 [London, 1835]): 70.

30. See the issues of April 20 and June 22, 1805.

31. See Henriques, *Religious Toleration in England,* 175.

32. Grande, *William Cobbett, the Press and Rural England*, 51–59. The exact date of his move is unknown, but in August 1805 he mentioned it enthusiastically in a letter to his publisher, John Wright, and in another letter to William Windham; see ibid., 52, n. 51.

33. William Cobbett, *Paper against Gold*, vol. 1 (London, 1815), letter 9 (October 2, 1810), 138–39 (italics in original).

34. *Cobbett's Weekly Political Register* 18 (October 3, 1810): 524

35. *Cobbett's Weekly Political Register* 40 (July 28, 1821): 89–111.

36. "We may number among the most striking of the traits which designate the Jewish character, the wonderful uniformity of views, which appears to have influenced the actions of this extraordinary people through the course of so many ages. Their history completely refutes the opinion, which has pretty generally been received, of the radical effect of climate (and, one might be tempted to add, of manners) upon national character. We have had occasion to observe their progress in the North and in the South, in the East and in the West" (*An Essay on the Commercial Habits of the Jews* [London, 1809], 5).

37. *An Essay on the Commercial Habits of the Jews*, 35, 5, 20, 34, 1, 45, 69 (italics in original).

38. *An Essay on the Commercial Habits of the Jews*, 7, 4, 10 (the quote is taken from 7); one of the means Jews use for that is their incomprehensible language, which they use as a secret code (see 17–18).

39. *An Essay on the Commercial Habits of the Jews*, 22. Jonas Hanway, *A review of the proposed naturalization of the Jews* (London, 1753).

40. *An Essay on the Commercial Habits of the Jews*, 11–12, 19–20, 37.

41. *An Essay on the Commercial Habits of the Jews*, 70–71, 75. It might be indicative that the *Anti-Jacobin Review and Magazine*, a conservative periodical, published a review of the *Essay on the Commercial Habits of the Jews* in sequence with a review on a work relating to the convening of the French Sanhedrin by Napoleon and another one on Jewish history; see *The Anti-Jacobin Review* 38 (February 1811): 170–86.

42. *An Essay on the Commercial Habits of the Jews*, 76–7.

43. *An Essay on the Commercial Habits of the Jews*, 39.

44. *An Essay on the Commercial Habits of the Jews*, 42–4.

45. Endelman, *The Jews of Georgian England*, chap. 2, esp. 78–9.

46. In June 1827, before the introduction of the bill, a petition by members of the conversionist Philo-Judaean Society which opposed Jewish disabilities was read in the House of Commons, and a year later, a petition by one Moses Levy was read in the Commons. In the Lords sitting of April 28, 1828, Lord Holland proposed to open the new phrasing of the oath to Jews, but his proposal failed. On the process of emancipation, see Endelman, *The Jews of Britain*, 101–10; Salbstein, *The Emancipation of the Jews in Britain*.

47. For a concise history of the campaign for political equality in England, see David J. Sorkin, *Jewish Emancipation: A History Across Five Centuries* (Princeton, NJ: Princeton University Press, 2019), 210–12.

48. Consols (consolidated stock) were government debts issued by the Bank of England as perpetual bonds, with an annual interest of 3 percent. *Hansard's Parliamentary Debates*, New Series, vol. 23 (London 1830), 1287–1336.

49. *Hansard's Parliamentary Debates*, New Series, vol. 24 (London 1830), 787.

50. [Thomas McLean, publisher,] *The Looking Glass, or, Caricature Annual* 3 (1830). The caricature appears in Niall Ferguson, *The House of Rothschild: Money's Prophets, 1798–1848* (New York: Viking, 1998), 181.

51. *Hansard's Parliamentary Debates*, Third Series, vol. 17 (London 1833), 227–38.

52. *Hansard's Parliamentary Debates*, New Series, vol. 24 (London 1830), 802–7.

53. *Hansard's Parliamentary Debates*, Third Series, vol. 20 (London 1833), 221–55.

54. On Wilberforce's exceptional attack on the Jews, see Frances Knight, "The Bishops and the Jews, 1828–1858," *Studies in Church History* 29 (1992): 392.

55. Good Friday of 1833 occurred on April 5. The early publication of the piece can be explained, I suggest, by the debate in the Commons on March 1, following the reading of a petition in favor of Jewish emancipation, a debate in which Cobbett was very active. The second attempt at passing a Jewish emancipation bill was soon to come, and Cobbett's sermon, plausibly, aimed to influence public opinion before it took place.

56. William Cobbett, *Good Friday, or the Murder of Jesus Christ by the Jews* (London, 1833), 5, 16–18. This text casts doubt on William Rubinstein's assertion that the radical populist strand in British antisemitism was secular in nature, Cobbett being a marked representative of it. William D. Rubinstein, *A History of the Jews in the English-Speaking World: Great Britain* (London: Macmillan, 1996), 54.

57. David Feldman, *Englishmen and Jews: Social Relations and Political Culture, 1840–1914* (New Haven, CT: Yale University Press, 1994), chap. 1; Cesarani, "British Jews."

58. His fortune rose from £90 thousand in 1815 to £1.142 million in 1825. On Nathan's undertakings during the war, see Ferguson, *The House of Rothschild*, chap. 3; for the estimation of Nathan's capital, see 269.

59. Ferguson, *The House of Rothschild*, 14–22. Georges Dairnvaell's 1846 defamatory pamphlet, *Histoire édifante et curieuse de Rothschild Ier, roi des juifs*, was a cornerstone of anti-Jewish conspiracy theories hinging on the Rothschilds.

60. For examples of such criticism in the 1820s, see Ferguson, *The House of Rothschild*, 143–49.

61. In general, there was no significant public resistance to Jewish emancipation, nor an anti-Jewish backlash following it, in contrast to the case on the Continent. See, for instance, Sarah K. Cardaun, *Countering Contemporary Antisemitism in Britain: Government and Civil Society Responses Between Universalism and Particularism* (Leiden: Brill, 2015), chap. 2; Anthony Julius, *Trials of the Diaspora*, 256; David Vital, *A People Apart: The Jews in Europe, 1789–1939* (Oxford: Oxford University Press, 1999), 178–80. Apparently, Disraeli attracted much stronger public criticism than Lionel de Rothschild; see Richard W. Davis, "Disraeli, the Rothschilds, and Anti-Semitism," *Jewish History* 10, no. 2 (1996): 9–19.

62. Felsenstein, *Anti-Semitic Stereotypes*, 184–85; Page, *Imperfect Sympathies*, chap. 3.

63. Emma Rothschild, "Political Economy," in *The Cambridge History of Nineteenth-Century Political Thought*, ed. Gareth Stedman Jones and Gregory Claeys (New York: Cambridge University Press, 2011), 753–60.

64. Alex Preda, "The Rise of the Popular Investor: Financial Knowledge and Investing in England and France, 1840–1880," *Sociological Quarterly* 42, no. 2 (2001): 205–32; Alex Preda, *Framing Finance: The Boundaries of Markets and Modern Capitalism* (Chicago: University of Chicago Press, 2009), chap. 3; David C. Itzkowitz, "Fair Enterprise or Extravagant Speculation: Investment, Speculation, and Gambling in Victorian England," *Victorian Studies* 45, no. 1 (2002): 121–47.

65. A third of those investors had a modest investment of £5 or less and another 15 percent had an investment of £6 to £10. Francis Playford, *Practical Hints for Investing Money* (London, 1855), 43; quoted in Preda, "The Rise of the Popular Investor," 208.

66. George Robb, *White-Collar Crime in Modern England: Financial Fraud and Business Morality, 1845–1929* (Cambridge: Cambridge University Press, 1992), introduction.

67. Mary Poovey, *Genres of the Credit Economy: Mediating Value in Eighteenth- and Nineteenth-Century Britain* (Chicago: University of Chicago Press, 2008), chaps. 2 and 4; Patrick Brantlinger, *Fictions of State: Culture and Credit in Britain, 1694–1994* (Ithaca, NY: Cornell University Press, 1996), chap. 4.

68. *The Art of Stock-Jobbing Explained* [. . .], 5th ed. (London, 1816).

EPILOGUE

1. For historical descriptions and explanations of Jewish economic exceptionalism, see Maristella Botticini and Zvi Eckstein, *The Chosen Few: How Education Shaped Jewish History, 70–1492* (Princeton, NJ: Princeton University Press, 2012); Muller, *Capitalism and the Jews*.

2. For more background on that, see Endelman, *The Jews of Georgian England*, chaps. 5–7.

3. Larry Neal, *The Rise of Financial Capitalism: International Capital Markets in the Age of Reason* (Cambridge: Cambridge University Press, 1990), chap. 2; Carruthers, *City of Capital: Politics and Markets in the English Financial Revolution*, 168–70.

4. Coffeehouses and print were inherently related, as people frequented them also to read the recent newspapers and pamphlets. Wennerlind, *Casualties of Credit*, 169–72; Alex Preda, "In the Enchanted Grove: Financial Conversations and the Marketplace in England and France in the 18th Century," *Journal of Historical Sociology* 14, no. 3 (2001): 276–307; Steve Pincus, "'Coffee Politicians Does Create': Coffeehouses and Restoration Political Culture," *Journal of Modern History* 67, no. 4 (1995): 807–34. The theme of disinformation is fundamental in contemporary writings on the market. See, for instance, Thomas Mortimer, *Every man his own Broker* (London, 1761), chap. 2.

5. It is not altogether clear however whether this was a real Jew or a designation for a non-Christian from the Mediterranean. Brian Cowan, *The Social Life of Coffee: The Emergence of the British Coffeehouse* (New Haven, CT: Yale University Press, 2005), 90.

6. Edward Ward, *The republican procession; or, the tumultuous cavalcade* (London, 1714).

7. Adam Anderson, *An historical and chronological deduction of the origin of commerce* [. . .], vol. 1 (London, 1764), 133; *Morning Post and Daily Advertiser*, August 14, 1786 (issue 4209).

8. *The grand question debated* [. . .] *whether it would be expedient to abolish the public debt* (London [1755?]), 22. One can clearly sense the correlation with modern anti-Jewish (conspiracy) theories regarding their sophisticated world power that evolves from an underground network. This deserves a serious discussion, beyond the scope of mine here.

9. *The Spectator*, no. 495 (September 27, 1712).

10. Richard Braverman, "Spectator 495: Addison and 'The Race of People Called Jews,'" *Studies in English Literature, 1500–1900* 34, no. 3 (1994): 537–52.

11. *The Spectator*, no. 495.

12. Matthew 21:12–17, Mark 11:15–19, and Luke 19:45–48; and a different version in John 2:13–16.

13. See his commentary on John 2, Matthew 21, and Mark 11. In a similar vein, Bishop Joseph Hall commented that Jesus rebuked the "fraudulent bargaines and griping transactions" that took place in the temple, and Edward Leigh noted that "under a pretence of buying and selling, [the priests] did nothing but cheate and cosen the poore people, and did in overreaching and circumventing the poore buyers, steale." See Joseph Hall, *A plaine and familiar explication* [. . .] (London, 1633); Edward Leigh, *Annotations Upon all the New Testament* [. . .] (London, 1650), both on Matthew 21.

14. Matthew Henry, *An exposition of All the books of the Old and New Testament* [. . .], vol. 5, 3rd ed. (London, 1725), 146, 444–45.

15. Henry Hammond, *A paraphrase and annotations upon all the books of the New Testament* [. . .], 2nd ed., (London, 1659), 168. See also the annotations on the NT of Edward Wells (1717), Matthew Henry (1725), John Gill (1746), William Dodd (1770), as well as Dodd's *Discourses on the miracles and parables* [. . .], vol. 2 (London, 1757), discourse 17.

16. See also *The Assembly's Annotations* and the commentaries of David Dickson (1651), Matthew Poole (1688), Daniel Whitby (1703), and William Burkitt (1707). Some English commentators maintained the traditional one and some combined the two aspects: For instance, Richard Baxter and Thomas Haweis stuck with the traditional interpretation; Edward Wells, John Gill, and William Dodd combined the two. Waterman, *Political Economy and Christian Theology*, chap. 7.

17. Trivellato, *The Promise and Peril of Credit*; for a description of the operation of early modern bills of exchange, see 24–27. Estienne Cleirac, *Us et coustumes de la mer* [. . .] (Bordeaux, 1647); Jacques Savary, *Le parfait négociant* [. . .] (Paris, 1675).

18. The Scottish jurist John Spotiswood stated that "some learned Men derive [the invention] from the Customs of the Hebrews" and quoted Molloy's passage as their proof. See John Spotiswood, *An introduction to the knowledge of the stile of writs, simple and compound* [. . .] (Edinburgh, 1752), 33–35, especially footnote a. Others combined a discussion of the exchange in the temple with the attribution of the invention to medieval Jews. See William Stevenson, *A full and practical treatise upon bills of exchange* [. . .] (Edinburgh, 1764); Edward Manning, *The Law of Bills of Exchange* [. . .] (London, 1801).

19. Charles Molloy, *De Jure Maritimo et Navali* (London, 1676), 259–60. For a short discussion on Molloy, see above at the end of Chapter 1. Molloy borrowed this passage from Thomas Godwin's *Moses and Aaron* (1625), the English seventeenth-century textbook on Jewish matters, which referred to the exchange in the temple regarding the annual contribution of the half shekel for the maintenance of the temple. See Thomas Godwin, *Moses and Aaron* (London, 1625), 270. For writers who adopted Molloy's account, see, for instance, John Spotiswood, *An introduction to the knowledge of the stile of writs* (Edinburgh, 1707); Timothy Cunningham, *The Law of Bills of Exchange* (London, 1760), 5–6; Timothy Cunningham, *The merchant's lawyer* (London, 1762), 65–66; William Stevenson, *A full and practical treatise upon bills of exchange* (Edinburgh, 1764); Edward Windham Manning, *Law of Bills of Exchange* (London, 1801), 1–2.

20. Malachy Postlethwayt, *The universal dictionary of trade and commerce* [. . .], vol. 1 (London, 1757), 253–54; compare to Jacques Savary des Brûlons, *Dictionnaire universel de commerce* (new ed.), vol. 3 (Paris, 1748), 67.

21. Hammond, *A paraphrase and annotations upon all the books of the New Testament* [. . .], 2nd ed. (London, 1659), 103–4. See also the interpretation of Daniel Whitby that the monetary transaction in the temple consisted chiefly of "the Return of Money from remote Places," so that "they who came to Jerusalem to worship, paying it to Merchants at home, might have it safe from Thieves, and from the trouble of Carriage, at Jerusalem." Daniel Whitby, *A paraphrase and commentary on the New Testament*, vol. 1 (London, 1703), 173 (Matt. 21:12).

22. Indeed, as many ancient sources indicate, the temple functioned as an economic center of the first order.

23. For an explanation of the working of dry exchange, see Trivellato, *The Promise and Peril of Credit*, 29–30. Charles Molloy, *De Jure Maritimo et Navali*, chap. 10. Molloy refers to Coke's *Institutions*, but Coke does not mention such a thing. This point was a conscious disagreement with Malynes, who ascribed the invention of this "biting manner of exchange" to

bankers in Henry VII's time; see *Lex Mercatoria* (London, 1622), 380–81. Other writers adopted Molloy's claim; see, for instance, Timothy Cunningham, *The law of bills of exchange*, 2nd ed. (London, 1761), 6–7.

24. Thanks to bills of exchange, commerce "became capable of eluding violence," and consequently "it became necessary that princes should govern with more prudence." Montesquieu, *The Spirit of the Laws* (London, 1750), book 21, 20.

25. Stewart Kyd, *A treatise on the law of bills of exchange* (London, 1790), 1–2; Edward Windham Manning, *The Law of Bills of Exchange* [. . .] (London, 1801), 1–2.

26. John Francis, *History of the Bank of England, its Times and Traditions*, vol. 1 (London, 1847), 3. It was sometimes argued that money itself was invented by the Jews; see Wyndham Beawes, *Lex mercatoria rediviva* (London, 1773 [1751]), 358; Thomas Mortimer, *A new and complete dictionary of trade*, vol. 1 (London, 1766), under "bills of exchange." English writers commonly mentioned Abraham as an early example of the use of money.

27. Nirenberg, *Anti-Judaism*. The quote is taken from 471.

28. Peter Stallybrass, "Marx's Coat," in *Border Fetishisms: Material Objects in Unstable Spaces*, ed. Patricia Spyer (New York: Routledge, 2013 [1998]), 183–207.

29. Karl Marx, "On the Jewish Question" (1844), in *The Marx-Engels Reader*, ed. Robert C. Tucker, 2nd ed. (New York: Norton 1978).

Index

Abravanel, Isaac, 45

Addison, Joseph, 139, 191

Addison, Lancelot, 62–63, 215n23, 216n31

agriculture, 237n45; ancient Israelite society as agrarian autarky, 16, 31, 33, 42, 44, 48, 49, 51, 63, 64, 66, 67, 68; Christian agrarianism, 50; subsistence agriculture, 3, 64

Ainsworth, Henry, 39–40, 209n9

"allosemitism," 14

ancient Israelite society, 30; as agrarian autarky, 16, 31, 33, 42, 44, 48, 49, 51, 63, 64, 66, 67, 68; commerce, 33; contemporary issues and, 48–49, 50–51, 68; detachment from and defamiliarization of, 70–71; economic ethnography of, 62–67; economic and spiritual twofold role of, 193–94; Financial Revolution and, 69; French model of, 49–51; historical analytical perspective on, 16, 33–35, 36, 37, 39, 51, 67, 70, 169; importance for current discussions of socioeconomic questions, 169; Israelites/Jews ethnological distinction, 48, 54, 68, 211n41, 217n54; theatrical representations of, 109, 226n5

ancient Israelite society and usury, 16, 30–35, 45, 49, 169; ban on usury, 34, 42–43, 45, 63, 64–65, 66–67; contemporary economic issues and, 35, 44; economic system/geographic organization connection, 45; historical analytical perspective on, 42, 43, 45, 47, 48–49, 50–51, 54; social structure and usury, 32–33, 34, 42, 43–45, 47; usury, regulation of, 31–32

anthropology, 1, 54

Anti-Jacobin Review and Magazine, 240n41

antisemitism, 13–14, 19, 196. *See also* Judeophobia

Appleby, Joyce, 69–70

Assembly's Annotations, 40, 46, 209n9

Babington, Gervase, 40–41

Bacon, Phanuel: *The Taxes* (play), 119–20, 122, 229n37

Baddeley, Robert, 142

Baker, Thomas: *Hampstead Heath* (play), 110, 113–14, 227n12

Bank of England, 3, 8, 219n11; 1797 Bank Restriction Act, 167, 202n49; consols, 240n48; Gideon, Samson and, 82; interest, 8; Jewish shareholders in, 9, 81, 220n27

Baring, Francis, 177

Barlow, Thomas, 25, 26, 204n19

Barnard, Sir John, 89, 91, 102, 132, 222n19, 231n9

Basnage, Jacques: *History of the Jews*, 62

Bauman, Zygmunt, 14

Baxter, Richard, 47–48, 211n37

"Benevolent Jew, The" (song), 126

Bible: sixteenth century, 40, 208n2; seventeenth century, 37, 38–41, 53; eighteenth century, 48; Bible commentaries, 37–48, 50, 52, 53, 70, 191–92, 208n4, 210n23, 210n24, 210n27; biblical historicism, 51–52, 53, 69; commercialism/biblical discourse relation, 38, 70–71; cultural impact on early modern England, 37; Dutch Bible exegesis, 33, 43, 47, 49, 51, 69; in early modern discourse, 33; English Bible, 4, 37, 52, 208n2, 213n3; English biblical discourse, 36, 37, 45, 70; exegetical shift, 48; French Bible exegesis, 50; historical thinking on usury as part of Bible exegesis, 47, 54; identity and, 4, 52; influence on ethnology, 218n56; political economy and, 51, 53; usury, 5, 7, 15–16, 24–25, 38, 52, 53, 69; usury, arguments for the acceptance of, 32, 35, 39, 40–45, 46–47, 51, 59; usury, ban of, 4, 15, 16, 32, 34, 38–43, 45–47, 48, 59, 67, 68. *See also* New Testament; Old Testament

Acknowledgments

This project has been a long time in the making, and throughout this time I have incurred numerous debts of gratitude. The first of them is to Dror Wahrman, a model of bright thought, imagination, and intellectual energy. He was (and still is) an unfailing source of insight and inspiration. I am also deeply grateful to Dana Rabin and Jonathan Karp, who have offered valuable critiques, suggestions, and support, and whose own scholarship was a source of insight for this work. Naomi Tadmor has read and commented on pieces of this project, while still unripe, and her patience for that deserves special gratitude, beyond her learned comments and guidance. Nathan Marcus, Daniel Ussishkin, Johann Somerville, Richard Ross, and Julie Mell all read and shared their ideas on various parts of the project, and for that I am deeply thankful. My profound thankfulness to Richie Cohen, who has been a rock of support, encouragement, and advice for many years. It has been an honor to work with such generous scholars.

This project spanned various academic institutions and countries, where I was privileged to have warm, generous, and supportive hospitality both intellectually and socially. I was fortunate to be a fellow at the Vidal Sassoon International Center for the Study of Antisemitism; a fellow at the Safra Center for Ethics at Tel Aviv University; Lady Davis Fellow at the Hebrew University of Jerusalem; and, when finishing up the work, a postdoctoral fellow at Haifa University. I deeply thank Manuela Consonni and Nicole Hochner at Hebrew University, Hanoch Dagan at Tel Aviv University, Zoe Beenstock at Haifa University, and Ann Blair at Harvard University for their efforts and support on all fronts. My sincere gratitude to the donors of these various institutions for the generous support that enabled me to carry out this work. At Haifa University, an ISF grant, number 624/21, assisted me in finishing the book. I am also thankful to the Kurt Grunwald Fund for Jewish Economic History, of the Cherrick Center for the Study of Zionism, the Yishuv, and the State of Israel at Hebrew University of Jerusalem, for granting support for the project.

Throughout the years I have benefited from the help of numerous friends and colleagues, whose friendship and intellect helped this project materialize.

Very heartfelt thanks go to Uri Erman, Ray Shrire, Boaz Berger, Alex Kerner, Sarah Mandel, Yakir Paz, and Marc Volovici, whose insightful comments and criticism on parts of the work have greatly improved it. Ami Asher meticulously not only worked on improving style and clarity, but also engaged with the arguments in the book and forced me to clarify them, and deserves my deep gratitude.

I am fortunate to have this book published as part of the Jewish Culture and Contexts series. I am truly grateful to the editorial staff at Penn Press, especially Jerome Singerman and Elisabeth Maselli, senior humanities editors, who spared no effort in bringing this book to press, as well as to the editorial board of the series. I wish to thank the anonymous reviewers for their thorough and engaging comments. They have certainly made this book a better one.

Some of the materials in Chapter 1 have been published in 2017 in the *Journal of Early Modern History* 21, no. 6 (2017): 489–515. A version of Chapter 5 was published in 2018 in the *Journal of British Studies* 57, no. 3 (July 2018): 467–92. Both are included here with permission.

My family has been an enduring source of support throughout the years. My sincere thanks go to Eliezer Schwartz, and to my beloved parents and parents-in-law—Shlomo and Hava Naeh, Israel and Esther Yuval—for their encouragement and belief in the project, their thoughtful comments, and, not least, their endless and exceptional support on all levels. My wonderful children, Ayala, Avigail, and Nadav, have grown alongside this project, reminding me—without their knowing—of priorities in life (priorities too often neglected in the course of long-term academic writing projects). Their bright personalities and joyful presence were a driving force during these years.

My debts, then, go to many people. But of all, the one without whom nothing would have come about, is my wife, Naomi Yuval-Naeh. Having watered seeds of vague ideas I had in mind, and cultured their fragile sprouts, she constantly helped me find my own way through the difficulties of early academic life and of this project. With her sharp, thorough, and penetrating thought, she treated every idea and passage with challenging criticism—and love. The inescapable moments of intellectual and mental deadlocks over the course of the years I have been working on this book were made manageable with her advice. To a great degree, she shaped this book into what it is, much more than she imagines. But far more than for this book, I thank her for her close and daily love, friendship, support, and understanding. This book is dedicated to her, and in memory of my dear grandparents, Miriam and Moshe Schwartz, z"l.

Printed and bound by CPI Group (UK) Ltd, Croydon, CR0 4YY

16/04/2025

14658413-0001